THEODORE ROOSEVELT AND THE JAPANESE-AMERICAN CRISES

THEODORE ROOSEVELT

AND THE

JAPANESE-AMERICAN CRISES

An Account of the International Complications Arising from the Race Problem on the Pacific Coast

By THOMAS A. BAILEY

Assistant Professor of History
Stanford University

GLOUCESTER, MASS.
PETER SMITH
1964

PREFACE

CERTAIN aspects of the foreign policy of Theodore Roosevelt have already been treated exhaustively. In 1925 Dr. Tyler Dennett published *Roosevelt and the Russo-Japanese War,* which was followed in 1927 by Professor Howard C. Hill's *Roosevelt and the Caribbean.* Up to the present time, however, no writer has attempted a detailed study of Japanese-American relations from 1905 to 1909, the years from the close of the Russo-Japanese War to the end of the Roosevelt administration. Yet during this period there occurred developments of such great significance as to mark a turning-point in the history of the two nations and to foreshadow difficulties that have continued to this day.

The Russo-Japanese War ended the golden age in Japanese-American relations. From the time of Commodore Perry's historic mission of 1853–1854 to the outbreak of this conflict the United States had evidenced an almost parental pride in the amazing transformation of her Far Eastern protégé. But as a result of the astonishing victories of 1904–1905 Japan emerged as a world power, and a tinge of jealousy, not unmingled with suspicion and fear, began to affect the traditional friendship between the two peoples. This changed attitude aggravated a growing friction on the Pacific Coast of the United States between the Americans and their Japanese immigrant neighbors, and during the ensuing years a half-dozen crises arose which taxed the conciliatory powers of the two governments and which on several occasions came uncomfortably near to precipitating war.

v

The purpose of the present volume is to examine critically the causes, course, and results of these developments in Japanese-American relations. Such a task will involve a consideration of so many different factors that at times the narrative will bear little direct relation to Theodore Roosevelt. But so completely did he dominate the foreign policy of the United States during this period and so definitely did he shape the course of Japanese-American relations that it has seemed proper to include his name in the title.

This study, then, is basically a chapter in American diplomacy. The writer has consequently limited any necessary excursions into Far Eastern history to the briefest possible compass. And with diplomacy primarily in mind he has made an effort not to wander too far into the by-paths which are continually tempting one interested in race relationships, international and constitutional law, mob psychology, yellow journalism, or military and naval strategy.

Whatever contributions this volume may make to the history of the period will in large part be due to unpublished manuscript materials which the writer was privileged to use. Of indispensable value were the Roosevelt Papers, which are deposited in the Library of Congress, and which have been partially opened to only a limited number of investigators. No less important was the diplomatic correspondence to be found in the Division of Communications and Records of the Department of State and referred to in the footnotes of this study by the file numbers. These documents had never before been consulted by the historian; and only by securing special permission was the author privileged to examine them.

For substantial favors in connection with the use of the Roosevelt Papers and the Department of State files, as well as other manuscript sources, the writer is deeply indebted to the Honorable Elihu Root; to Mr. Maxwell M. Hamilton, assistant chief of the Division of Far Eastern Affairs of the Department of State; to Mr. William R. Langdon, also of the Division of Far Eastern Affairs; to Dr. J. Franklin Jameson, Dr. Thomas P. Martin, and Dr. Curtis Garrison of the Division of Manuscripts of the Library of Congress; to Mrs. Maddin Summers, of the Department of State archives; and to Mrs. David Starr Jordan of Stanford University.

The writer's colleague, Professor Payson J. Treat, has read the manuscript and offered valuable suggestions for its improvement. Professor John C. Parish, managing editor of the *Pacific Historical Review,* permitted the author to use, in revised and expanded form, certain materials which originally appeared in an article in that journal entitled, "The World Cruise of the American Battleship Fleet, 1907–1909." Mr. Manoel Cardozo, Mr. Daniel Gage, and Mr. Olaf Amdahl, all of Stanford University, rendered useful service in preparing the manuscript for publication.

T. A. B.

STANFORD UNIVERSITY
May 30, 1934

CONTENTS

"I am being horribly bothered about the Japanese business."—Roosevelt to Kermit Roosevelt, October 27, 1906.

"As for the San Francisco incident, it caused me more concern than you can imagine . . . ."—Roosevelt to Takahira, April 28, 1907.

"Nothing during my Presidency has given me more concern than these troubles."—Roosevelt to Kaneko, May 28, 1907.

"The Newfoundland business and similar matters are mere child's play compared with this Japanese business . . . ."—Roosevelt to Root, July 13, 1907.

"My chief concern in foreign affairs now is over the Japanese situation."—Roosevelt to Whitelaw Reid, July 26, 1907.

"I cannot give in public my reasons for being apprehensive about Japan, for of course to do so might bring on grave trouble . . . ."—Roosevelt to Kermit Roosevelt, April 19, 1908.

"The whole business has been most unfortunate, and I am more concerned over it than any of the other rather stormy incidents during my career as President."—Roosevelt to William Kent, January 22, 1909.

". . . . the troubles I have with Congress don't count at all when compared with the trouble I am having with California over Japan."—Roosevelt to Theodore Roosevelt, Jr., February 6, 1909.

CHAPTER I

The Beginnings of Anti-Japanese Agitation

"The feeling on the Pacific slope . . . . is as
foolish as if conceived by the mind of a Hottentot."—Roosevelt to Lodge, June 5, 1905

OUR STORY is one of race prejudice. A certain element on
the Pacific Coast did not care to live cheek by jowl with
the masses of the Orient—and they did not hesitate to say
so. Whether this feeling was justified or unjustified, or as
"foolish as if conceived by the mind of a Hottentot," is
not the primary concern of the historian. For him the
significant thing is that race hostility existed and that it
took certain unreasoning forms which came uncomfortably
close to precipitating war between two powers whose historic friendship had become a byword among nations. An
understanding, however, of these basic developments will
take us back to a brief consideration of the status of the
Japanese in the United States prior to 1906.

In 1880, there were only about one hundred and fifty
Japanese in the United States, but beginning with 1891
they began to come in at the rate of about 1,000 a year, a
figure which had increased by 1900 to 12,000. The Californians, in this case largely San Franciscans, whose ideas
as to the undesirability of large masses of unassimilable
Orientals[1] had been crystallized by a violent twenty-year

[1] R. L. Buell, "The Development of the Anti-Japanese Agitation in
the United States," *Political Science Quarterly,* XXXVII (1922), 606 ff.
See also Yamato Ichihashi, *Japanese in the United States* (Stanford
University, 1932), pp. 230 ff.

campaign against the Chinese, consequently became uneasy and took steps in 1900 which resulted in the first considerable protests against the Japanese. Wishing to do what it could to quiet such agitation, the Japanese government announced in August, 1900, that henceforth no passports would be issued to laborers desiring to go to the mainland of the United States. As a result of this voluntary limitation, which certain writers have called the first Gentlemen's Agreement, the influx of coolies fell off one-half in 1901. Such an arrangement, however, was but a palliative, and in 1905 there occurred the first vigorous movement against the Japanese on the Pacific Coast.[2]

The primary cause of the outburst of 1905 was the failure of the first Gentlemen's Agreement satisfactorily to exclude the Japanese. Largely as a result of graft in the passport administration, laborers were still coming in from Japan in disconcerting numbers. More serious was the inapplicability of the arrangement to Hawaii, which thousands of coolies were using merely as a stepping-stone to the mainland. The California agitators might have viewed this situation with more equanimity had there been any immediate prospect of obtaining Japanese exclusion legislation from Congress; but that body was indifferent.[3]

[2] Buell, *loc. cit.*, p. 609. For the announcement of the suspension of immigration, see Buck to Hay, Aug. 13, 1900, Department of State, *Despatches*, Japan, Vol. 74.

[3] In May, 1900, shortly after the first considerable difficulties with the Japanese in San Francisco, there was some little stir in Congress over the situation. In that month four different resolutions were introduced and adopted requesting the secretary of the treasury to provide information as to the numbers and the status of Japanese immigrants. This sudden display of interest in Congress was, however, only temporary. Ensuing proposals for Japanese exclusion were completely ignored. Between June, 1902, and December, 1905, four Japanese exclusion bills were introduced in the House, two by Robinson, of Indiana, one by McKinlay, of

Indeed, there was a growing belief on the Atlantic Coast that American treatment of the Chinese had been unwise and that it might not be inadvisable, in view of the existing labor shortage, to consider modifying the Chinese exclusion law.[4] Furthermore, it was obvious that President Theodore Roosevelt would veto any Japanese exclusion measure that should pass Congress, for in his annual message of December, 1904, he had squarely opposed a discriminatory immigration policy, a view which he was known to have expressed with even greater force in private.[5] On May 15, 1905, for example, he wrote to Henry Cabot Lodge:

Meanwhile, I am utterly disgusted at the manifestations which have begun to appear on the Pacific slope in favor of excluding the Japanese exactly as the Chinese are excluded. The California State Legislature and various other bodies have acted in the worst possible taste and in the most offensive manner to Japan. Yet the Senators and Congressmen from these very States were lukewarm about the Navy last year. It gives me a feeling of disgust to see them challenge Japanese hostility and justify by their actions any feeling the Japanese might have against us, while at the same time refusing to take steps to defend themselves against the formidable foe whom they are ready with such careless insolence to antagonize. How people can act in this way with the Russo-Japanese war going on before their eyes I cannot understand. I do all I can to counteract the effects, but I cannot accomplish everything.[6]

California, and one by Hayes, of California; but none of them occasioned any discussion or was even reported out of committee. *Congressional Record*, 56 Cong., 1 sess., pp. 4956, 5381, 5454, 5582, 5704; *ibid.*, 57 Cong., 1 sess., p. 7615; *ibid.*, 58 Cong., 1 sess., p. 516; *ibid.*, 59 Cong., 1 sess., pp. 115, 569.

4 *Outlook,* Dec. 29, 1906, p. 1051; New York *Times,* Oct. 27, 1906; San Francisco *Chronicle,* Jan. 11, Feb. 11, 1907.

5 *Congressional Record,* 58 Cong., 3 sess., p. 17.

6 *Selections from the Correspondence of Theodore Roosevelt and Henry Cabot Lodge, 1884–1918* (New York, 1925), II, 122. Hereafter cited as *Lodge Letters.*

But the antipathy of certain Californians to the Japanese was not based alone upon differences of race. Organized labor, which already professed to feel the pinch of Japanese competition and which feared a lowered standard of living, was quick to espouse the cause of exclusion. Nor was this reaction confined to San Francisco, as has sometimes been assumed, for the American Federation of Labor, at its annual convention held in that city during November, 1904, demanded that the Chinese exclusion law be applied to the Japanese.[7] But since labor was probably more strongly organized in San Francisco than anywhere else in the state, it was not unnatural that this city should have become the hotbed of anti-Japanese feeling. In addition, probably as a result of economic fear if not racial antipathy, stories were widely circulated throughout California which tended to discredit the Japanese—reports of their general untrustworthiness in financial matters and of their activity as spies for the Mikado.[8]

The factor behind the anti-Japanese movement of 1905–1906 which was most easily understood in the East (used hereafter to refer to the eastern United States) and which probably did more than anything else ultimately to enlist the acquiescence of that section in a policy of exclusion was the outcome of the Russo-Japanese War. When this struggle broke out the sympathies of America, despite the fact that Russia was her traditional friend and a white, Christian nation, turned overwhelmingly to Japan. Ever

---

[7] Buell, *loc. cit.*, p. 609.

[8] *Ibid.*, pp. 611 ff. The *Chronicle* remarked: "The Japanese who come here remain Japanese. Their loyalty is to the Japanese Emperor. Every one of them, so far as his service is desired, is a Japanese spy." San Francisco *Chronicle*, Nov. 14, 1906.

since Commodore Perry's memorable visit the United States had regarded Japan not only as a friend but to some extent as a protégé, and had shown a disinterestedness in dealing with her that is noteworthy in the history of international relationships.[9] Furthermore, Japan had seen to it that her case against Russia was presented to the press of the United States in its most favorable light. In launching this campaign of propaganda she stole a march on Russia, and, in the words of Dr. Tyler Dennett, "built up an opinion that she was fighting for the independence of Korea and the return of Manchuria to China. She had presented herself as an unoffending David attacked by a brutal Goliath and possessed of no purpose save to battle for justice and right."[10]

In these circumstances, American public opinion, naturally friendly to the under dog, turned to the nation which appeared to be backed to the wall without just cause by a big bully. During the war the Japanese government, through censorship and through personally conducted tours of the battlefields, was able to suppress reports unfavorable to Japanese conduct. But during the peace conference at Portsmouth, the Russians, now alive to the value of American public opinion, turned the tables on Japan[11] and manipulated the press in such a way as to tear from Japanese motives and aspirations much of the altruism with

[9] Note particularly the return of the $785,000 Shimonoseki indemnity to Japan in 1883. Payson J. Treat, *The Far East* (New York, 1928), p. 224.

[10] Tyler Dennett, *Roosevelt and the Russo-Japanese War* (Garden City, 1925), pp. 238–39.

[11] *Ibid.*, pp. 248–49; Henry F. Pringle, *Theodore Roosevelt: a Biography* (New York, 1931), p. 387; Payson J. Treat, *Japan and the United States, 1853–1921* (Stanford University, 1928), p. 185.

which they had been clothed by a gullible and admiring American public. The resulting disillusionment brought about a reaction in the United States against the original sympathy for Japan, and this feeling was not improved when reports came of riots that had occurred in Tokyo as a result of Japanese displeasure with the terms of peace, outbursts which in a number of instances resulted in damages to the property and indignities to the persons of Americans.[12]

The astonishing victories of Japan awakened within the United States a feeling of uneasiness if not of jealousy. Newspapers and men in public life began to speak freely of the irrepressible conflict with Japan.[13] In describing this change of attitude the *Japan Weekly Mail* later remarked: ". . . . America began by regarding Japan as an interesting curiosity; then she learned to look at her with some admiration; then followed a sentiment of surprise; then a feeling of alarm; and finally a mood of jealousy."[14] Within a period of six years both the United States and Japan had become world powers. To the farsighted it seemed inevitable that their interests would clash in the Pacific at some time in the not distant future. Perhaps Japan, recently wedded anew to England by the Anglo-Japanese Alliance of 1905, would actually menace the territorial possessions of the United States. It was not unnatural, then, that the two powers should have regarded each other differently. As the *Japan Weekly Mail* put it:

The truth is that for many years the United States and Japan lived in a kind of diplomatic Utopia. The cause was plain. Neither of

12 See *Lodge Letters,* II, 192.   13 See Buell, *loc. cit.,* pp. 614–15.
14 *Japan Weekly Mail,* April 6, 1907, p. 358.

the friends had become a world Power. Both from their high places of peaceful domestic development, looked out calmly on the armour-clashing world around them. But within a very brief space both have stepped down into the arena, and so they can no longer regard each other with quiet eyes of trust and faith. The change was bound to come. We may lament it but we must bow to it.[15]

Like the Americans in 1848 and 1898, the Japanese evidenced a pronounced exaltation of spirit as a result of their remarkable successes. During the Russo-Japanese War reports came to Roosevelt that the Japanese in Hawaii, who far outnumbered the whites, were showing an insolent temper, and on February 9, 1905, the President wrote to Secretary of War Taft suggesting that the latter communicate with the governor of Hawaii "and see if he needs a regiment or two of troops in the islands."[16] Roosevelt, however, was not surprised by these evidences of an inflated national pride, for he wrote to Lodge:

That Japan will have her head turned to some extent I do not in the least doubt, and I see clear symptoms of it in many ways. We should certainly as a nation have ours turned if we had performed such feats as the Japanese have in the past sixteen months; and the same is true of any European nation. Moreover, I have no doubt that some Japanese, and perhaps a great many of them, will behave badly to foreigners. They can not behave worse than the State of California . . . .[17]

After the peace Roosevelt observed—and Lodge agreed with him—that the outburst "in Tokio is unpleasant evidence that the Japanese mob—I hope not the Japanese people—had had its head completely turned . . . ."[18]

---

[15] *Ibid.*, Feb. 9, 1907, p. 136.   [16] Dennett, *op. cit.*, p. 160.

[17] Roosevelt to Lodge, June 5, 1905, *Lodge Letters,* II, 134.

[18] Roosevelt to Lodge, Sept. 6, 1905, *ibid.,* p. 190. See also Lodge to Roosevelt, Sept. 14, 1905, *ibid.,* p. 193.

More specific information concerning the conduct of certain Japanese appears in a letter in which Roosevelt repeated what two American correspondents, originally pro-Japanese, had related to him upon returning from the Far East.

Moreover, they [the correspondents] said that under the stress of victory the Japanese grew exceedingly insolent to the foreigners, and, curiously, particularly to the Americans; a latent feeling that I had not in the least expected becoming evident as to our having thwarted Japan's hopes not merely in the Philippines but in Hawaii. [One man reported] that toward the end of his stay the Japanese soldiers would sometimes threaten the various foreigners (the English and Americans just as much as the Germans or Frenchmen) if they met them alone, and that the tone of the Japanese officers was often insolent; in some cases to an almost unbearable extent. In short, the Japanese army showed a disposition to lump all white men together and to regard them with a common hatred.[19]

The reports of returning war correspondents, however, must be taken with a grain of salt. Many of these men had had unpleasant experiences with Japanese officials, who not unnaturally sought to guard their military secrets and to present to the world the best possible front. A group of these disgruntled correspondents left Japan in 1905 vowing, as they expressed it, "to get their knives into Japan" sooner or later.[20] When, after the San Francisco school incident, a considerable number of newspapers made obvious attempts to misinterpret Japan's position and to aggravate the situation by unfounded reports of impending hostilities, it was suspected both in the United States

19 Dennett, *op. cit.*, p. 48. The date of this letter is not clear.
20 *Japan Weekly Mail*, Oct. 27, 1906, p. 542.

and in Japan, although it could not be proved, that this was the deliberate work of these same correspondents.[21]

However natural and explainable the so-called cockiness of the Japanese may have been, it was particularly irritating to those on the Pacific Coast who were anxious not only to exclude Japanese but also to keep those already there in what was regarded as their proper place. In fact, one member of the Board of Education that passed the segregation order of 1906 later testified that the victories of Japan, which had definitely aroused anti-Japanese feeling on the Pacific Coast, had to some extent been responsible for the action of that body.[22]

Another result of the Russo-Japanese War which had a definite bearing upon the situation in California was the widespread belief that a large number of former Japanese soldiers, tired of the war, unwilling to return home and shoulder the new economic burdens imposed by the conflict, and aroused by their experiences to seek additional adventure and a new scene, would pour into the United States.[23] When, in later months, it became evident that considerable groups of these discharged soldiers actually were emigrating to Hawaii, Mexico, and California,[24]

[21] The *Japan Weekly Mail* thought that this explanation was much more agreeable than to think that a friend, long loved and trusted, was deliberately turning away from the Japanese. *Ibid.* See also New York *Times*, Oct. 30, 1906; Herbert B. Johnson, *Discrimination against the Japanese in California* (Berkeley, California, 1907), p. 31.

[22] Arthur G. Butzbach, "The Segregation of Orientals in the San Francisco Schools" (unpublished Master's thesis, Stanford University, 1928), p. 19.

[23] San Francisco *Chronicle*, Feb. 23, 1905.

[24] Speck von Sternberg to Roosevelt, July 14, 1907; Roosevelt to von Sternberg, July 16, 1907; von Sternberg to Roosevelt, July 19, 1907; Roosevelt to von Sternberg, July 24, 1907. Roosevelt Papers, Library of Congress. Hereafter cited as Roosevelt Papers.

Roosevelt refused to be alarmed, attributing this phenomenon to perfectly natural and understandable causes. Nevertheless, the people of California were uneasy, and the ground was well prepared for the flare-up of 1905.

On February 23, 1905, just before the battle of Mukden, the San Francisco *Chronicle* formally launched the anti-Japanese campaign of that year by printing a nine-column article, flamboyantly headlined, on the menace of Japanese immigration. Among the numerous arguments advanced in support of its stand this newspaper devoted particular attention to the expected influx of discharged soldiers at the close of the war. Why the *Chronicle,* which was far from being recognized by the labor unions as their organ,[25] should have taken the lead in this spectacular manner was a matter of conjecture. One explanation was that the anti-Japanese cause, which was popular among the labor element in San Francisco, would enable the *Chronicle* to outdistance its rival, the *Examiner,* in the competition for subscribers.[26] The other explanation, and one widely believed, was that the proprietor of the *Chronicle,* Michel Harry deYoung, was hoping that the issue would carry him into the Senate of the United States.[27] This charge cannot be substantiated, but De Young's activity in state politics and his candidacy for the United States Senate in 1892 added strength to the rumor. President Roosevelt was acquainted with this situation, for he later characterized the "course of De Young's paper thruout" as "in-

[25] San Francisco *Chronicle,* Dec. 10, 1906.

[26] London *Times,* Dec. 8, 1906.

[27] *Senate Documents,* 59 Cong., 2 sess., no. 147, p. 27. Hereafter cited as *Metcalf Report.* New York *Nation,* Nov. 1, 1906.

famous," and added that he "understood all about it, and the reasons."[28]

On March 1, 1905, less than a week after the *Chronicle* outburst and probably as a direct result of it, a resolution was introduced into the state legislature which outlined ten reasons why the Japanese laborer was undesirable and which called upon the California delegation in Congress to make representations to the secretary of state and to President Roosevelt looking to the limiting or diminishing, by treaty or otherwise, of the influx of Japanese laborers. Most of the ten points had to do with the economic effects of Japanese penetration, particularly as they related to white labor. But the tenth and climactic point was:

. . . . we cannot but regard with the greatest sense of danger and disaster the prospect that the close of the war . . . . will surely bring to our shores hordes, to be counted only in thousands, of the discharged soldiers of the Japanese army, who will crowd the State with immoral, intemperate, quarrelsome men bound to labor for a pittance, and to subsist on a supply with which a white man can hardly sustain life. . . . .[29]

Although the resolution was crudely worded and was an intemperate if not unfair presentation of the case against the Japanese, the state senate adopted it on the same day by a 28 to 0 vote.[30] It is significant that in supporting the resolution Senator Wolfe, of San Francisco, emphasized the crowding of Japanese children into the schools and the consequent inconvenience to the white pupils.[31] The assembly acted with dispatch, and on the

[28] Roosevelt to Edwin Emerson, May 8, 1907, Roosevelt Papers.
[29] *Senate Journal* (California), 1905, p. 1165.
[30] *Ibid.*, p. 1166.
[31] San Francisco *Chronicle*, Mar. 2, 1905.

next day, March 2, 1905, approved the resolution, likewise by a unanimous vote, 70 to 0.[32] This remarkable display of unanimity was doubtless due in no small measure to the agitation of the *Chronicle,* and the next day that journal remarked editorially, with evident satisfaction, that its position had been sustained.

Certain writers have fallen into the error of stating that the Japanese and Korean Exclusion League, which had not been organized as yet, was responsible for the rise of the anti-Japanese agitation of 1905–1906; that this movement was confined solely to California; that in California the anti-Japanese feeling was to be found only in the cities; and that in the cities it was supported almost entirely by the labor union element. Several of these misapprehensions will be corrected at the proper point, but it is evident that by March, 1905, there was a formidable anti-Japanese movement under way in the state of California. If the agitation was limited solely to the cities, it must be observed, as the unanimous vote of the legislature would indicate, that the movement had the sympathy if not the active support of the other sections of the state. Nor was hostility toward the Japanese at this time to be found only in California. Between December 5, 1901, and December 11, 1905, the legislatures of three other Western states, Idaho, Montana, and Nevada, petitioned Congress for legislation limiting or excluding Japanese laborers.[33] Sentiment against the Japanese, then, was neither a sudden development nor a localized prejudice.

[32] *Assembly Journal* (California), 1905, p. 1554. This was not a record vote. For those voting see San Francisco *Chronicle,* Mar. 3, 1905.

[33] *Congressional Record,* 57 Cong., 1 sess., pp. 135, 306, 536; *ibid.,* 59 Cong., 1 sess., p. 267.

It should further be noted that, contrary to a popular belief, the segregation order of 1906 was not an altogether unexpected move on the part of the San Francisco Board of Education. Even as far back as 1892 there had been some agitation to establish a separate school for Japanese children.[34] More significant was the action of the Labor Party in 1901. In that year their candidate for mayor was elected on a platform which advocated, among other things, "that all Asiatics, both Chinese and Japanese, be educated separately from other children in schools exclusively for themselves."[35] For various reasons, however, no action was taken on this platform pronouncement. But with the outburst of 1905 attention was directed to the increasing number of Japanese in the public schools. Since 1859 the Chinese children had been housed in a separate building in their own quarter, and it seemed to many only natural that the Japanese, now that they were coming to school in numbers, should be segregated in like fashion. The Japanese consul in San Francisco, learning that the chief objection to these pupils was their advanced age, suggested to the Japanese newspapers in San Francisco, in March, 1905, that they advise their readers voluntarily to withdraw their older children. These journals followed his advice, and a number of the more mature Japanese pupils discontinued attending the schools.[36]

[34] Ichihashi, *op. cit.,* p. 230.

[35] San Francisco *Chronicle,* Sept. 7, 1901.

[36] George Kennan, "The Japanese in San Francisco Schools," *Outlook,* June 1, 1907, p. 247. Kennan was a correspondent for the *Outlook* in the Far East during the Russo-Japanese War and in Roosevelt's opinion was taken into camp by the Japanese. Dennett, *op. cit.,* p. 19. After the school incident he was sent to San Francisco, where he made a thorough investigation and wrote this penetrating article for the *Outlook.*

The first significant move in the direction of segregation was made on April 1, 1905. On that day, a year and a half before the final order, the San Francisco Board of Education presented to the Board of Supervisors a budget which provided for the construction of added facilities at the Chinese school, which, it was proposed, all the Japanese children throughout the city should attend. But since the Board of Supervisors could not overstep the one-dollar tax-rate limit imposed by the charter, the money for this purpose was not made available.[37] Yet the Japanese government, showing further evidence of a desire to avoid trouble, endeavored to quiet the growing agitation by limiting the number of Japanese emigrants to Hawaii, the way station to California, to 500 per ship; and, finally, in April, 1905, by temporarily suspending all such emigration.[38]

Nothing daunted by this obstacle in the way of its first step toward segregation, the Board of Education passed a resolution on May 6, 1905, which read:

Resolved, That the board of education is determined in its efforts to effect the establishment of separate schools for Chinese and Japanese pupils, not only for the purpose of relieving the congestion at present prevailing in our schools, but also for the higher end that our children should not be placed in any position where their youthful impressions may be affected by association with pupils of the Mongolian race.[39]

Because of the inability of the Board to translate its objective into action this resolution elicited little comment at the

37 San Francisco *Chronicle*, Oct. 30, Dec. 19, 1906. Kennan's theory was that the municipal government was so busily engaged in grafting that it was indifferent to this proposal. Kennan, *loc. cit.*, p. 247.

38 Buell, *loc. cit.*, p. 617.

39 *Metcalf Report*, p. 3.

time and was generally overlooked when the segregation ordinance of October, 1906, was passed. But in view of the general impression that the segregation order was an unexpected development, it is well to keep these preliminary steps in mind.

In the meantime, the leadership of the anti-Japanese movement in San Francisco had fallen into the hands of union labor, which then held the city in its grip. Meetings were called, and the boycotting of Japanese or those who employed them was urged. On May 7, 1905—a day of great significance in the history of Pacific Coast anti-Japanese agitation—a mass meeting was held at which the Japanese and Korean Exclusion League was launched. The major objective of this organization was to secure, through propaganda and various other kinds of pressure, an extension of the Chinese exclusion laws to the Japanese. Late in 1906 the League claimed a membership of 78,500 in California alone, three-fourths of whom were said to live in San Francisco.[40] This organization also worked for a boycott of the Japanese, and on October 22, 1905, instructed its executive committee to appear before the Board of Education and petition that body to carry out the League's avowed policy of segregating the Mongolian children of the city.[41]

During all this time Roosevelt had been watching the situation in California with deep interest. On June 3, 1905, Lodge wrote to him and suggested that the solution of the Japanese difficulty lay in "an arrangement with Japan by which she excludes our labor and we exclude

[40] *Ibid.*
[41] San Francisco *Chronicle*, Oct. 23, 1905.

hers."[42] This statement is of significance as suggesting the nucleus of the Gentlemen's Agreement of 1907 and phrasing an idea which was to crop up repeatedly in the President's correspondence during the ensuing months. Two days later Roosevelt wrote regarding the evident turning of the Japanese head by the recent victories, and added:

They [the Japanese] can not behave worse than the State of California, through its Legislature, is now behaving toward the Japanese. The feeling on the Pacific slope, taking it from several different standpoints, is as foolish as if conceived by the mind of a Hottentot. These Pacific Coast people wish grossly to insult the Japanese and to keep out the Japanese immigrants on the ground that they are an immoral, degraded and worthless race; and at the same time that they desire to do this for the Japanese and are already doing it for the Chinese they expect to be given advantages in Oriental markets; and with besotted folly are indifferent to building up the navy while provoking this formidable new power— a power jealous, sensitive and warlike, and which if irritated could at once take both the Philippines and Hawaii from us if she obtained the upper hand on the seas. Most certainly the Japanese soldiers and sailors have shown themselves to be terrible foes. There can be none more dangerous in all the world. But our own navy, ship for ship, is I believe at least as efficient as theirs . . . . At present we are superior to them in number of ships, and this superiority will last for some time . . . . I hope that we can persuade our people on the one hand to act in a spirit of generous justice and genuine courtesy toward Japan, and on the other hand to keep the navy respectable in numbers and more than respectable in the efficiency of its units. If we act thus we need not fear the Japanese . . . . In any event we can hold our own in the future . . . . only if we occupy the position of the just man armed. . . . .[43]

---

[42] Lodge to Roosevelt, June 3, 1905, *Lodge Letters,* II, 127.

[43] Roosevelt to Lodge, June 5, 1905, *ibid.,* pp. 134–35. On June 18, 1905, Lodge wrote to Roosevelt: "The attitude of the Pacific Slope toward the Japanese seems incomprehensible at this time from every

The Exclusion League, ignorant of Roosevelt's views, went ahead with its plans and persuaded two California Congressmen to introduce anti-Japanese legislation in the next session of Congress, which was to convene in December, 1905. The President's annual message, however, which strongly opposed discriminatory legislation, was disquieting to the League, and to a delegation of California Congressmen Roosevelt expressed himself with such vehemence that efforts to secure exclusion of the Japanese by act of Congress were temporarily abandoned.[44]

The unfriendly attitude of the federal administration led the Exclusion League to intensify its efforts. A monster mass meeting was called for May 6, 1906.[45] But before it could be held there occurred the appalling earthquake and fire of April, 1906, a catastrophe which had much to do with the later treatment of the Orientals in San Francisco. The Japanese, in spite of the financial exhaustion occasioned by their recent war, responded magnificently to the cry for help that went up from the stricken city, and their government and Red Cross promptly contributed $246,000, more than all of the other foreign nations of the world combined.[46] This generous outpouring on the part of Japan made the subsequent action of the San Franciscans, particularly the Board of Education, appear all the more reprehensible.

The several thousand Japanese affected by the earth-

point of view. We must treat the Chinese more civilly too. I am heartily in favor of barring out coolie labor whether Chinese or Japanese but it must be done discreetly and reasonably—in fact there is no other way in which it can be done." *Ibid.*, p. 157.

[44] Buell, *loc. cit.*, pp. 619–20.

[45] *Ibid.*, p. 620.   [46] Kennan, *loc. cit.*, p. 246.

quake and fire naturally flocked together for mutual succor and, through their ability to secure funds, took on an appearance of prosperity in advance of the Americans.[47] This circumstance in itself was not pleasing to many of the San Franciscans, but vastly more irritating was the Japanese invasion of what had long been regarded as the better white residential district—a movement which was to some extent caused by the dearth of houses elsewhere. Not only was this seeming aggressiveness objectionable but since many of the San Francisco Japanese were of the well-to-do merchant class, as compared with their poorer countrymen in the agricultural districts of the state, they were frequently able to outbid the whites in competition for housing. In fact, landlords insisted upon and obtained higher rentals from the Japanese in order to compensate for the opprobrium that they incurred, with the result that a number of Americans were evicted to make room for Orientals.[48] This situation naturally increased the existing bitterness of feeling.

In the general disorder that followed the earthquake, lawlessness lurked on every hand among the ruins of San Francisco. Undesirable characters came from afar to batten on the prostrate city, and the local newspapers were filled with the exploits of gas-pipe thugs and other ruffians.[49] The San Francisco police records showed that between May 6 and November 5, 1906, there occurred two hundred and ninety cases of assault, many of them

[47] *Japan Weekly Mail,* Oct. 27, 1906, p. 543.

[48] *Ibid.,* Aug. 25, 1906, p. 183.

[49] A correspondent of the *Japan Weekly Mail* reported that the police force had been reduced as a result of the necessity for economy. Nov. 17, 1906, p. 632.

resulting in death. This crime wave, which the authorities seemed powerless to stop, even spread across San Francisco Bay to Oakland.[50]

It was inevitable that a certain number of Japanese should be among the victims of these assaults. The San Francisco newspapers, however, repeatedly denied that the attacks were manifestations of race feeling and pointed out that the Orientals did not suffer any more in proportion to their numbers than did the whites.[51] In his unusually thorough investigation of the San Francisco situation late in 1906, of which more will be said later, Secretary of Commerce and Labor Victor H. Metcalf found no cases of assaults on Japanese before the earthquake, but he discovered nineteen after the disaster, most of them in August and September, 1906. Practically all of the attacks upon whites had been made with robbery as the obvious motive; but in the case of the Japanese, as Metcalf pointed out with damaging directness, only one assault appears to have been made with a view to robbery.[52] Nor do these figures take into account minor attacks and annoyances, such as stonings, for most of which boys and young men were responsible.[53] The obvious conclusion .is that, with robbery excluded as a motive, the Japanese were attacked simply because they

[50] *Metcalf Report*, p. 16.

[51] See San Francisco *Argonaut*, Dec. 15, 1906.

[52] *Metcalf Report*, pp. 12–16.

[53] An attack was made in one instance upon a group of Japanese Christians on their way to church. Early in 1907 a Japanese was arrested for carrying a club and was fined, apparently with unnecessary severity, the sum of sixty dollars. In his defense he said, probably truthfully, that he carried this weapon because he had been frequently stoned. Kennan, *loc. cit.*, p. 246; San Francisco *Chronicle*, Feb. 13, 1907.

were Japanese. Metcalf was convinced that this activity against the Orientals was the result of a race hostility which had been inflamed by newspaper accounts of anti-Japanese meetings.[54]

The most unfortunate of these assaults were those upon the persons of two distinguished visiting scientists. Shortly after the earthquake the Japanese government sent Dr. F. Omori, of the Imperial University at Tokyo, an eminent seismologist, to make observations. He was accompanied by Professor T. Nakamura, professor of architecture in the same institution. Dr. Omori and his party were repeatedly stoned and otherwise annoyed while pursuing their investigations, the most serious demonstration occurring on June 9, 1906.[55] In May, 1906, Professor Nakamura was assaulted by hoodlums in Golden Gate Park, San Francisco, and on June 8, 1906, he was covered with dust and ashes thrown by boys while he was making observations in the burned district.[56] Early in June, 1906, Dr. Omori was again attacked, this time by a labor union man on the streets of Eureka, in northern California.[57] Such exhibitions as these, which undoubtedly were the results of race prejudice, would have been resented by the Japanese in any circumstances, but they seemed all the more inexcusable in view of the distinguished character of the visitors and the recent generosity of Japan toward the unfortunate city. Japanese in public life expressed profound displeasure, and a press dispatch from Kobe reported that public opinion regarding the United States was undergoing a marked change as a

54 *Metcalf Report*, p. 16.
56 Kennan, *loc. cit.*, p. 246.
55 *Ibid.*, pp. 15, 38–39.
57 *Ibid.*; *Metcalf Report*, p. 15.

result of recent disturbances in California and elsewhere on the Pacific Coast.[58]

It is not to be assumed, however, that a majority of the people of San Francisco approved of these assaults. Boys and irresponsible young men, inflamed by the words of their elders, appear to have been responsible for most of them. Neither Dr. Omori nor Professor Nakamura made any formal complaint or sought any official recognition of the indignities they had suffered, but the Japanese consul brought the outrages to the attention of the San Francisco authorities. The postmaster of the city wrote a letter of apology to Dr. Omori inasmuch as several postal delivery boys had been recognized among his assailants. An apology was also forthcoming from the mayor of Eureka, who explained—Metcalf thought rather lamely—that the attack had grown out of labor difficulties.[59] The mayor of San Francisco and the governor of California likewise expressed their deep regrets in letters to Dr. Omori.[60] Even the San Francisco *Chronicle,* which was now witnessing some of the fruits of its intemperate campaign, deplored these unhappy developments.[61] In his biennial message to the legislature of California, on January 10, 1907, Governor Pardee stated that California deprecated indignities to Japanese and Chinese, just as the latter would deprecate them if they had occurred to Americans in their own countries, and he hoped "that

[58] *Japan Weekly Mail,* Nov. 3, 1906, p. 570; Sacramento *Union,* Oct. 17, 1906.

[59] *Metcalf Report,* pp. 15 ff. It was widely stated that Dr. Omori was mistaken in Eureka for a strike-breaker. Johnson, *op. cit.,* pp. 74–75.

[60] *Metcalf Report,* p. 39.

[61] San Francisco *Chronicle,* Dec. 20, 1906.

the Japanese and Chinese governments also know, that it is only the irresponsible and vicious who, in America, insult and injure the subjects of these two great nations. All good Americans frown upon such indecencies here . . . ."[62] Indeed, Metcalf was convinced after his investigation that, although California was in favor of the exclusion of coolies, the overwhelming sentiment of the state was for law and order and that the assaults on the Japanese were condemned by all respectable citizens.[63]

The Japanese in San Francisco were further annoyed by boycotts which the unions instituted against Japanese restaurants. Before the earthquake there had been only eight of these establishments which served food to Americans, but following the fire about thirty of them opened and for a while did an excellent business among the workingmen engaged in rebuilding. As early as June 25, 1906, the Exclusion League protested that many union men were patronizing these places, and it began a vigorous campaign against them.[64] From October 3 to October 24, 1906, as a consequence of this feeling, the Cooks' and Waiters' Union, assisted and encouraged by the Carpenters', Masons', and Cabmen's unions, maintained a

[62] *Assembly Journal* (California), 1907, p. 73.

[63] *Metcalf Report*, p. 16. San Francisco officials promised Metcalf that they would do everything within their power to protect the Japanese. The *Chronicle* asserted that no member of any race was surer of official protection than the Japanese. It did not want them to come in masses but while they were in America they were entitled to protection and decent treatment. This they were getting. San Francisco *Chronicle*, Nov. 8, 1906.

[64] Buell, *loc. cit.*, p. 621. The whites claimed that the Japanese undersold them and drove them out of business. Devlin to Bonaparte (copy), Nov. 23, 1906, in file 1797, Division of Communications and Records, Department of State. All file numbers hereafter cited, unless otherwise indicated, refer to this source.

boycott against the Japanese.[65] The official Japanese conception of the subsequent disorders is best illustrated by the statement of Ambassador Aoki to Secretary of State Root, dated October 25, 1906. Aoki had obtained his information from the Japanese consul in San Francisco.

The restaurants which have thus been made victims of boycott, are ones in which the food served is not cooked in the Japanese style but the cuisine is entirely European or American, although the proprietors and cooks and other employees are exclusively Japanese. Those restaurants are thus patronized no less by Americans than by the Japanese and other foreign residents of San Francisco. The boycotters linger about the restaurants and accost all customers who approach, giving them small match-boxes bearing the words "White men and women patronize your own race." When this is not effective, they frequently stand in front of the doors of the restaurants so as to bar the entrance and prevent customers from going in.

On a number of occasions the windows of the restaurants have been stoned, and groups of boycotters have gathered about the entrance in a threatening manner so as to frighten the customers away. A case which occurred on the 18th instant, and in which a Japanese restaurant trading under the name of "Golden Bay Restaurant" . . . . was a victim of organized attack, has attracted particular attention owing to the size of the crowd which assembled to enforce the boycott on the premises of that restaurant. In that case, an American customer, who had just finished his lunch and came out from the restaurant, was attacked no less than the proprietor himself.[66]

The boycotting of the Japanese restaurants was less clearly a case of racial discrimination than the numerous

---

[65] For example, Branch A, Amalgamated Society of Carpenters and Joiners, at a meeting held on October 22, 1906, agreed that a fine of $14 (the maximum allowed by the laws of the society) should be imposed upon every member who directly or indirectly patronized a concern conducted by or employing Japanese or other Mongolians. San Francisco *Chronicle*, Oct. 23, 1906.

[66] Aoki to Root, Oct. 25, 1906, in file 1797.

cases of assault. For the previous five or six years, as Metcalf pointed out, there had been boycotts of non-union white restaurants by union men and their families in San Francisco, Oakland, and other cities in California. These boycotts had been maintained for weeks at a time and had not infrequently been accompanied by acts of violence.[67] It was the contention of the San Franciscans that many more white than Oriental restaurants were thus affected, and in a large number of these cases there were grounds for contending that the Japanese were being discriminated against not because they were Japanese but because they were non-union.[68] Yet however circumspectly the adults may have conducted themselves, the numerous occasions when stones were thrown by boys and young men, to say nothing of other demonstrations, were clearly manifestations of race feeling.

During the first seven months of 1906 there occurred several developments in a larger theater which had no little effect in preparing the San Franciscans for drastic action. On July 16 and 17, 1906, the American authorities on St. Paul Island, in repelling a series of raids on the seal rookeries by Japanese poachers, killed five of them, wounded two, and captured twelve.[69] Outside of San Francisco this unfortunate incident does not appear to have measurably aroused public opinion in the United States against Japan.[70] It was readily recognized, as

67 *Metcalf Report,* p. 11.

68 *Argonaut,* San Francisco, Jan. 5, 1907.

69 For an official account of these raids, see report of Edwin Sims, solicitor of the Department of Commerce and Labor, who was sent to St. Paul Island to investigate the situation. *House Documents,* 59 Cong., 2 sess., no. 251.

70 Boston *Evening Transcript,* Oct. 25, 1906.

Roosevelt pointed out to his friend Baron Kaneko, that such piratical forays were not representative of or sanctioned by the Japanese people.[71] The Japanese government certainly had no desire to defend the work of these outlaws, and, after the usual representations from the Department of State, provided assurances that Japan would take all practicable measures to prevent a recurrence of the outrage.[72] The incident, then, did not become even a minor diplomatic problem. Nevertheless, it is significant to note, particularly in connection with the subsequent world cruise of the American fleet, that Roosevelt's firm belief in the wisdom of keeping his powder dry led him to take every precaution. On August 10, 1906, he wrote to Secretary of the Navy Charles J. Bonaparte that, although he did not for a moment anticipate trouble from the Japanese over the poachers, he felt that the navy should have possible contingencies clearly in view. He was particularly concerned over the Asiatic fleet, which was too weak to resist attack but too strong to throw away, and he was anxious that the General Board should be ready with advice in the event of hostilities. His own idea was that in case of war the Asiatic squadron should retreat hastily across the Pacific and join the main fleet,

[71] After the segregation of the Japanese children in the San Francisco schools had been ordered, Roosevelt wrote: "The action of these people in San Francisco no more represents American sentiment as a whole than the action of the Japanese seal pirates last summer represents Japanese sentiment." Roosevelt to Kaneko, Oct. 26, 1906, Roosevelt Papers.

[72] See Roosevelt's annual message, *Congressional Record*, 59 Cong., 2 sess., p. 34. Aoki was reported as having said that the Japanese poachers were clearly in the wrong, but that there was some doubt as to whether or not the punishment inflicted had been unnecessarily severe. Boston *Evening Transcript*, Oct. 25, 1906. See also San Francisco *Chronicle*, Oct. 25, Dec. 9, 1906; London *Times*, Oct. 26, 1906.

either in the Atlantic or at San Francisco.[73] These views were naturally kept secret, but Roosevelt did give notice that he would send a warship to Alaska waters during the coming summer.[74]

However indifferent the rest of the United States may have been to this incident, it served further to inflame the minds of many San Franciscans, especially when reports began to come in describing the barbarity attending the work of the poachers. Subsequent investigations showed that most of the seals killed were females, that many of them apparently were skinned while alive, and that a number of them were found half-skinned and still living.[75] It was not unnatural, then, that the anti-Japanese element in San Francisco should have professed to see in this incident confirmation of its views regarding the lawlessness and general undesirability of the Japanese. The San Francisco *Chronicle* stated baldly: "The lower classes of Japanese . . . . are born thieves."[76]

Further developments during the months preceding October, 1906, had a direct or indirect bearing on the state of mind that was responsible for the action of the San Francisco Board of Education. During the first six months of 1906 the excess of Japanese arrivals over departures in San Francisco alone was 5,772, or almost

[73] Roosevelt to Bonaparte, Aug. 10, 1906, Roosevelt Papers.

[74] Roosevelt to H. G. Otis, Jan. 8, 1907, Roosevelt Papers. In this same letter, written after the school incident, Roosevelt added: " . . . . I served notice on Japan that where she did what was wrong we would instantly resent it. On the other hand, where we have been wrong I shall do my best to see that we right the wrong."

[75] See Roosevelt's description in his annual message of 1906. *Congressional Record,* 59 Cong., 2 sess., p. 34.

[76] Quoted in Buell, *loc. cit.,* p. 621.

1,000 a month. Annoying, also, was the fact, which was becoming more and more evident, that Japan was preparing to exploit Korea and Manchuria without much consideration for American business interests. Then, events of the fall of 1906 further indicated that the feeling against the Japanese was not confined to San Francisco. Into the statewide political campaign which was then being waged was injected the Japanese issue, and it proved to be a popular one. The Democrats and the Republicans of California, meeting in their respective conventions, declared unmistakably for Japanese exclusion. And on September 16, 1906, the Exclusion League held a mass meeting in San Francisco which was addressed by the candidates for Congress, and it was announced, probably with exaggeration, that the League membership had reached 78,500 and that its program had been endorsed by organizations numbering four and one-half million members.[77] Exaggeration or no exaggeration, the stage was obviously set for serious trouble, and that trouble came when the San Francisco School Board, in October, 1906, passed its famous segregation order.

[77] *Ibid.*, pp. 621–22.

CHAPTER II

The San Francisco School Order of 1906

". . . . the labor unions bid fair to embroil us with Japan."—Roosevelt to Lodge, October 27, 1906

EVENTS were now moving rapidly to a climax. On August 23, 1906, the Exclusion League again made representations to the Board of Education, on this occasion protesting against the alleged crowding of white children in the schools by the Japanese. The Board replied that every effort was being made to seat the whites first but that a lack of funds prevented the erection of a separate building for the Japanese.[1] Then it was that the Chinese school, which had been rebuilt after the fire, provided the Board with an opportunity to take the action that it had long been contemplating. When this school was reopened, fewer Chinese children enrolled than had previously done so.[2] There was room, apparently, for the ninety-three Japanese pupils elsewhere in attendance at the public schools of the city. Accordingly, at its meeting of October 11, 1906, the Board passed the following resolution, which was soon to produce international repercussions:

[1] Butzbach, "Segregation of Orientals in San Francisco Schools," p. 24, citing Board of Education minutes for Aug. 23, 1906.

[2] San Francisco *Chronicle*, Oct. 30, 1906. Dr. Jordan learned that when the teacher of this school found she had so few pupils she asked the school authorities to transfer to her jurisdiction those Japanese pupils living in the adjoining district. She appears to have feared that she was in danger of losing her position. The Board then decided upon complete segregation. (Undated memorandum in Jordan Papers, Stanford University. Confirmation of this interpretation is lacking.)

Resolved, That in accordance with Article X, section 1662, of the school law of California, principals are hereby directed to send all Chinese, Japanese, or Korean children to the Oriental Public School, situated on the south side of Clay street, between Powell and Mason streets, on and after Monday, October 15, 1906.[3]

It is of the first importance to observe what the four leading San Francisco newspapers had to say immediately following the passage of the resolution. Their accounts not only provide an index to public interest in the matter but also shed light upon the reasons that the Board gave at the time, as distinguished from reasons given later, for its action. The San Francisco *Bulletin* did not mention the subject at all until October 18, seven days later, when the incident had become an international issue. The *Examiner* presented a brief statement of the resolution, with no explanation for its passage, on page eleven of the next morning's edition, October 12. On this same day the *Call,* likewise on page eleven, printed a bare account of the Board's action, and added: "The resolution is the result of an agitation that has been waged against the intermingling of the Asiatic races with the Caucasian. Director Altmann has made a study of conditions and he is determined that the races shall be kept separate." On October 12 the *Chronicle,* as befitted its interest in the subject, published the fullest account, but even this column appeared on its last page. The Board felt, it was stated, that the pupils could obtain better instruction if housed separately, and that it was for the best interests of the schools that such a policy be adopted. The reporter for the *Chronicle,* strangely enough, was the only one of the

[3] *Metcalf Report,* p. 3.

four who remarked that the resolution was more than a purely local matter, for he observed that the opposition of the Japanese, Korean, and Chinese consuls might be aroused "and questions may arise which will call for an inquiry by the Department of State." At the time none of the four newspapers commented editorially on the action of the Board.

The Board of Education consistently maintained that in passing the order it had acted in good faith. It is difficult to associate such a quality with a part of a municipal administration so notoriously corrupt, but in all fairness it must be noted that something can be said in support of this contention. The Board repeatedly asserted that its action was not sudden or unexpected, as indeed it was not. In April, 1905, as has been shown, the Board asked for an appropriation for a Japanese school, and on May 6, 1905, it stated its position in a resolution. Again, when the budget was being prepared in 1906, the Board requested funds for separate housing, but before the Board of Supervisors had time to consider the matter the earthquake came. The Board further contended that it had acted because of the numerous requests that had come in from parents who for some reason or other did not want their children to sit in the same room with Japanese, especially adults. As Alfred Roncovieri, San Francisco superintendent of schools, later insisted: "It was purely a local regulation for the good of the San Francisco children, whose parents urged us to action and which was much easier to enforce after the fire than before."[4] Further-

4 William Inglis, "The Width of a School Bench," *Harper's Weekly,* Jan. 19, 1907, pp. 83–84. On the other hand, Colonel John P. Irish, a

more, the Board permitted those Japanese who were about to graduate to finish their term in the schools which they were attending in order that they might go on to high school without interruption. And when the matter of distance came up, which will be discussed later, the Board informed the Japanese consul that an Oriental primary school would be established elsewhere in the city so that the children of tender years would not have to go inconveniently or dangerously far.[5] There were many who believed that this statement of the Board was but an idle gesture, but proof of such a contention is lacking.[6]

So much, then, for the evidence in support of the Board's good faith. It now becomes necessary to analyze a number of so-called reasons for the resolution, some of which were obviously the product of rationalization and some of which were plain excuses. Throughout the controversy the Board stoutly maintained that it had acted in pursuance of section 1662 of the school law of California, and that the provisions of that statute were mandatory.[7] Representative Hayes, of California, to say nothing of others, upheld this view on the floor of Congress.[8] If it

former San Francisco editor and a politician of considerable influence, wrote in January, 1907: "I state as a fact that no teacher nor school principal ever protested against the Japanese pupils in the San Francisco schools. I state as a fact that no oral or written protest was ever made against the Japanese pupils by the parents of white pupils in those schools." Quoted in Johnson, *Discrimination against Japanese in California*, p. 23. This is a sweeping statement, obviously difficult to prove. Metcalf was later informed that when these complaints became known to the Japanese some of the older pupils were withdrawn from the primary grades. *Metcalf Report*, p. 4.

[5] San Francisco *Chronicle*, Dec. 6, 1906.

[6] See San Francisco correspondent of London *Times*, Dec. 20, 1906.

[7] San Francisco *Chronicle*, Oct. 30, Nov. 10, 1906.

[8] *Congressional Record*, 59 Cong., 2 sess., p. 1581.

was true that the Board had no volition in the matter, the blame for its action could well be laid at the door of the state legislature, which had passed the statute in question. Reference to the law itself will clear up this point:

> Trustees shall have the power to exclude children of filthy or vicious habits, or children suffering from contagious or infectious diseases, and also to establish separate schools for Indian children and for children of Mongolian or Chinese descent. When such separate schools are established, Indian, Chinese, or Mongolian children must not be admitted into any other school . . . .[9]

Even to the layman it is evident that the Board—and that body must have known this—was under no obligation to provide for a separate school unless it wanted to; but once the school was established the Oriental children had to attend it. In this sense alone the law was mandatory. A recognition of this fact was seen in an attempt in the state senate, on January 21, 1907, to amend the statute so as to make it mandatory in the first instance.[10] Furthermore, the original law had been passed many years earlier to deal with the Chinese (or Mongolian) children, and the courts had not yet decided whether or not Japanese were Mongolians. In fact, a good case could be made out in support of the contention that they were not.[11]

An argument used with considerable effect, before and after the passing of the resolution, was that the Japanese pupils were crowding the whites out of certain schools. Several months after the segregation order, Mayor Schmitz was quoted as having said that this was the only

---

[9] *School Law of California* (Sacramento, 1902), p. 37.
[10] Johnson, *op. cit.*, p. 22.
[11] See *Japan Weekly Mail*, No. 4, 1906, p. 571.

reason for the action of the Board.[12] The *Chronicle* did not hesitate to say that the Japanese had no right to deprive native white children of their rights;[13] and the *Bulletin* asserted, "American mothers and fathers have made stubborn efforts to keep the Japanese children from crowding their own boys and girls out of their seats in the overflowing public schools, and they have at length succeeded. . . . ."[14] But when the facts were made known in the Metcalf report, it was discovered that only ninety-three Japanese children, twenty-five of whom were American citizens, were enrolled in twenty-three San Francisco schools on October 11, 1906. It was unfair, however, to point out, as certain commentators did, that the Japanese children averaged a little more than one pupil to a school building (there were seventy-two San Francisco schools in all), for nineteen of the group attended one grammar school, and twenty-three one primary school.[15] It is quite possible that in several of these already crowded buildings the addition of even two or three Japanese children may have worked some hardship, but it is evident that the overcrowding problem was greatly exaggerated.

Another argument, equally specious, was that a considerable number of the Japanese who crowded into the public schools were young men, and that it was highly undesirable that white girls of tender years should sit

[12] San Francisco *Chronicle*, Feb. 12, 1907. It will be remembered that the crowding argument was presented in the state senate in March, 1905, and undoubtedly it had something to do with the creation of a hostile state of mind in San Francisco.

[13] San Francisco *Chronicle*, May 7, 1905.

[14] San Francisco *Bulletin*, Oct. 18, 1906.

[15] *Metcalf Report*, pp. 17–18; George Kennan, "The Japanese in the San Francisco Schools," *Outlook*, June 1, 1907, p. 249.

beside them in the classrooms.[16] It is probably fair to say that the members of the Board most frequently justified their action by asserting that a number of parents had written to them objecting to the presence of adult Japanese in the schools.[17] So strongly did the dramatic possibilities of this argument appeal to the local press, that the most obvious exaggerations resulted. The *Examiner* reported, probably incorrectly, that the superintendent of schools had said that ninety-five per cent of the Japanese were young men;[18] and the *Bulletin* echoed this charge when it stated that they were "nearly all young men . . . ."[19] Even more specifically the *Call* asserted that "they were not children in the true sense" but ranged "in age from fifteen to twenty-five."[20] These exaggerations were printed elsewhere in California and in the East as true, and it is important to note that much of the strong public support which San Francisco received in California and in the other Western states was probably due to convictions resulting from a reading of these false statements.[21]

The merits of the over-age argument may be briefly considered. It was admittedly undesirable, from a good

16 The impression frequently given by the word "beside" was that whites and Japanese were forced to share the same seats. Dr. Jordan learned that grown Japanese boys were brought over from the upper classes and seated in the kindergarten, where photographs of them were taken and used by the Board. Undated memorandum, Jordan Papers, Stanford University.

17 See San Francisco *Chronicle*, Oct. 30, Nov. 6, 1906.

18 Quoted in Kennan, *loc. cit.*, p. 248.

19 San Francisco *Bulletin*, Dec. 6, 1906.

20 San Francisco *Call*, Nov. 13, 1906.

21 Metcalf reported that he found sentiment in the state very strong against seating adult Japanese with white pupils. *Metcalf Report*, p. 6.

many points of view, that adults and children should sit in the same classroom. Metcalf readily acknowledged this. But it would have been a simple matter, as was later done, for the Board to establish a maximum age limit for all nationalities, thereby making segregation unnecessary. The facts in regard to this situation are clear. Only thirty-three Japanese in the San Francisco schools were over fifteen years of age, and the two oldest were twenty. Furthermore, twenty-eight of the ninety-three pupils were females; and in no case was it reported that a Japanese boy sat in the same seat with a white girl.[22] Nevertheless, since a number of the older Japanese attended the lower grades, it is not difficult to understand why the parents of the San Francisco white children, already inflamed over the immigration problem, should have envisaged the worst possible results from these contacts.

It is probably true that parents objected to over-age Japanese in the schools not so much because they were adults as because these older Japanese pupils were liable to have all the vices commonly attributed to their elders. The press of San Francisco regarded the Japanese, particularly when compared with his Chinese brother, as tricky and dishonest. The constantly recurring canard that only Chinese were employed in Japan in places of responsibility was repeated, and the *Chronicle* stated baldly that "there is not the slightest trust to be placed in one of them [Japanese]."[23] Attention was directed to legalized prostitution in Japan, and it was widely rumored that the Japanese children carried loathsome diseases to school.[24] The

[22] *Ibid.*, pp. 4 ff.   [23] San Francisco *Chronicle*, Nov. 14, 1906.
[24] *Argonaut*, San Francisco, Dec. 20, 1906, p. 340.

Call regarded the public schools "as an extension of the home" and remarked that "Californians do not desire to meet the Japanese or the Chinese on equal terms in the home . . . ."[25] The *Chronicle* observed editorially:

> Whatever the status of the Japanese children while still young and uncontaminated, as they grow older they acquire the distinctive character, habits, and moral standards of their race, which are abhorrent to our people. We object to them in the familiar intercourse of common school life as we would object to any other moral poison.[26]

The stories of disease, immorality, and misconduct were effectively disproved during the investigation that followed the order. The testimony of the teachers as to the exemplary conduct of the Japanese pupils and their general desirability was so overwhelming as to banish all doubts on that score. One teacher, in fact, thought that the Japanese were a good influence because their studiousness and perfect decorum set a model for the white children to follow. Even the president of the Board of Education and the superintendent of schools testified as to the unobjectionable deportment of the Japanese pupils.[27] In fact, not a single dissenting voice on this point appears to have been raised by anyone in a position to know what he was discussing.

It is evident, thus far, that the state law under which the Board had acted was not mandatory, that the Japanese were not crowding the whites out of the public schools, that only an inconsiderable number of the Japa-

25 San Francisco *Call,* Nov. 15, 1906.
26 San Francisco *Chronicle,* Nov. 6, 1906.
27 For a discussion of this point see Kennan, *loc. cit.,* p. 250.

nese were adults, and that, far from being diseased, immoral, and otherwise undesirable, they were generally regarded as model pupils. At the time it took action the Board may have thought that the reasons which it gave were valid, but this explanation does not seem a sound one, for that body undoubtedly was in possession of enough of the facts to know how flimsy were the grounds for such charges. The parents of San Francisco, however, may have been sufficiently misinformed to believe that a real menace existed, and this probably accounts for the pressure, if any, they brought to bear on the Board. But even this interpretation strikes one as inadequate. Other reasons must be sought.

In October, 1906, San Francisco was wallowing in a cesspool of corruption seldom, if ever, equaled in the none too savory history of the American city. A correspondent of the London *Times,* then on the ground, wrote that if one-quarter of the current reports could be believed, the state of things was worse than any other American municipality had ever experienced.[28] The mayor, Eugene Schmitz, then absent in Europe, and his henchman, Abe Ruef, had both been indicted by a grand jury for extortion shortly before the passing of the segregation order. It is significant that the Board of Education was composed of men every one of whom owed his appointment to this corrupt régime, and the entire body was admittedly but a rubber stamp for the Schmitz political machine.

It was not unnatural, then, that the segregation order should have been interpreted in certain quarters as an attempt on the part of the municipal administration to stir

[28] London *Times,* Nov. 24, 1906; see also issue of Dec. 20, 1906.

up a cloud of dust that would postpone or avert the day of reckoning.[29] More than one writer since then has credited this explanation. But such a theory, tempting though it is, encounters several serious obstacles. In the first place, if we may judge from the inconspicuous place, if any, accorded the action of the Board in the San Francisco newspapers, few people believed that the order would create a storm, let alone one violent enough to enable Schmitz and Ruef to escape their prosecutors. The rank and file of the San Franciscans, as will be shown, were indifferent to the order, and it is difficult to believe that the Board expected an uproar to follow its action. Moreover, Schmitz was in Europe at the time, and the net had not yet begun to tighten sufficiently to cause the administration any apparent disquietude.[30] Even more damaging to the cloud-of-dust theory is the fact that the Board had put itself on record as favoring segregation long before the scandals developed. Whatever the motives of the Board, then, there seems little reason for disagreeing with the conclusion of the San Francisco *Bulletin* that the order was passed without "any foresight of the uproar that the act would cause."[31] Perhaps no other group in

---

[29] San Francisco *Chronicle*, Oct. 27, 1906.

[30] Not until October 20, 1906, did it become evident that the prosecution was to be formidable. On that day the district attorney appointed Francis J. Heney as an assistant in the prosecution, and on the same day it was announced that the famous William J. Burns had been enlisted to dig up the evidence. San Francisco *Bulletin*, Oct. 21, 1906.

[31] *Ibid.*, Feb. 1, 1907. The *Chronicle* noted that when the order was passed "there was not any idea that it would lead to international discussion." San Francisco *Chronicle*, Oct. 30, 1906. Congressman Hayes, of California, said that if the Board had known that it was going to insult a foreign nation it would never have passed the order. *Ibid.*, Feb. 12, 1907.

the city was more surprised at the result than the Board itself.[32]

Another widely accepted explanation of the segregation order was that it was a political maneuver to be viewed in the light of the impending elections.[33] A correspondent of the London *Times* hastened out to San Francisco and reported:

The whole agitation against the Japanese here is causeless, artificial, and wicked. Coming here with an open mind on the question, and honestly endeavoring to learn the truth, I found that almost every one with whom I talked gave a different explanation of the situation. The truth is that the people have been worked up to a high pitch of excitement by politicians who believed that by raising the Japanese issue they could increase their own popularity.[34]

A correspondent of the *Japan Weekly Mail* reported substantially the same thing, remarking that every year or so the Japanese in San Francisco had to fight the "peanut politicians" who sought to curry favor with the laboring class by raising this ever-popular issue.[35] George Kennan, the well-known Russo-Japanese War correspondent, investigated the situation in person and concluded that the Exclusion League and the labor leaders saw in the school question an excellent opportunity for exciting prejudice against the Japanese and securing political support for

---

[32] The superintendent of schools was quoted as saying: "We had no conception when we endeavored to force this rule that it would cause any national commotion. It was purely a local regulation for the good of San Francisco children, whose parents urged us to action and which was much easier to enforce after the fire than before." Inglis, *loc. cit.*, p. 83.

[33] See *Literary Digest*, Nov. 3, 1906, p. 621.

[34] London *Times*, Dec. 8, 1906.

[35] *Japan Weekly Mail*, Nov. 17, 1906, p. 632.

themselves.[36] Later, when the Board of Education showed a willingness to recede from its position, certain observers in the East professed to see in this change of heart a lack of sincerity and further evidence that the whole movement was agitation for purely political purposes.[37]

But this interpretation leaves out of consideration several factors of prime importance. If the school resolution had been passed for immediate political gain it would doubtless have been given what it did not receive—effective publicity. As far back as 1901, it will be remembered, the Labor Party had put itself on record as favoring segregation, and the fulfillment of this pledge in 1906 can hardly be regarded as a sudden maneuver designed to carry the election of that fall. Yet if the political explanation is viewed apart from any immediate gain, it begins to take on a certain degree of plausibility. Segregation was undoubtedly approved, although perhaps not actively supported, by the rank and file of the Labor Party, and the municipal administration may well have had in mind, as a secondary consideration, strengthening itself with the electorate. In the words of John P. Irish, a prominent San Franciscan, the order could be interpreted "as a part of its [the Labor Party's] policy to make itself solid with the vote which put it in power."[38]

Another explanation which contained a large measure of truth, but not the whole truth, attributed the resolution to the influence of the labor unions in San Francisco. The shortage of living accommodations since the earthquake

---

[36] Kennan, *loc. cit.*, p. 251.
[37] *Literary Digest*, Feb. 23, 1907, p. 276.
[38] Irish to Root, Oct. 26, 1906, in 1797.

had forced rents up, and labor had girded itself to raise wages correspondingly.[39] Economic conditions were at best chaotic, and the unions, which had never evidenced any love for the Japanese, were in an ugly temper. The London *Times* correspondent wrote that "the Japanese situation in San Francisco is intimately connected with Labour Unionism. I asked a Labour Union leader what would happen if, say, a thousand Japanese were set to work helping clear away the *débris*. He replied, 'A thousand murders.'" And yet, continued this writer, San Francisco was in dire need of labor, skilled and unskilled.[40] The *Japan Weekly Mail* remarked that there could "be no doubt that the labour element is at the bottom of the whole agitation," and later added that the school question had the labor problem "for its main if not its sole basis."[41] Even President Roosevelt accepted this interpretation, for late in October, 1906, he wrote that "the labor unions bid fair to embroil us with Japan."[42]

For several reasons the labor union explanation is not altogether satisfying. Jerome Hart, editor of the *Argonaut*, a San Francisco weekly which was bitterly anti-union, wrote: "The labor unions have nothing whatever to do with the school question. The crisis there was brought about by the objections of the parents to the presence of adult Japanese in schools with their young children. The

[39] Even white laborers from other parts of the United States who had their union cards were in some cases refused permission to work. See London *Times*, Oct. 30, Dec. 10, 1906; *Literary Digest*, Oct. 27, 1906, p. 572.

[40] London *Times*, Dec. 10, 1906.

[41] *Japan Weekly Mail*, Oct. 27, 1906, p. 543; Feb. 9, 1907, p. 136.

[42] Roosevelt to Lodge, Oct. 27, 1906, Roosevelt Papers.

action of these parents had nothing to do with labor unions."[43] The *Chronicle,* by no means a union organ, supported the action of the Labor Party Board of Education with great enthusiasm, and regretted that the impression would go out through the East that only labor was opposed to the presence of the Japanese in California.[44] The other three leading dailies of San Francisco, the *Examiner,* the *Call,* and the *Bulletin,* although flaying the Labor Party administration, energetically defended the action of the Board of Education.

To brush aside all arguments, excuses, and half-truths, it seems clear at this distance that the basic reason for segregation was race prejudice. Unquestionably the action of the Board was discriminatory and the Japanese as a race were ordered set apart because the white parents of San Francisco did not want their children to associate with them. The *Chronicle* let the cat out of the bag when it remarked, "Just now our race feeling has shown itself in the provision that the children of the races shall be kept separate in the schools."[45] The *Call* was even more outspoken: "We regard the public schools as part of the home, and we are not willing that our children should meet Asiatics in intimate association. That is 'race prejudice,' and we stand by it."[46] Edward J. Livernash, who had

[43] *Argonaut,* San Francisco, Jan. 5, 1907, p. 355. Several weeks later Hart wrote: "Most of the labor unions were ignorant of the fact that the Japanese children were in the public schools with the white children. Had they been conversant with that fact, they would beyond question have protested long before." Jerome Hart, "The Oriental Problem, as the Coast Sees It," *World's Work,* XIII (Mar., 1907), 8692.

[44] San Francisco *Chronicle,* Dec. 23, 1906.

[45] *Ibid.,* Nov. 11, 1906.

[46] San Francisco *Call,* Dec. 1, 1906.

recently completed a term in Congress as a member of the
Labor Party, wrote in February, 1907:

No matter what is said or unsaid at this stage of the case, it
was generally known here [San Francisco] that the principle on
which the Japanese were thus excluded had no relation to the
state of their knowledge of English, and not much to their age,
but a very great deal to this—that they were ASIATICS, and because of RACE should be educated apart from the children of our
own people. This was not meaning that they were INFERIOR, but
that they were DIFFERENT.[47]

The Japanese children were set apart because the whites
were prejudiced against them, and the root of this prejudice, at least in San Francisco, appears to have been the
belief that coolie labor was thwarting the work of the
unions and lowering the American standard of living.
Intermittently since 1900 the unions had been working for
exclusion, and part and parcel of their campaign was the
cry that the Japanese should be segregated in the schools.
The *Coast Seamen's Journal,* a labor organ, stated frankly
that "the school question is a mere incident in our campaign for Japanese Exclusion."[48] The San Francisco
Chronicle declared that the controversy was worse than a

[47] San Francisco *Bulletin,* Feb. 23, 1907.

[48] *Coast Seamen's Journal,* Feb. 20, 1907, quoted in Ruth Haines
Thomson, "Events Leading to the Order to Segregate Japanese Pupils
in the San Francisco Public Schools" (unpublished doctoral dissertation,
Stanford University, 1931), p. 133. The Washington correspondent of
the London *Times* (Feb. 11, 1907) remarked that the "school question
is undoubtedly a secondary matter." Dr. Jordan wrote that the school
question was "a side issue of the greater one of immigration." Boston
Evening Transcript, Dec. 29, 1906. Mayor Schmitz stated that the Californians did not "care a rap about the school question, but were opposed
to the admission of coolies." San Francisco *Chronicle,* Feb. 12, 1907.
The *Chronicle,* striking back at its Eastern critics, remarked that "thus
far and with some reason" they had connected the school affair with
California's desire for a complete exclusion of coolies. *Ibid.,* Nov. 8,
1906.

school problem—it was one involving the civilization of
the Pacific Coast.[49] Early in 1907, this newspaper put the
whole matter in a nutshell when it said that what the Coast
was after was the exclusion of coolie labor, and with that
demand satisfied the school question would take care of
itself, for no more adult Orientals would be seeking admission to the public schools. The *Chronicle* concluded,
"There would be no fuss made about the small number of
Japanese children here, if assured that the State would not
be overrun."[50] And five months after the event Roosevelt
testified in support of this view:

> I was informed very early, by men professing to speak for,
> and as I have every reason to suppose actually speaking for, the
> labor organizations of San Francisco, that the real objection was
> to the incoming of Japanese laborers—this meaning of course, to
> the incoming of the great mass of Japanese. They asserted un-
> equivocally that the trouble was not with the attendance of the
> Japanese at the schools; that this was merely a symptom of the
> irritation. They exprest their entire willingness to support any
> arrangement which would secure the exclusion of all Japanese
> laborers.[51]

It is clear, then, that the school incident may be regarded
as intimately associated with the campaign for Japanese
exclusion, and subordinate to it. This, rather than the
excuses advanced at the time and later by the Board of
Education and its supporters, was the real source of the
difficulty. It would doubtless be going too far to say that
the Board acted in order to create a situation that would
force the federal government to take steps in the direction
of exclusion, for such an interpretation would presuppose

[49] San Francisco *Chronicle*, Feb. 14, 1907.   [50] *Ibid.*, Feb. 1, 1907.
[51] Roosevelt to Gillett, Mar. 11, 1907, Roosevelt Papers.

that this body expected an uproar to follow its action—
and it is clear that the Board was not prepared for the
violent discussion that ensued. But it is probably true, as
Roosevelt later wrote in his *Autobiography*, that this action was taken "to show . . . . disapproval of the Japanese coming into the State. . . . ."[52] It was an attempt
to put the Japanese in his place, even as the Chinese had
long before and without audible protest been put in his.
Excluding the Japanese child from the same school with
the white was certainly approaching the problem of excluding coolie labor from the wrong end. Nevertheless,
illogical though it may have been, segregation set in train
a series of events which in a short time brought to the
Pacific Coast its first effective exclusion of Japanese.

[52] Theodore Roosevelt, *An Autobiography* (New York, 1916), p. 393.

CHAPTER III

The International Crisis of 1906

"I am being horribly bothered about the Japanese business. The infernal fools in California . . . . insult the Japanese recklessly and in the event of war it will be the Nation as a whole which will pay the consequences."— Roosevelt to Kermit Roosevelt, October 27, 1906

THERE IS no evidence that anyone connected with the passing of the school order entertained the thought that Japan would take serious offense at what was clearly discriminatory action. Why the Board of Education could not have foreseen that this proud and sensitive people, recently emerged from a victorious war, would rise up in resentment is a question which cannot be definitely answered. Perhaps the parochial nature of the problem, the small number of children involved, and the often demonstrated capacity of the Chinese to accept similar discriminations, to say nothing of indignities, without effective protest may suggest the correct answer. But even if the Board had anticipated some international friction—and a member or two may have glimpsed the future dimly—there is no reason to believe, especially in the light of later developments, that it would have done differently.

The order was not passed, however, without efforts on the part of the Japanese consul in San Francisco to prevent it. When he discovered the purpose of the school authorities, he remonstrated verbally; and when the Board acted in spite of his representations, he immediately lodged a formal written protest.[1] In addition, he urged the Japanese children to refrain from attending the so-called Oriental school—an injunction which they faithfully observed.[2] On October 18, 1906, the Board permitted an attorney for Consul Uyeno, as well as other persons interested in the Japanese, to appear before it and present arguments for rescinding the order. Mr. G. Ikeda, speaking for the consul, directed attention to the hardship the order would work on the small children, who would have to walk many miles through falling ruins, and he stated bluntly that if the order was persisted in he would carry the case into the courts.[3] After being advised that the Board would not reverse its decision, Uyeno wrote to that body on October 23, 1906, and informed it flatly that the plan that had been suggested for establishing a special school for the smaller Japanese children nearer their places of residence failed to remove the more serious objection that the order was "a species of discrimination which is offensive to the Japanese national spirit."[4]

Little notice was taken of the segregation resolution in the San Francisco press, and consequently none in newspapers elsewhere in the United States; but the news was quickly sent on to Japan by interested persons. Mr. G. Ikeda, secretary of the Japanese Association of America, promptly communicated, as he himself later testified, with "the papers throughout Japan."[5] The parents of some of

---

[1] *Japan Weekly Mail,* Oct. 27, 1906, p. 543.
[2] San Francisco *Chronicle,* Oct. 18, 1906.
[3] *Ibid.,* Oct. 19, 1906.　　　　　[4] *Ibid.,* Oct. 25, 1906.
[5] Interview quoted in San Francisco *Call,* Feb. 1, 1907.

the children affected immediately sent cables to the home-
land newspapers, appealing to them to arouse public opinion in their behalf. It must be noted, however, that many
of the statements which first reached Japan regarding the
situation were greatly exaggerated if not actually false.
The *Japan Weekly Mail* reported that the expulsion "of
all Japanese children from the California schools" had
"created much excitement and indignation in Japan."[6]
The Japanese were soon to learn that the order affected
only San Francisco; but a great many of them continued
to believe that the segregation resolution, instead of establishing public school facilities elsewhere in the city, was
an exclusion order suddenly depriving Oriental pupils of
all educational privileges. Many Americans were to fall
into this same error.

Even if the action of the Board of Education had been
correctly reported, there doubtless would have been a serious outburst in Japan. The segregation order, as the Japanese themselves noted, came with poor grace after Japan's
generous outpouring to the earthquake sufferers of San
Francisco.[7] Then, too, the resolution was particularly
offensive to a people who not only are deeply attached to
children but who place a high value upon education. Most
severe of all, perhaps, was the blow to Japanese pride. The
recent exhilarating successes in the war with Russia, a
climax to a long struggle to secure international recognition on a basis of equality, had made Japan particularly
sensitive to anything savoring of discrimination. As the
London *Times* remarked editorially: "The insult was

6 *Japan Weekly Mail,* Oct. 27, 1906, p. 542.
7 *Ibid.,* Nov. 3, 1906, p. 570.

naturally felt very keenly in Japan, whose people justly consider that they have abundantly proved their right to equal treatment among civilized nations."[8]

The school order was passed on October 11, 1906, but the news leaked back to Japan so slowly that it was not until about October 20 that people there began to evidence nation-wide concern. The more excitable newspapers expressed themselves with great bitterness, and there swept over the country a wave of resentment against what was commonly spoken of as both a treaty violation and an insult at the hands of the United States. In obvious alarm the Tokyo correspondent of the New York *Sun* wired that during his nineteen years of residence in Japan he had "never seen the Japanese press so agitated against the Americans."[9] Even the *Jiji Shimpo,* an independent newspaper, perhaps the most influential journal in Japan,[10] was astounded, for it had not thought it possible that a country which prided itself on principles of freedom could be guilty of such action. The *Jiji* had for some time noticed evidences of anti-Japanese sentiment in the United States, but because of Japan's debt to America and the long-continued traditional friendship had refrained from comment. As long as this feeling was shown only by individuals, asserted the *Jiji,* their opinions could be ignored, but the latest act of San Francisco compelled Japan to protest.[11] The editor of the *Kokumin Shimbun,* a government organ, later stated in an interview that the segregation order had

[8] London *Times,* Oct. 30, 1906.

[9] Washington *Herald,* Oct. 22, 1906.

[10] The estimates of the newspapers that follow are those of Ambassador Luke Wright. Wright to Root, Oct. 22, 1906, in file 1797.

[11] Quoted in *Japan Weekly Mail,* Oct. 27, 1906, p. 542.

come like a thunderclap out of a blue sky. He had known that there was discontent in California over the coolie question, but he had not been prepared for the action of the Board of Education. It was like being suddenly slapped in the face by one's best friend. This made it hurt all the more. Japan was stunned by the attack; but she was sad rather than angry.[12] The *Hochi Shimbun,* which was often sensational, advocated reprisals;[13] and the *Mainichi Shimbun,* a reputable Tokyo journal owned and edited by one of the ablest members of the Diet, wrote in a most inflammatory vein:

The whole world knows that the poorly equipped army and navy of the United States are no match for our efficient army and navy. It will be an easy work to awake the United States from her dream of obstinacy when one of our great Admirals appears on the other side of the Pacific . . . . the present situation is such that the Japanese nation can not rest easy by relying only upon the wisdom and statesmanship of President Roosevelt. The Japanese nation must have a firm determination to chastise at any time the obstinate Americans.

Stand up, Japanese nation! Our countrymen have been HUMILIATED on the other side of the Pacific. Our poor boys and girls have been expelled from the public schools by the rascals of the United States, cruel and merciless like demons.

At this time we should be ready to give a blow to the United States. Yes, we should be ready to strike the Devil's head with an iron hammer for the sake of the world's civilization . . . . Why do we not insist on sending ships?[14]

12 Quoted by William Inglis, "Japan's Preference for Peace with America," *Harper's Weekly,* Mar. 2, 1907, p. 298.

13 Sacramento *Union,* Oct. 21, 1906.

14 Translated inclosure from issue of Oct. 22, 1906, in Wright to Root, dispatch number 90, in file 1797. A contributor to the Tokyo *Yorodzu* wrote that he had often wished that he were a mighty monarch and could blow up the whole city of San Francisco. Quoted in *Literary Digest,* Dec. 1, 1906, p. 797.

It would be a mistake, however, to assume that the Japanese press was preponderantly alarmist, particularly after it had recovered from the first shock. The passage just quoted is by no means representative but illustrates the jingo press at its worst. Indeed, counterparts of this statement could easily be found in the yellow journals of the United States. The Tokyo correspondent of the London *Daily Telegraph* protested against the sensational misrepresentation of the actual state of Japanese feeling, and, although he admitted that the Japanese were "intensely pained," he declared that they were sensible enough to realize that the trouble was purely local.[15] The Tokyo correspondent of the London *Times* asserted that "the leading journals decline to regard the action of the Pacific Slope as an index of the great heart of the American nation, and declare that such unworthy and unmanly incidents cannot shake Japan's steadfast faith in her proved and constant friend America."[16] And Baron Kaneko, a friend of Roosevelt, gave out an interview in Tokyo in which he applauded the moderate tone of the Japanese press.[17]

One has merely to turn to the leading journals of Japan for confirmation of these views. The *Jiji Shimpo,* one of the best-known newspapers in Japan, printed a long anonymous article which was known to have emanated from a member of the government, attempting to explain away the acts which had offended the Japanese.[18] In a later issue

[15] Quoted in Boston *Evening Transcript,* Oct. 27, 1906.
[16] London *Times,* Oct. 22, 1906.
[17] Boston *Evening Transcript,* Oct. 26, 1906.
[18] *Ibid.,* Oct. 22, 1906.

this same journal went so far as to contend that the Japanese in San Francisco were partly to blame for their troubles because they did not assimilate American ways and customs.[19] The *Asahi Shimbun* and the *Kokumin Shimbun*, which together with the *Jiji Shimpo* were probably the most influential newspapers in Japan, pleaded for moderation, warning their readers not to interpret the attitude of the Californians as representing that of America, and advising them to trust the liberal sentiments of the United States to avert a rupture of friendly feelings. The *Kokumin Shimbun* in particular took a strong pro-American position and urged confidence in the justness of Roosevelt, Root, and Taft; but it confessed that the exclusion of the children, plus Congressman Kahn's recent unfriendly remarks, had been a severe shock to the Japanese nation.[20] So, on October 26, when the effect of the suddenness of the blow had partially worn off, the Tokyo Associated Press correspondent could report that public opinion was sobering down and that thoughtful Japanese could see that if the country allowed itself to be carried away it would merely play into the hands of its enemies, who were anxious to alienate foreign sympathy from Japan.[21]

One of the most unhappy aspects of this outburst remains to be considered. The *Japan Weekly Mail* stated frankly that the segregation order was viewed as the culmination of a number of recent unpleasant developments,

[19] Boston *Evening Transcript,* Oct. 27, 1906, quoting Tokyo correspondent of London *Daily Telegraph.*

[20] *Ibid.,* Oct. 22, 1906, quoting New York *Sun* correspondent.

[21] *Ibid.,* Oct. 26, 1906.

many of which would have been practically overlooked had not the school incident come as a climax. This journal would have liked to believe that the source of these earlier and minor irritants had been the disgruntled war correspondents, but such an explanation did not account for a number of alleged grievances, a list of which it gave as follows: (1) a pronouncement by the United States Minister to China to the effect that Japan was seeking to monopolize everything in Manchuria to the exclusion of other nations; (2) a statement of the United States consul general at Yokohama to the effect that Japan's recent tariff changes were due to a desire to discriminate against foreign nations; (3) a report of a United States consul to the effect that the great decline in the trade of the United States with China was due to anti-American prejudice fostered by Japan; (4) advices from the United States attributing the decrease in American trade in the Far East to Japanese competition; (5) statements from Washington officials to the effect that the Japanese in Hawaii were planning to supplant the whites there. From the American point of view several of these charges could be explained away, but it is important to note that after the segregation order they were conspicuously referred to by the Japanese newspapers, and it was easy to see, in the words of the *Japan Weekly Mail,* that there had grown up in Japan "a feeling of profound sorrow and astonishment."[22]

Other developments of recent months took on a new significance in the eyes of the Japanese press. The Tokyo correspondent of the New York *Sun* summed them up in

[22] *Japan Weekly Mail,* Oct. 27, 1906, pp. 542–44.

his alarming cable, which was clipped from the Washington *Herald* of October 22, 1906, annotated by A. A. Adee, second assistant secretary of state, and filed away in the records of the Department of State.

It would be difficult to overestimate the gravity of the situation caused by the anti-Japanese feeling that has been given voice to in the United States . . . . At a dinner last night, attended by 150 prominent bankers and business [men] at the Imperial Hotel, deep feeling was expressed that America should regard with indifference acts that are tantamount to actual war.

Little was said regarding the American protest against the Japanese programme in Manchuria, the killing of Japanese sealers, the murder of the Japanese banker in San Francisco, the attack by John D. Rockefeller on the Japanese commercial treachery, the Hawaiian exclusion policy, the public insults to Prof. Omori, and Congressman Kahn's war threats . . . . but the exclusion of Japanese children from the public schools of California [*sic*] cuts this child-loving nation to the quick.

The references to several incidents in the above cablegram require a word of explanation. On October 3, 1906, during a crime wave of great violence in San Francisco, a Japanese banker was killed in his own bank and the sum of $4,000 was carried away. This was one case in which robbery was obviously the primary motive, but the incident was widely heralded in Japan and in the eastern part of the United States as further evidence of race hatred.[23] Then, early in October, 1906, John D. Rockefeller was quoted as having said that "in view of the rise of Japan and her hostility to foreign nations generally, American

[23] This was but one of a number of atrocious murders, yet the *Chronicle* believed that in no case had the police expended so much effort to apprehend the murderers, and that in no instance had public expression of horror been more outspoken, or a desire for vengeance more evident. The murderers were caught and speedily brought to justice. San Francisco *Chronicle*, Oct. 21, Nov. 8, 1906.

business interests must unite against any rash attempt to curb their legitimate power." The oil magnate's reported statement was attributed in Japan to a recent increase of the Japanese duties on kerosene, one of a number of steps made necessary by straitened finances, and it struck Japan as inconsistent that the United States, the leading tariff nation of the world, should take offense at this adjustment. The *Japan Weekly Mail,* though admonishing its readers not to regard Rockefeller's voice as that of the nation, wrote:

But we venture to affirm that, could her [Japan's] heart be laid open for inspection, no incident of modern times would be found to have pained it so much as this accusation coming from a leading citizen of the United States. It is upon the United States that Japan's affection has been fixed for the past thirty years . . . . Therefore it will shock her profoundly to find a charge of hostility fastened on her by one of the leading men of the nation she regards with so much friendliness and trust.[24]

On November 17, 1906, however, there appeared in the *Japan Weekly Mail* a copy of a telegram which the head of the Standard Oil interests in Japan had received on October 29 from the New York office. It contained a categorical denial of the statements attributed to Mr. Rockefeller and asserted that his remarks, correctly interpreted, were a high tribute to the commercial genius of Japan and a prophecy as to her future industrial development. The *Japan Weekly Mail* thereupon admitted that it had been wholly deceived and fully expressed its regret for the statements made.[25] But the damage had already been done.

[24] *Japan Weekly Mail,* Oct. 13, 1906, pp. 489, 507.
[25] *Ibid.,* Nov. 17, 1906, p. 619.

Ambassador Wright, representing the United States in Japan, summed up the situation in his telegram of October 21, 1906. He noted that the more conservative newspapers, including government and independent organs, had evidenced "surprise and regret" but had also pointed out that the agitation was local "and not indicative of American feeling generally." Expressing confidence in the President and the administration, they had declared that this unhappy development should not impair the traditional friendship existing between the United States and Japan. On the other hand, certain newspapers, particularly those of the opposition party, were "more radical and denunciatory" and strongly urged "retaliation and the holding of public meetings to take action." Wright had interviewed some of the leading officials and he had concluded that they were "reasonable and doing all in their power to control the situation, but are evidently nervous and fear an anti-American agitation among the people with disagreeable consequences, as I do." The American ambassador was endeavoring to minimize and explain away recent unhappy developments, but he felt that the situation would be improved by some kind of reassuring statement from the President and from Secretary of State Root.[26]

On the day following, October 22, 1906, Ambassador Wright elaborated his telegraphic report in a detailed dispatch to Secretary Root, beginning: "The facts, as set forth in my telegram, form a conservative view of the situation. There can be no question that there has developed in the popular mind here a marked feeling of irritation against the United States . . . ." Wright then

26 Wright to Root, Oct. 21, 1906, in file 1797.

went on to say that there had recently been so many unfavorable reports regarding America, many of them from
London through Reuter's news agency, as to suggest that
they were "intended to generate suspicion if not ill-will in
the Japanese mind, whether for commercial or political
reasons can only be surmised." "It may be proper to add
in this connection," he continued, "that the entire foreign
press of the Orient (with one possible exception) is under
inspiration and control which is politically and commer-
cially critical of the United States." Wright further noted
that there had "also been published several telegrams indicating that the United States was largely reinforcing its
fleet in Oriental waters." He was of the opinion, however, that "the Japanese authorities and the people generally, have apparently not been seriously disturbed by
these publications and the more responsible newspapers
have made them the basis of editorial comment expressive,
as a rule, of friendship and regard for the American people
and of confidence in their good intentions." Then followed several significant observations:

My personal conviction is that whilst the Japanese have a formal alliance with England, they in reality have a more disinterested regard for Americans than for any other foreigners, and
that this sentiment is sincere, genuine and general. Such publications, however, cannot but have their effect, and when coupled
with positive acts of hostility by Americans against Japanese,
such as are reported here from San Francisco, may be considered
largely responsible for the many evidences of annoyance and irritation now in the Japanese mind. I do not mean to convey the
idea that this feeling is general, or that as matters stand, there is
probability of serious trouble, certainly so far as the Japanese
authorities are concerned; but a few more such incidents as those
which are alleged to have occurred are not incapable of causing
a total change of sentiment which might result in a boycott or

some other form of retaliation. It should not be forgotten that the Japanese are an emotional, proud people, who just at this time have a very considerable opinion of themselves, and who are neither as phlegmatic nor as long-suffering as the Chinese.

As stated in my telegram, the reported seclusion or segregation of Japanese children in the public schools of San Francisco provokes the most criticism and indignation: first, because it appears to be the deliberate action of responsible Government officials, and, not the result of a mere labor dispute, and, second, because it is taken to indicate racial hostility. I am inclined to think, from a remark made to me by Viscount Hayashi, Minister for Foreign Affairs, that there is especial sensitiveness upon this latter point.

I have been endeavoring to explain and minimize these incidents, wherever possible, by confidential talks with prominent men, including several newspaper editors who are inclined to be friendly toward us. The Foreign Office is, I think, also exerting its influence with the press friendly to it, in the same direction. There is, however, a strong opposition party in Japan, who control newspapers of wide circulation and who are no more disinclined to embarrass the administration here than in the United States; and from the tone of their editorials, it is evident they are quite willing to put the Government in the position of submitting tamely to indignity, if they can do so.[27]

It is a curious yet significant fact that the Eastern press of the United States learned of the school imbroglio, not from San Francisco, but indirectly through Japan. When telegrams began to arrive from Tokyo describing the outburst there, the Eastern newspapers suspected that something important had occurred in San Francisco. The necessary inquiries were then made, and on October 22, 1906, eleven days after the event, the New York press for the first time printed reports of the affair and of the events leading up to it.[28] Largely because of the obviously pa-

[27] Wright to Root, Oct. 22, 1906, in file 1797.
[28] See London *Times*, Oct. 23, 1906.

rochial nature of the incident and the absence of any considerable concern in the United States, the Department of State refused to be alarmed by the reports sent in by Ambassador Wright. A. A. Adee noted, in a memorandum for Secretary Root, that it would seem as if Wright had sent his telegram of October 21 after a disquieting talk with the Tokyo correspondent of the New York *Sun*.[29] Secretary Root reflected the attitude of Adee when he cabled a reply to Wright's telegram on October 23, 1906:

Troubles your despatch of twenty-first are so entirely local and confined to San Francisco that this Government was not aware of their existence until the publication in our newspapers of what had happened in Tokyo.

The best information we have been able to obtain indicates that there is nothing even in San Francisco but an ordinary local labor controversy excited by the abnormal conditions resulting there from the earthquake and fire.

We cannot prevent men desirous of a labor vote from making speeches in favor of excluding any kind of competition. This does not seem to have gone beyond irresponsible agitation to which no attention can be paid by this Government or should be by the people of Japan. The trouble about schools appears to have arisen from the fact that the schools which the Japanese had attended were destroyed at the time of the earthquake and have not yet been replaced.

You may assure the Government of Japan in most positive terms that the Government of the United States will not for a moment entertain the idea of any treatment towards the Japanese people other than that accorded to the people of the most friendly European nation, and that there is no reason to suppose that the people of the United States desire our Government to take any different course.

The President has directed the Department of Justice to make immediate and full investigation and take such steps as the facts

29 This memorandum is in file 1797 and is appended to a clipping of the Tokyo correspondent's report as it appeared in the Washington *Herald* for Oct. 22, 1906.

call for, to maintain all treaty rights of Japanese subjects in the spirit of the friendship and respect which our people have so long entertained. The purely local and occasional nature of the San Francisco school question should be appreciated when the Japanese remember that Japanese students are welcomed at hundreds of schools and colleges all over the country.[30]

The day before Root's reassuring telegram was sent, the New York *Sun* printed another statement from its Tokyo correspondent to the effect that a "prompt repudiation of the anti-Japanese sentiment by the United States at large is necessary to avert a crisis here that would result in the destruction of the historic friendly political, financial, and commercial relations between the two nations."[31] This repudiation was almost immediately forthcoming, for the Japanese government promptly gave Root's telegram to the press, and Wright could report that it had "been received with satisfaction by the Japanese people and has had a very quieting effect."[32] Particularly comforting were the assurances that the friendship of the United States for Japan was unaffected, and that the federal government was doing everything in its power to protect the Japanese in their rights. Then, on October 26, came further evidence of the solicitude of the American government, for on that day Roosevelt let it be known that his secretary of commerce and labor, Victor H. Metcalf, would proceed to San Francisco[33] to investigate the situa-

---

30 Root to Wright (telegram), Oct. 23, 1906, in file 1797.

31 Quoted in Boston *Evening Transcript,* Oct. 22, 1906.

32 Wright to Root (telegram), Oct. 28, 1906, in file 1797.

33 New York *Times,* Oct. 27, 1906. A Reuter dispatch from Tokyo stated that the "acute stage in the American-Japanese difference is now considered to have been passed," and that a favorable result was confidently expected from the Metcalf mission. London *Times,* Oct. 31, 1906.

tion, an announcement which naturally had a happy effect on the Japanese mind. Thus passed the first phase of the San Francisco school incident, and the tension, which for a time had been acute, was appreciably relieved.

After the first reports from Japan began to arrive, the press of the United States recognized that a crisis had occurred and that the situation was fraught with danger. It was generally understood in Washington that the officials of the federal government were greatly concerned.[34] The possibility of war was widely discussed in the American newspapers, and some comfort was derived from the fact that Japan had not yet recovered sufficiently from the financial prostration of her recent struggle with Russia to welcome the prospect of fighting the United States.[35] Not the least among the disagreeable features of the crisis was the possibility that the Japanese might institute a boycott against the United States. Sentiment in this direction, although expressed occasionally, was not widespread in Japan;[36] it was not until after repeated grievances at the

[34] Boston *Evening Transcript,* Oct. 25, 26, 1906 ; London *Times,* Oct. 26, 1906. The sensational press of the United States made much of the fact that just at this time a Japanese student at Annapolis left the Naval Academy. This action was regarded as further evidence of the gravity of the crisis, but the withdrawal appears to have had nothing to do with the international situation. See Boston *Evening Transcript,* Oct. 25, 30, 1906 ; New York *Times,* Oct. 25, 1906.

[35] New York *Times,* Oct. 28, 1906.

[36] The United States was particularly concerned over the possibility of a boycott, for one instituted by the Chinese on no large scale in the winter of 1905–1906 had proved exceedingly annoying. The sensational *Hochi Shimbun* was one of the few Japanese journals that spoke openly of retaliation. American newspapers took what comfort they could from the fact that the balance of trade was such that Japan would lose more heavily than the United States from a boycott. *Japan Weekly Mail,* Oct. 27, 1906, p. 542; London *Times,* Oct. 26, 30, 1906; San Francisco *Chronicle,* Oct. 26, 1906.

hands of the San Franciscans that the movement in this direction gained any real momentum.[37]

If the press of the United States had needed any further proof of the gravity of the situation, the action of Ambassador Aoki would have been convincing. On October 25, 1906, two days after Secretary Root's reassuring telegram to Wright, Aoki called at the Department of State to make the expected representations. The conference between him and Root was prolonged, and, although the press could do no more than guess as to the nature of the conversation, it was remarked that the Ambassador's manner and language had betrayed deep concern and that he had impressed the American officials with the seriousness of Japan's reaction.[38] After his visit with the secretary of state, Aoki gave out a statement to the press in which he asserted that the action of San Francisco was "resented very bitterly by all Japanese"; and the New York correspondent of the London *Times* added that the Ambassador had "made no attempt to minimize the gravity of the present anti-American agitation in Japan."[39]

It was widely reported that Aoki had made no official protest, merely representations, and he was quoted as having said that in view of the extremely friendly relations between the two powers any formal action would be out of place.[40] The evidence, as will be noted, tends to

[37] In December, 1906, there was some talk in Japan of instituting a boycott against the city of San Francisco alone. San Francisco *Chronicle*, Dec. 2, 1906.

[38] New York *Times*, Oct. 28, 1906; Boston *Evening Transcript*, Oct. 25, 1906; London *Times*, Oct. 26, 29, 1906.

[39] London *Times*, Oct. 26, 1906.

[40] *Japan Weekly Mail*, Nov. 3, 1906, p. 570; Boston *Evening Transcript*, Oct. 25, 1906.

support this view. In the files of the Department of State there are to be found three communications on the stationery of the Japanese embassy dated October 25, 1906, the day on which Aoki called.[41] They are not formally addressed to the secretary of state and none of them bears a signature. Although Root later referred to one of these communications as a note, they resemble memoranda in form and suggest the *note verbale* rather than the severely formal note of protest. The first of these documents, and the most important of the three, is a paraphrase of instructions received from the imperial Japanese government by Aoki. It begins:

> You are instructed to call the serious attention of the Secretary of State to the condition of affairs in San Francisco. The Imperial Government learned with great regret and concern of the anti-Japanese movement in that city and of the action of the local authorities concerned. It has, however, refrained thus far from bringing the matter to the attention of the Government of the United States, hoping that the necessary measures of prevention and remedy would be adopted in the usual course. Much to the disappointment of the Imperial Government the situation in San Francisco is evidently growing worse and worse. Japanese children are now arbitrarily excluded from ordinary public schools by the action of the municipal authorities. Japanese restaurant keepers are boycotted and all possible annoyances and obstacles are placed in their way, including acts of personal violence to persons patronizing such restaurants.

Attention was then directed to the treaty of 1894 with the United States and to the rights of the Japanese under it:

> It is unnecessary to recall that the Japanese subjects are by Treaty not only entitled to full and perfect protection in their

[41] All three of these communications are to be found in file 1797.

persons and property, but are assured, in matters connected with
the rights of residence, both national and most favored treatment.
It is sufficient to observe that the equal right of education is one
of the highest and most valuable rights connected with residence.

The Imperial Government is not aware whether the special
schools, which the authorities of San Francisco propose to provide for the accommodation of Japanese children of school age,
are equally good as the schools established and maintained for
the instruction of the children generally of that city; but even if
they were equally good, the fact that Japanese children, because
of their nationality, are segregated in special schools and not permitted to attend the ordinary public schools, constitutes an act of
discrimination carrying with it a stigma and odium which it is
impossible to overlook.

The paraphrase closed with a reference to the historic
friendship between the two nations and to the faith of the
Japanese nation in the high purposes of the United States.

In their eventful history of the last fifty years the people of
Japan have not only learned to look upon the people of the United
States as their warm friends in whom they could with justice
place unbounded confidence, but to look with admiration to the
high ideals of their national life. The hostility demonstrated
against Japanese residents in San Francisco has, therefore, produced among all classes of people in Japan a feeling of disap-
pointment and sorrow which is all the more intense because of
the high regard in which they hold the people of the United States.
The Imperial Government placing explicit confidence in the high
sense of liberty, equality and justice, which guides the destinies
of the American people, looks to the Government of the United
States for the speedy and spontaneous action to correct the injustice and abuses complained of.

The second communication consisted of a page of notes
on the boycotting of Japanese restaurants and the assaults
on Japanese residents in San Francisco. This information
had apparently been secured from Consul Uyeno, and the
essential portions of it have already been paraphrased or

quoted in connection with the earlier discussion of these subjects.[42] It may occasion some surprise that the Japanese government, at a time when public opinion was thoroughly aroused over the school imbroglio, should have seen fit to confuse the issue with these other grievances. The obvious answer is that Japan was so profoundly stirred that she desired to direct the attention of the United States government to incidents which had formerly been ignored; and, as Consul Uyeno pointed out, the school question was intrinsically a minor one when compared with indignities to Japanese and damage to their property.[43]

The third communication related directly to the action of the Board of Education. Aoki noted that the Oriental school was located "in the burned district and far removed from the portion of the city in which the Japanese children and their parents live." He continued:

Mr. Uyeno . . . . reports that to reach the school in question, children must pass through congested streets littered with débris or travel on crowded cars, thus exposing themselves, under the material and social conditions actually prevailing in that city, not only to accidents and danger from physical causes but to cruel maltreatment at the hands of misguided youths and other undesirable elements that constitute social dangers in any community. Hence, apart from a stigma which is unavoidably associated with an act of discrimination and segregation, the Consul is convinced that many parents will hesitate to expose their children to such possibilities of harm, more especially as many of the children are of tender years and their homes widely scattered.

Then followed a recital of the attempts of the Japanese consul to prevail upon the school authorities to rescind the order. Reference was made to the offer of the Board to

[42] See *supra*, p. 23.
[43] San Francisco *Chronicle*, Dec. 20, 1906.

establish another school for the younger children which
would be nearer their places of residence, and to the reply
of Uyeno that this step would "not meet the essential
. . . . grievance complained of," but that the "point to
which the serious attention of the Board is invited consists in the discriminatory character of the order of the
Board." And in conclusion Aoki made himself unmistakably clear: "The exclusion of children from ordinary
public schools, because of their Japanese origin, is based
on racial distinction and is as such resented by the Japanese people as derogatory to their dignity."

Not the least among the disquieting aspects of the crisis
was the attitude of the Japanese in San Francisco, whose
protests against discrimination reached the high-water
mark on the very day that Aoki made his representations
to Secretary Root. Unlike the Chinese, who had long
attended without remonstrance a separate school conven-
iently located in their quarter, the Japanese in San Francisco were not disposed to submit tamely to the segregation order. From their point of view it was humiliating
enough to be regarded as unfit to associate with the Americans, but to be branded as Mongolians and relegated to
the company of Chinese and Koreans was a heavy cross
to bear. In addition, the blow fell with all the more force
because of the recent exaltation of the Japanese national
spirit. When the order became effective, therefore, the
Korean and Chinese children obeyed; but it was characteristic that the Japanese, almost as a unit, kept their children at home.[44] A few days later, on October 25, 1906,

[44] The Japanese-language press in San Francisco strongly protested
against the action of the Board. See *Metcalf Report*, pp. 19 ff. Uyeno
later reported that he had visited the Oriental school twice and that on

the Japanese of San Francisco gathered, 2,500 strong, to consider their grievances and to raise money for pressing the test case in the courts. Although one speaker warned the white people of the city that they were making a great mistake and were "merely driving trade to Puget sound," the meeting adjourned without untoward incident.[45]

Now that we have considered the reaction of the Japanese, as expressed through the channels of public opinion and diplomacy, it will be profitable to turn to the press of the United States for the American point of view. When the news of the school incident was finally relayed to the Atlantic Coast, the newspapers there immediately adopted an attitude almost uniformly unsympathetic toward San Francisco. The prospect of war was alarming, and to the Easterner it seemed highly reprehensible that a single state, in blind and unreasoning race prejudice, should provoke a war which would involve all of her sister states.[46] The Cleveland *Plain Dealer* was but one of a number of journals which, to put it mildly, regretted that "California is beyond reach of the paternal slipper of the national administration";[47] and many other Eastern newspapers were bitter in their strictures.

both occasions he had found only one Japanese present. San Francisco *Chronicle,* Dec. 20, 1906. See also *ibid.,* Oct. 19, 1906; San Francisco *Bulletin,* Oct. 18, 1906.

[45] San Francisco *Chronicle,* Oct. 26, 1906.

[46] The New York correspondent of the London *Times* wrote: "There is absolutely no sympathy in the Eastern States with the anti-Japanese agitation in California. Most of the afternoon papers here comment on the despatches from Tokyo, and all the comment is unfavorable towards the people of San Francisco." London *Times,* Oct. 23, 1906. See also San Francisco *Chronicle,* Nov. 7, Dec. 31, 1906; *Literary Digest,* Nov. 3, 1906, p. 622.

[47] Quoted in San Francisco *Call,* Dec. 4, 1906.

These criticisms aroused the ire of the San Francisco editors. The *Call* described the tone of the Eastern press as that "of the person in authority lecturing an unruly child as to what is good for it . . . ."[48] This journal later asserted: "It is a strange but instructive fact that . . . . the miles and miles of editorials we have seen in the Eastern press . . . . decided the issue by the rule that the West is always wrong, and the farther west the more wrong."[49] The *Chronicle* likewise was disgusted:

> There is an astonishing disposition shown by Eastern editors to crawl on their bellies when discussing the Japanese question. Is it really a fact that the prowess displayed by the little brown men in their recent war with Russia has so frightened them that they feel compelled to ask whether American polity must be governed by fear of the consequences of the wrath of foreigners?[50]

There was a tendency on the part of the San Francisco press to advise the East to mind its own business. Smarting under the strictures of unsympathetic editors, the *Chronicle* asserted that the "anti-Japanese feeling which exists in this city would be just as strong in Boston or any other Eastern city under the same conditions," and that there were more outrages against Negroes in a single year in New York than against Orientals in the whole history of California.[51] The San Francisco *Bulletin* was no less emphatic when it stated:

48 San Francisco *Call*, Nov. 13, 1906.   49 *Ibid.*, Dec. 4, 1906.

50 San Francisco *Chronicle*, Nov. 7, 1906. Such extravagant statements led to some speculation in the East as to the possibility of California's seceding from the Union. See *ibid.*, Dec. 1, 1906.

51 *Ibid.*, Nov. 10, 1906; Jan. 3, 1907. On another occasion the *Chronicle* said: "The people of this city have reason to complain of the attitude of the majority of the Eastern press. We are accused of bigoted and unreasoning race hatred. It is not true." *Ibid.*, Nov. 29, 1906.

It is a misfortune that the Eastern people, who are not acquainted with conditions here, are rushing in to solve this problem. Local issues should be frankly met by the local authorities. New York cannot settle San Francisco issues. San Francisco cannot run New York institutions. California can settle this matter with Japan if let alone by the great American public and the nations of Europe.[52]

A most galling feature of Eastern criticism had to do with the possibility of injuring commercial relations with the Orient. Secretary of Commerce and Labor Straus, who had succeeded Metcalf, warned California that there was danger of losing all or part of its flourishing trade with Japan. The San Francisco *Bulletin* replied that California would like to hold that trade, but that there were worse calamities than losing it, one being a degradation of white labor to the coolie level.[53] In commenting upon a statement recently printed in the New York *Tribune,* the *Chronicle* observed: "That is a fair sample of the spirit displayed by the crawling degenerates of the East who would endure anything from aliens able to buy calico rather than lose the sale of a yard of it."[54] And again it wrote: "The only trouble is in the sordid character of Eastern people, who would wreck our civilization if thereby they could sell calico, and our pig-headed national administration, which is much of the same character. We have more hopes of convincing the Japanese statesmen of the wisdom of keeping the races apart than of convincing Eastern manufacturers and fool sentimentalists."[55]

It must not be assumed, however, that the press of the East was unanimous in upbraiding California. A number

---

[52] San Francisco *Bulletin,* Dec. 3, 1906.   [53] *Ibid.,* Jan. 17, 1907.
[54] San Francisco *Chronicle,* Jan. 3, 1907.   [55] *Ibid.,* Nov. 30, 1906.

of editors regretted the action of the Board, but rather than direct their criticisms against the Californians they deplored that defect in the structure of the government which denied to the federal arm the power to reach out to the states in such cases.[56] The *Review of Reviews* was disposed to view the situation with some equanimity, pointing out that the Japanese might at some time in the future find it desirable to send the American children in Tokyo to separate schools.[57] Of the prominent Eastern journals of opinion, the *Outlook* was perhaps the only one that defended the action of California with any degree of warmth. It was not convinced that the order was solely the result of prejudice but felt that the action of the Board might have been in the interests of all the pupils concerned. These, it added, were matters that the local authorities were best able to decide.[58] In a later issue, even after it had been amply demonstrated that hostility to the Japanese had been behind the segregation movement, the *Outlook* stated:

We may provide only for the education of white children, as some of the Southern states formerly did; or for education in the religion of the Episcopal Church, as England practically does; or in that of the Roman Catholic Church, as most Latin countries formerly did; or in no religion at all, as the United States does; and no other nation would have any right to complain. . . . . That Japan should declare war against the United States because California does not make the kind of school provision for Japanese children that Japan desires is a preposterous notion. It is no business of any other nation what provision America makes for the education of children residing within her territory. People

[56] *Literary Digest,* Nov. 3, 1906, p. 621.
[57] *Review of Reviews,* XXXIV (Dec., 1906), 645.
[58] *Outlook,* Nov. 3, 1906, p. 538; Dec. 15, 1906, p. 900.

who migrate to America must take the school provisions which they find here.[59]

Unlike the East, the South was generally sympathetic with the position taken by San Francisco. This section had a race problem of its own, and it had long followed the practice of sending the Negro children to separate schools.[60] It was difficult, therefore, for the South to understand why there should be such a great commotion over the segregation of a handful of Japanese in one city. Furthermore, Southerners regarded the school incident as a local problem involving the right of a municipality to manage its own affairs, and with their traditional views on such matters they not unnaturally interpreted the position of the federal government as another of the increasingly numerous assaults of the Roosevelt administration on the rights of states—and resented it accordingly.[61]

After Secretary Root came forward with the contention that a city could not segregate children of a foreign power if such action conflicted with established treaty rights, the Southerners recognized dangerous implications in this doctrine. Particularly vigorous were the objections of Southern Congressmen in discussing this matter, some of whom professed to see in the position of Root and Roosevelt a movement to break down the whole system

[59] *Ibid.*, Feb. 9, 1907, pp. 301, 302.

[60] But the *Chronicle* denied that this was a matter of race hatred: "There is nothing of the kind and has not been. There is fear of a vicious economic contest probably leading to race hatred if the Oriental labor is freely admitted." San Francisco *Chronicle*, Mar. 2, 1907.

[61] Senator Morgan, of Alabama, doubtless expressed a prevalent view when he remarked that California had as much right to segregate the Japanese and other races as it had to segregate the males from females in the schools. Boston *Evening Transcript*, Oct. 30, 1906.

of separate schools for Negroes in the South. If the federal government could win the day in this case, it might, after negotiating the proper treaty with Great Britain or France, force the black subjects of these powers into the white public schools of the South. Senator Rayner, of Maryland, and Representative Garrett, of Tennessee, expressed such fears with considerable force on the floor of Congress.[62] Representative Williams, of Mississippi, asserted: ". . . . I stand with the State of California . . . . in opposition to mixed schools. [*Applause.*] I stand with Californians in favor of the proposition that we want a homogeneous and assimilable population of white people in this Republic [*applause*] . . . ."[63]

It is a popular belief—although it may not be sound meteorology—that at the center of every storm there is an area of calm. In the midst of the international storm aroused by the school order the center of calm was the city that had caused the difficulty. The action of the Board, as has been noted, was inconspicuously reported in the local press, if at all; and when the news of the outburst in Japan was printed it was not even regarded by the San Francisco *Chronicle* as front-page news.[64] San Francisco would doubtless have regarded the school matter as a purely local problem in any event, but at this time an orgy of murders and the beginnings of the spectacular graft prosecutions occupied the space of the dailies as well as the attention of

[62] *Congressional Record,* 59 Cong., 2 sess., pp. 297, 1235. See also San Francisco *Chronicle,* Dec. 2, 1906.

[63] *Congressional Record,* 59 Cong., 2 sess., p. 3218. On this same day Representative Burgess, of Texas, served notice that the Texans in Congress were ready to vote with California for the exclusion of the Japanese. *Ibid.,* p. 3224.

[64] San Francisco *Chronicle,* Oct. 22, 1906.

the people. The press was not so much concerned with the
prospect of a foreign war as with the existing war on the
grafters. And, late in October, after the campaign against
the corrupt city officials had gathered momentum, even
less interest was evidenced in the international crisis. Ex-
emplifying the "can't be bothered" attitude of the San
Francisco press was an editorial appearing in the *Bulletin*:

San Francisco has other fish to fry besides being drawn into a
controversy with Japan or the Federal Government about Japan.
. . . . Secretary Metcalf . . . . will doubtless be impressed with
the rather indifferent attitude of the people toward the whole
matter. . . . . He has probably learned that San Francisco is
concerned about another matter which is purely local but of immense significance. One trouble at a time is enough. After some
of the city officials are put in prison there will be opportunity to
answer for not giving the Japanese children a square deal in the
public schools.[65]

Nevertheless, an occasional reference to the situation
did appear from time to time in the comments of the San
Francisco dailies. The *Bulletin* entitled its first editorial
on the subject: "Japanese School Question a Tempest in
a Teapot." It then went on to say: "Certain agitators
who are glad to seize upon such a pretext are making a
mountain out of a mole hill and trying to make an international issue out of a local condition which has no significance whatever than that the Japanese children have
been put in separate schoolhouses as a matter of expediency,
owing to our overcrowded condition." The editorial further observed that there was no "heated race prejudice in
this matter" and that there was "no desire to violate the
treaty. . . . . There will be no international conflict

[65] San Francisco *Bulletin*, Nov. 14, 1906.

over the matter, and our Eastern friends need not feel alarmed."[66] A little later a statement appeared in a news column of the *Chronicle* to the effect that the difficulty, which had begun as "a squabble between the Board of Education and the Japanese residents of the town," had actually "assumed the nature of an international affair, calling for diplomacy and tact."[67] A month later the *Bulletin* remarked, with a touch of nonchalance, that "the people of California . . . . feel that this whole affair is over-emphasized."[68]

The press of San Francisco generally regarded as ridiculous the apprehension that war with Japan could develop out of such a trifling affair. "We are not greatly alarmed at the outlook," the *Call* observed, "notwithstanding the inky disturbance of the Eastern mind. There is about as much chance of war with Japan as there is of General de Young's going to the Senate."[69] The *Bulletin* was convinced that if "Japan wishes to find a pretext for a war with the United States, the action of the Board of Education . . . . will not afford a sufficient cause."[70] The *Call* elaborated this idea: "We do not share the apparent apprehension which this clash of opinion inspires in the East. Japan is not going to fight about so small a matter unless that nation is spoiling for a fight, right or wrong. In that case, one pretext for offense would serve as well as another, and we should not escape by playing the cow-

66 San Francisco *Bulletin*, Nov. 1, 1906.
67 San Francisco *Chronicle*, Nov. 3, 1906.
68 San Francisco *Bulletin*, Dec. 3, 1906.
69 San Francisco *Call*, Nov. 13, 1906.
70 San Francisco *Bulletin*, Dec. 3, 1906.

ard. If the Japanese want to fight about trifles they can be accommodated. It might do them good."[71] P. H. McCarthy, president of the San Francisco Building Trades Council, echoed this thought at a mass meeting of the Exclusion League, when he was reported to have said that "the States west of the Rockies could whip Japan at a moment's notice."[72]

The *Call* insisted that the demand of the Japanese to be admitted to the same schools with the whites was "nothing less than impudent." It asserted that the Board had "treated the Japanese more liberally than they deserve when a special school was provided which they are at liberty to attend along with other Mongolians. It is not at all clear that they are entitled to so much consideration."[73] A few weeks later the same newspaper thought it more than "commonly impudent" that the Japanese, after being offered a free education, should insist that it be given their way. "The answer is that if they don't like it they can leave it."[74] About a month later this journal was even more emphatic: "The Japanese are not here by invitation, but on sufferance, and if they make themselves obnoxious they will be put out."[75]

The *Chronicle* was more than annoyed at the Eastern contention that the Japanese should have a voice in the manner of their education in San Francisco, and observed that there was "no power on earth which could compel the people of this State to tax themselves against their will to

[71] San Francisco *Call,* Dec. 1, 1906.

[72] Quoted in George Kennan, "The Japanese in the San Francisco Schools," *Outlook,* June 1, 1907, p. 249.

[73] San Francisco *Call,* Oct. 22, 1906.

[74] *Ibid.,* Nov. 15, 1906.   [75] *Ibid.,* Dec. 9, 1906.

educate aliens whom we do not want here at all."[76] This journal felt that such an imposition would be inhuman, and that if coolie immigration was to be continued unchecked nothing could prevent the Hawaiianization of the Pacific Coast "except revolution and massacre, which would be certain."[77] The *Bulletin* asserted that San Franciscans would not object to extending educational advantages to the Japanese, "but as to the conditions under which this instruction is to be given the California people claim the right to decide a local matter, even if it involves international issues."[78] A few weeks later this same newspaper observed that the Board "was supported by public opinion unanimously," for its action involved the principle of state sovereignty. "Diplomatically they may not have acted prudently," the *Bulletin* concluded, "but they acted within their rights."[79]

After Roosevelt's annual message of December, 1906, as will be noted, the sympathy of California was unquestionably strongly behind San Francisco in its handling of the Japanese problem. Before then, however, the evidence is not so clear. We have already observed that a majority of the Californians were probably hostile to Japanese coolie immigration at this time, and when it is borne in mind that the school question was but one aspect of the race problem there would seem to be grounds for concluding that the people of the state generally approved of or

[76] San Francisco *Chronicle*, Oct. 26, 1906.   [77] *Ibid.*, Nov. 11, 1906.
[78] San Francisco *Bulletin*, Dec. 3, 1906.

[79] *Ibid.*, Feb. 1, 1907. The *Examiner*, which in its editorials practically ignored the controversy, observed that the people of the state had merely dealt with a municipal problem in a manner which seemed to them wise, and it asserted that no "treaty rights are involved, much less violated." San Francisco *Examiner*, Dec. 13, 1906.

acquiesced in the stand taken by the San Francisco authorities.[80] Yet it must be noted again that much of this support was doubtless based upon exaggerated stories then current as to the number, age, and general undesirability of the Japanese children in San Francisco. Indicative of feeling elsewhere in the state was the action of the authorities of Sacramento, the capital city, who about a year prior to October, 1906, had seriously discussed the desirability of segregating the Japanese children from the whites in the schools.[81] Indeed, there are indications that even before the intervention of Roosevelt San Francisco's handling of the school matter had met with such favor elsewhere in the state as to provide a stimulus to further anti-Japanese agitation.

Nevertheless, there is abundant evidence that a considerable number of influential Californians were opposed to the action of the Board. The Fresno *Republican* wrote: "The majority of the thoughtful people of California are not in sympathy with the agitation of the demagogues of the cities against the Japanese. . . . ."[82] If this generalization is confined to the "thoughtful people" of the state, it is probably correct; but thoughtful people were in a minority at this time. Chambers of commerce, fearing possible injury to trade relationships, strongly opposed

[80] Several of the San Francisco journals assumed that the rest of the state was with them on this issue, but their testimony was not unbiased. See San Francisco *Bulletin,* Dec. 3, 1906; San Francisco *Call,* Jan. 19, 1907.

[81] The matter was brought to a head by an increasing number of Japanese children and by the complaints of the white parents. Although the school authorities, after an investigation, recommended separate schools, the proposal was shelved on the ground of expense. San Francisco *Chronicle,* Nov. 21, 1906.

[82] Quoted in Johnson, *Discrimination against the Japanese,* p. 42.

anti-Japanese activity; and the Los Angeles Chamber of Commerce sent a telegram to Roosevelt in which it asserted that the general trend of public opinion in southern California was decidedly averse to any discrimination against the Japanese in the matter of school privileges.[83] Prominent educators throughout the state voiced their disapproval, among them David Starr Jordan, president of Stanford University, and Benjamin Ide Wheeler, president of the University of California. They were joined by school principals in San Francisco itself and by the superintendent of the Los Angeles city schools. The state association of school superintendents, while in convention in San Diego, tabled without action a resolution calling for an endorsement of the stand of the San Francisco authorities.[84] Clergymen, missionaries, churches, and church journals were almost unanimously opposed to what they regarded as an un-Christian act.[85]

In those agricultural centers of California where cheap labor was in demand for harvesting crops the anti-Japanese agitation was deplored. This was especially true of the orange-growing district of the southern part of the state.[86] One Los Angeles newspaper, in fact, asserted that the anti-Japanese movement was largely the work of professional labor leaders who wanted to keep wages up.[87]

[83] Quoted in *Literary Digest,* Mar. 2, 1907, p. 320; see also R. L. Buell, "The Development of the Anti-Japanese Agitation in the United States," *Political Science Quarterly,* XXXVII (1922), 625.

[84] San Francisco *Chronicle,* Dec. 23, 1906; *Metcalf Report,* p. 7; Buell, *loc. cit.,* p. 625.

[85] Johnson, *op. cit.,* pp. 18 ff.

[86] San Francisco *Chronicle,* Oct. 9, 1906; *Japan Weekly Mail,* Oct. 27, 1906, p. 543.

[87] Quoted in Johnson, *Discrimination against the Japanese,* p. 58.

It is important to note in this connection that the state grange of California had passed a resolution at its last session to the effect that all races should be treated alike.[88]

Not without significance was the reaction of other nations, particularly those of Europe, to the school imbroglio. England was more than ordinarily interested in the situation, for there was even some apprehension that she might conceivably be forced into a war·on behalf of her ally, Japan, against the United States.[89] In certain portions of the empire, notably in Australia, where the white ideal was strong, and in British Columbia, where the Japanese were penetrating in numbers, the action of the San Francisco authorities was commended.[90] The following comment of the London *Times* is revealing: "Englishmen will extend to the Federal Government a sympathy all the more cordial because we may conceivably be involved in similar trouble by the headstrong action of a self-governing colony."[91] This prophecy was soon to be fulfilled at Vancouver, British Columbia, in September, 1907.

In continental Europe there was a considerable amount of derisive comment on the "all men are created equal" clause of the Declaration of Independence.[92] The *All-*

[88] J. P. Irish (Naval Officer of the Customs, San Francisco) to Root, Oct. 26, 1906, in file 1797.

[89] New York *Times,* Oct. 31, 1906; San Francisco *Chronicle,* Dec. 2, 1906.

[90] The Sydney *Bulletin,* the most widely circulated newspaper in Australia, spoke approvingly, as did the Vancouver *Province.* Quoted in Jerome A. Hart, "The Oriental Problem, as the Coast Sees It," *World's Work,* XIII (Mar., 1907), 8693. See also the *Argonaut,* San Francisco, Dec. 1, 1906, p. 267.

[91] London *Times,* Oct. 30, 1906; see also *Literary Digest,* Mar. 9, 1907, pp. 371–72.

[92] See *Literary Digest,* Nov. 24, 1906, p. 751.

deutsche Blätter, the organ of the Pan-Germanic Association, rejoiced at this "rift in the lute of Japan's friendship,"[93] and in St. Petersburg the leading journals discussed at length the prospects of an armed collision.[94] The Paris correspondent of the London *Times* reported that there was a noticeable sympathy in France for the Japanese, who in the arts, science, and war were regarded as the French of the Far East; and considerable condemnation of the United States, which was then unpopular because of alleged designs on Cuba. Although the Paris *Intransigeant* spoke of the "irrepressible conflict," the *Siècle* and the *Figaro* believed that the school incident would lead to no serious difficulty. The latter remarked that the whole controversy threw a "lurid light on the drawbacks of federalism."[95] The feeling of uncertainty in France was appreciably relieved, however, when the Japanese ambassador gave out an interview in which he denied that the situation was an alarming one. Robert S. McCormick, United States ambassador to France, testified as to the excellent effect of this statement in shutting off "any exaggeration as to possible strained relations between Japan and the United States."[96]

An examination of Roosevelt's private correspondence provides ample confirmation of the view of the press, both at home and abroad, that the chief executive and his advisers were deeply disturbed. On October 26, 1906, in

[93] Quoted in *Japan Weekly Mail,* Nov. 17, 1906, p. 627.

[94] The *Bourse Gazette* thought that if Japan wanted war she would precipitate it before the United States had time to complete her naval program and the Panama Canal. Cited in London *Times,* Dec. 8, 1906.

[95] Quoted in *ibid.,* Oct. 30, 1906; see also New York *Times,* Oct. 30, 1906; *Literary Digest,* Dec. 22, 1906, p. 932.

[96] McCormick to Root, Nov. 2, 1906, in file 1797.

response to a cable from his friend, Baron Kaneko, Roosevelt wrote:

The movement in question is giving me the gravest concern. It is so purely local that we never heard of it here in Washington until we got dispatches from Tokyo . . . . I shall exert all the power I have under the Constitution to protect the rights of Japanese who are here, and I shall deal with the subject at length in my message to Congress . . . . The action of these people in San Francisco no more represents American sentiment as a whole than the action of the Japanese seal pirates last summer represents Japanese sentiment.[97]

On October 27 Roosevelt wrote to Lodge in confidence, "Just at present the labor unions bid fair to embroil us with Japan";[98] and on the same day he asked the acting secretary of the navy, Truman H. Newberry, for an exact comparison of the Japanese with the American warships, including those that would be available within the next three years. Roosevelt also wanted to know if the General Board was studying the plan of operations to be followed in the event of hostilities with Japan.[99] More important than either of these communications was the letter which the President sent to Senator Hale, of Maine, chairman of the Senate Committee on Naval Affairs. After referring to the persecution of the Japanese in California and stating that he was doing all in his power to right these wrongs, Roosevelt continued:

Probably Root will have to communicate formally with the Governor of California. Exactly how much further I shall go I do

[97] Roosevelt to Kaneko (confidential), Oct. 26, 1906, Roosevelt Papers.

[98] Roosevelt to Lodge, Oct. 27, 1906, Roosevelt Papers.

[99] Newberry supplied the desired information. Newberry to Roosevelt, Oct. 30, 1906, Roosevelt Papers.

not know. It is possible I may have to use the army in connection with boycotting or the suppression of mob violence.

If these troubles merely affected our internal arrangements, I should not bother you with them; but of course they may possibly bring about war with Japan. I do not think that they will bring it about at this moment, but even as to this I am not certain, for the Japanese are proud, sensitive, war-like, are flushed with the glory of their recent triumph, and are in my opinion bent upon establishing themselves as the leading power in the Pacific.

Roosevelt then observed that, although his main motive in stopping the Russo-Japanese War had been humanitarian, he had also been influenced by the desirability of keeping Russia in the Far East to preserve the balance of power.

But the internal condition of Russia is now such that she is no longer in any way a menace to or restraint upon Japan, and probably will not be for a number of years to come; I do not pretend to have the least idea as to Japan's policy or real feeling, whether toward us or toward anyone else. I do not think that she wishes war as such, and I doubt if she will go to war now; but I am very sure that if sufficiently irritated and humiliated by us she will get to accept us instead of Russia as the national enemy whom she will ultimately have to fight; and under such circumstances her concentration and continuity of purpose, and the exceedingly formidable character of her army and navy, make it necessary to reckon very seriously with her. It seems to me that all of this necessitates our having a definite policy with regard to her; a policy of behaving with absolute good faith, courtesy and justice to her on the one hand, and on the other, of keeping our navy in such shape as to make it a risky thing for Japan to go to war with us.

In conclusion, the President urged upon Hale the necessity of building bigger, faster, and more battleships. "I most earnestly feel," he asserted, "that we can not afford to let our navy fall behind." Hence the United States should go ahead with an annual program of laying down "two ships the equal of any laid down by any nation."[100]

On the same day, October 27, 1906, Roosevelt wrote to his son, Kermit: "I am being horribly bothered about the Japanese business. The infernal fools in California, and especially in San Francisco, insult the Japanese recklessly and in the event of war it will be the Nation as a whole which will pay the consequences. However I hope to keep things straight." And then came this touch, characteristically Rooseveltian, "I am perfectly willing that this Nation should fight any nation if it has got to, but I would loathe to see it forced into a war in which it was wrong."[101]

Before we turn to a consideration of the steps that Roosevelt took to avoid such a conflict, it is well to determine how serious the crisis was before the acute stage had been passed. The Japanese were so completely stunned by the unexpectedness of the blow that even experienced observers in Japan, as we have seen, mistook their immediate reaction for unreasoning anger. But after the shock had worn off, the old confidence in the historic friendship of the United States began to assert itself, and the majority of the Japanese appear to have anticipated an equitable solution of the problem. If this affair had followed a series of incidents like those between 1906 and 1913, the outlook would have been somewhat different, for by 1913 Japanese patience had worn thin. But in 1906, since no other real disturbance had occurred in the relations between the two peoples, the Japanese could view the controversy with relative calm after they

100 Roosevelt to Hale, Oct. 27, 1906, Roosevelt Papers.
101 Roosevelt to Kermit Roosevelt, Oct. 27, 1906, Roosevelt Papers.

had recovered from their first reaction of surprise and sorrow. It would seem, then, that the situation with respect to Japan was less alarming during this acute stage than it was described as having been in the press of the United States, and that much of the concern caused in America was based upon what the Japanese said and did before recovering from the shock of the news. Nevertheless, the outlook at best was disconcerting, and it was evident that the utmost care would have to be exercised by the United States if more serious trouble was to be avoided.

CHAPTER IV

The Big Stick in Action

"To shut them [the Japanese] out from the
public schools is a wicked absurdity . . . ."
—Roosevelt's Annual Message to Congress,
December, 1906

PRESIDENT ROOSEVELT was temperamentally unable to
sit back and quietly watch the "demagogs" of San Francisco embroil the entire country in a war with Japan. He
was not one to chop logic about the rights of states and
twilight zones of federalism while the welfare of the nation was at stake. He therefore acted with promptness,
and his first move toward bringing pressure to bear on the
San Francisco authorities was to dispatch Metcalf to California on a mission which appears to have been at that
time without precedent in American history.[1] Metcalf
left Washington on October 26, 1906, the day following
Aoki's representations, with orders to make a thorough
investigation of the situation and to ascertain the facts.
In addition, he was specifically instructed by Roosevelt to
impress upon the school authorities "the grave risk they
are forcing the whole country to incur."[2] There was a
widespread belief, which the foregoing statement would
confirm, that Secretary Metcalf was to do what he could

[1] Metcalf was doubtless chosen for this task because he was a resi-
dent of Oakland, California, and was presumably already familiar with
the general situation. San Francisco *Chronicle*, Oct. 27, 1906.

[2] Roosevelt to Hale, Oct. 27, 1906, Roosevelt Papers. See also Boston *Evening Transcript*, Oct. 27, 1906; San Francisco *Chronicle*, Oct. 27,
1906.

to induce the Board to rescind its objectionable order; but it was generally felt in the East that the task was hopeless.[3]

In more ways than one the sending of Metcalf was an act of statesmanship. It demonstrated to the country as a whole that the federal government was thoroughly aroused to the seriousness of the controversy and was doing everything in its power to adjust matters. But more important was the effect on the Japanese mind. Metcalf's departure was convincing proof of the disinterestedness and sincerity of the Roosevelt administration, and it served to emphasize the purely local nature of the difficulty.[4] It is evident, therefore, that both the Root telegram and the announcement of Metcalf's mission contributed a great deal to tiding over the most acute phase of the international crisis.

The Japanese press, which had not as yet entirely recovered from the first shock, now began to assume "a conspicuously circumspect" tone, and the leading newspapers were confident that the Roosevelt administration would be able to iron out the difficulty with a minimum of friction.[5] Baron Kaneko wrote to Roosevelt on October 31, 1906, and stated that the President's attitude and sincerity were fully understood and appreciated by the government and people of Japan. "I am glad," he added, "to see the general tone of the papers quite moderate and unexcited, except one or two."[6] Ambassador Wright con-

3 See London *Times,* Oct. 29, 1906.

4 San Francisco *Chronicle,* Oct. 27, Nov. 1, 1906; Boston *Evening Transcript,* Oct. 27, 1906.   5 *Japan Weekly Mail,* Nov. 3, 1906, p. 570.

6 Kaneko to Roosevelt, Oct. 31, 1906, Roosevelt Papers. Roosevelt's private correspondence to Kaneko was handed on to high Japanese offi-

firmed the tendency of the influential newspapers to "reflect a more quiet tone of confidence in the lasting friendship of the American people, and the justice and good intentions of the American Government to right any local wrong." Yet he observed that "underneath all is a current of feeling which shows how nearly the implied racial discrimination has touched home." The suggestion of drawing "a color-line in America has created the deepest chagrin"; yet unless other events occurred "to strengthen and perpetuate ill-feeling, there seems little doubt that the resentment which so quickly came to the surface will soon be forgotten."[7]

Metcalf arrived in Oakland, California, on October 31, 1906, and on the following day began his work in earnest. The San Francisco *Chronicle,* which later criticized his report with the utmost severity, admitted at the time that his investigation was thorough.[8] Even before his arrival, he had arranged to have the acting commissioner of immigration make a preliminary report embodying all available information, including accounts in the local newspapers. Metcalf himself interviewed or had conferences with the United States attorney, with representatives of the Exclusion League, with the president of the Board of Education, with Consul Uyeno, and with Japanese restaurant-

cials, including the minister for foreign affairs, and doubtless had much to do with assuring the Japanese government of Roosevelt's intention to settle the difficulty amicably.

[7] Wright to Root, dispatch number 90, in file 1797. Even after the acute stage had been passed there was evidence that a considerable minority in Japan were refusing to be mollified. *Japan Weekly Mail,* Nov. 3, 1906, pp. 570–71; Boston *Evening Transcript,* Oct. 31, 1906; London *Times,* Oct. 27, 1906.

[8] San Francisco *Chronicle,* Nov. 4, 13, 1906.

keepers and others who had suffered indignities at the hands of the whites. He also visited the Japanese district and investigated in person the recently established Oriental school.[9] The press, however, was kept in the dark; and although Metcalf sent at least one preliminary report to Roosevelt on the legal aspects of the problem[10] he refused to drop any hint as to what would be the nature of his conclusions.

Any hope that the federal administration may have had of persuading the Board of Education to rescind the resolution was dispelled by statements which began to emanate from that body even before the arrival of Metcalf. The Board stoutly maintained that it had acted for the best interests of the white pupils and that it would stand firm. It professed to feel under obligations to comply with the state law and announced that if the Japanese had a grievance the proper legal channels were open to them.[11] Upon beginning his investigation, however, Metcalf had an interview with the president and with the legal adviser of the Board, at the conclusion of which he was obliged to write Roosevelt that it was hopeless to look for modification or repeal of the order.[12]

After "vicariously waving the big stick" in San Francisco for about two weeks,[13] Metcalf departed for Wash-

[9] San Francisco *Chronicle*, Oct. 30 to Nov. 13, 1906.

[10] Metcalf to Roosevelt (telegram), Nov. 3, 1906, in file 1797.

[11] San Francisco *Chronicle,* Oct. 26, 1906; Nov. 2, 10, 1906; London *Times,* Oct. 31, 1906.

[12] Metcalf to Roosevelt (copy), Nov. 2, 1906, in file 1797.

[13] Two weeks after Metcalf's departure the *Chronicle,* noting that "the presence of a Cabinet officer vicariously waving the big stick . . . . did not work," trusted that "he had a pleasant trip and enjoyed his visit." Nov. 27, 1906.

ington on November 13, 1906. There he spent some little time in getting his report in readiness for Roosevelt, who had left on November 8 to inspect the work on the Panama Canal. On the day after the President's return, November 27, Metcalf was closeted with Roosevelt for some time at the White House, presumably for a discussion of the San Francisco investigation.[14] Still no trustworthy information was forthcoming as to the nature of Metcalf's findings, and the press could do no more than indulge in guesses on this score.[15] But before the report in its final form was made public, Roosevelt entered the lists in a spectacular way with his resounding annual message of December 4, 1906.

Roosevelt's message to Congress contained a number of unusually forceful recommendations, but the most sensational passages had to do with problems arising from the San Francisco imbroglio. Although expressing himself less vigorously than in his private correspondence,[16] the President took the recalcitrant city to task in no uncertain terms. He began this portion of his message with an appeal for fair play toward the stranger within the gates, and observed that hostility toward Japan "may be fraught with the gravest consequences to the nation." He

14 *Ibid.,* Nov. 28, 1906.

15 From Tokyo Ambassador Wright wired: "Has a copy of Metcalf's report been sent to me? Newspapers here publish conflicting statements regarding its nature." Wright to Root, Dec. 1, 1906, in file 1797.

16 Pointing out that the Japanese did not average more than one *bona fide* child to a school in San Francisco, Roosevelt asserted that the "cry against them is simply nonsense." Roosevelt to H. G. Otis, Jan. 8, 1907, Roosevelt Papers. Writing also of the small number of Japanese children in San Francisco, Roosevelt stated: "It is surely a wicked thing for such an object to jeopardize the relations between Japan and the United States." Roosevelt to Jordan, Jan. 9, 1907, Roosevelt Papers.

paid a ringing tribute to Japan's remarkable development
in peace and war, and noted that the overwhelming mass
of Americans treated the Japanese as they deserved, but
that here and there an "unworthy feeling" had manifested
itself, as in shutting them out of the common schools.
This, asserted Roosevelt, was a "wicked absurdity," for
we have "as much to learn from Japan as Japan has to
learn from us; and no nation is fit to teach unless it is also
willing to learn." Americans were treated well in Japan,
and not to reciprocate "is by just so much a confession of
inferiority in our civilization." Where the federal government had power it would be exercised; where the states
had power they would be urged to use it wisely and
promptly, for "good manners should be an international
no less than an individual attribute." Roosevelt thereupon
recommended that Congress pass an act permitting naturalization of the Japanese so that they could become good
citizens; and he earnestly urged upon Congress that "the
criminal and civil statutes of the United States be so
amended and added to as to enable the President . . . .
to enforce the rights of aliens under treaties." In conclusion, he promised to use all the forces at his command
to protect the Japanese.[17]

As one reads the message today one is struck by its
spirit of fair play and its international outlook, qualities
which were quite inconsistent with the narrow nationalism
characteristic of the turn of the century. Although perhaps not pro-Japanese, the message was a bit effusive in
its praise of Japanese civilization and achievements. Nevertheless, as these sentiments are compared with Roosevelt's

[17] *Congressional Record,* 59 Cong., 2 sess., p. 31.

previously expressed views it becomes evident that the President was thoroughly sincere in what he said. Early in 1904 Roosevelt had become so deeply impressed with Japanese institutions that he had begun an investigation of jiujitsu and Bushido under the tutelage of Japanese friends.[18] It was not strange, then, that from the beginning of the Russo-Japanese War his sympathies should have been with Japan.[19] The key to his attitude is to be found in his statement to George Kennan: "I thoroughly admire and believe in the Japanese. They have always told me the truth, and the Russians have not. Moreover, they have the kind of fighting stock that I like . . . ."[20] To a man of Roosevelt's militaristic bent the amazing record of the Japanese armies was indeed a recommendation of the highest nature.

Throughout the Russo-Japanese War, passages appeared in Roosevelt's correspondence which, in their praise of Japan, clearly foreshadowed certain portions of the annual message of 1906.[21] Nor did the President's friendship for Japan stop with words. Although thoroughly misunderstood and widely blamed even by the Japanese people for his activity in connection with the Peace of Portsmouth, Roosevelt kept secret certain details which would have cleared himself but which would have made the Japanese officials appear in a less favorable light.[22]

[18] Dennett, *Roosevelt and the Russo-Japanese War*, p. 35.

[19] *Ibid.*, p. 27.   [20] Quoted in *ibid.*, p. 161.

[21] See *ibid.*, pp. 49, 166. In 1913, Roosevelt reiterated his stand: "I then had and now have a hearty admiration for the Japanese people. I believe in them; I respect their great qualities; I wish that our American people had many of these qualities." *Autobiography*, pp. 393, 395.

[22] Dennett, *op. cit.*, pp. 286, 339.

With good reason, therefore, could the President speak of his friendship for Japan.

It is now clear, as many suspected at the time, that the references to Japan in the annual message were deliberately inserted for the purpose of mollifying that nation and putting it in a more favorable mood for the settlement of the existing immigration difficulties. As we have seen, Roosevelt promised Baron Kaneko, as early as October 26, 1906, that he would "deal with the subject at length in my message to Congress."[23] On the next day Roosevelt sent a draft of his message to Dr. W. Sturgis Bigelow, stating: "I hope it will do good. I shall show it to the Japanese Ambassador in confidence within two or three days."[24] A month later the President informed Metcalf that he had "a talk with the Japanese Ambassador before I left for Panama; read him what I was to say in my annual message, which evidently pleased him very much . . . ." In the same letter Roosevelt wrote of his desire to persuade the Japanese government to accept a plan for the mutual exclusion of laborers, and he indicated that the great obstacle in the way of any such achievement was "the irritation caused by the San Francisco action." Roosevelt hoped that his message would "smooth over their feelings so that the Government will quietly stop all immigration of coolies to our country. At any rate I shall do my best to bring this about."[25]

Writing to J. St. Loe Strachey on December 21, 1906, two weeks after the message, Roosevelt stated his position

[23] Roosevelt to Kaneko, Oct. 26, 1906, Roosevelt Papers.
[24] Roosevelt to Bigelow, Oct. 27, 1906, Roosevelt Papers.
[25] Roosevelt to Metcalf, Nov. 27, 1906, Roosevelt Papers. This letter was printed in full in the New York *Times,* Jan. 11, 1922.

even more plainly. He explained that he had had "two especial purposes." First of all he "wanted to let not only the Californians but the rest of my countrymen know that no political considerations would interfere for a moment with my using the armed forces of the country to protect the Japanese if they were molested in their persons and property." Secondly, he wished "to show all possible consideration for the Japanese, so as to soothe their wounded feelings, and if possible get them into a frame of mind in consequence of which we may be able to get some mutual agreement between Japan and the United States reciprocally to keep the laborers of each country from the other."[26]

We have already observed that Roosevelt showed the Japanese ambassador the pertinent passages in his message at least four weeks in advance of its publication, and Aoki could scarcely have failed to send on such important information to Tokyo. Such assurances probably helped to fortify the Japanese government in its determination to go slowly, despite a considerable amount of pressure from the jingo press, and to rely upon the fairness and justice of Roosevelt and his advisers. This may partially explain why, three days before the submission of the message, the Associated Press was authorized to quote the Japanese Embassy in Washington as follows:

Japan has every confidence that President Roosevelt will adjust the California school controversy entirely to the satisfaction of both nations. Feeling this confidence, Japan has ceased to be agitated over the situation. The Japanese newspapers are emphatically moderate in all their notices of the affair, and so far as the Japanese nation is concerned, there is absolutely no reason for the revival of newspaper notoriety in this country.

[26] Roosevelt to Strachey, Dec. 21, 1906, Roosevelt Papers.

This statement further declared that there were no new developments of any character, that the matter was in the hands of Roosevelt, and that there was complete confidence in his willingness and ability to act.[27]

Although the message probably came as no surprise to the Japanese government, its mollifying effect on Japanese public opinion was so pronounced as doubtless to exceed the expectations of the President. So great was the interest in Roosevelt's pronouncement that several of the Tokyo journals went to the expense of having lengthy portions of the message cabled from America, even though such excerpts filled over four columns in the *Jiji Shimpo*.[28] Ambassador Wright forwarded a number of newspaper clippings illustrating the reaction of the Japanese, and added:

The newspapers were unanimous in their expressions of satisfaction at the forcible and sympathetic manner in which the President deals with the San Francisco school question, and in their admiration for, and absolute confidence in, his lofty personality as the determining factor in the present unpleasant complication. The President's recommendation to provide for the naturalization of Japanese subjects on the basis of equality with those of European nations is received with especial enthusiasm and, if carried into effect, would, in my opinion, do more than any other one thing to heal their wounded national pride.[29]

Praise of Roosevelt's message was not confined to the

27 San Francisco *Chronicle*, Dec. 2, 1906.

28 See *Japan Weekly Mail*, Dec. 15, 1906, p. 737.

29 Wright to Root, Dec. 11, 1906, in file 1797. Wright's analysis of public opinion is confirmed by a number of other sources. The Tokyo correspondent of the London *Times* wrote of the "profound satisfaction" that the message had caused, and of the feeling "entertained generally throughout the country since the beginning of the complication—namely, that Japan can trust her often-proved friend America to do her justice, and may confidently leave the matter in the hands of Washington." London *Times*, Dec. 10, 1906. See also *ibid.*, Dec. 7, 1906; San Francisco *Chronicle*, Dec. 8, 9, 1906.

Japanese press. In Tokyo, Baron Kaneko stated in an interview that he had known all along that the disturbance was purely local, an impression which was more than confirmed by Roosevelt's message, "which I consider to be the greatest utterance by an American President since Washington's farewell address." Kaneko added that if the question had arisen elsewhere than in the United States "loud defiance would have been uttered throughout the length and breadth of the empire. On the other hand the quiet tone of the Japanese press clearly demonstrates the confidence which is reposed in President Roosevelt and American sentiment generally."[30] Replying to an interpellation in the lower house on January 29, 1907, Viscount Hayashi, Japanese minister for foreign affairs, stated that the President's message "showed that the American government was sincerely endeavoring to arrive at an amicable settlement of the question."[31]

The Japanese in America likewise rejoiced. The consul at Seattle announced that Roosevelt was the "best friend Japan ever had," and the Seattle Japanese Business Men's Association telegraphed its thanks to the President.[32] The Japanese in San Francisco were naturally pleased over this verbal chastisement of their white neighbors, and Consul Uyeno described the message in superlatives.[33] Ambassador Aoki made a personal call on the President to thank him warmly for what he had done.[34] It is evident, then,

30 London *Times*, Feb. 4, 1907.
31 Wright to Root (translation), Feb. 8, 1907, in file 1797.
32 San Francisco *Chronicle*, Dec. 6, 1906.
33 *Japan Weekly Mail*, Dec. 29, 1906, p. 819.
34 San Francisco *Chronicle*, Dec. 6, 1906.

that Roosevelt had been extraordinarily successful in his efforts to quiet the Japanese mind. The Washington correspondent of the London *Times* observed that the "Japanese could hardly expect more outspoken condemnation of the acts complained of or more energetic promises to punish wrongdoers," and he reported that "thoughtful people agree that, had the President not taken this attitude, the Government would have had serious trouble with Japan."[35]

But Roosevelt's message was a two-edged sword. If it had the effect of mollifying public opinion in Japan, it had precisely the opposite effect on the people of San Francisco.[36] That city, which up to this point had viewed the school difficulty with a considerable measure of complacency, was rudely jarred from its attitude of indifference and was suddenly awakened to the fact that the Board had stirred up a hornets' nest. Indeed, for the first time the San Francisco press began to feature the school controversy. The *Call* spoke sarcastically of this "outburst of august and Jovian wrath," and asserted that the message was "based on misinformation, and, apparently, was conceived in a fit of bad temper."[37] The *Chronicle* came out flatly and stated, "Our controversy is not with them [Japanese] but with the President." It further observed that when the coolies were excluded the school problem would disappear, and that there was no reason at all, "except the President," why all this should not be quietly and

---

[35] London *Times,* Dec. 6, 1906.

[36] The Connecticut *Courant* remarked that not since the days of Andrew Jackson had such a rebuke been administered to an American city. Quoted in *Current Literature,* XLII (Jan., 1907), 5.

[37] San Francisco *Call,* Dec. 6, 1906.

peacefully accomplished.[38] A few days later the *Chronicle* was even more emphatic: "Our feeling is not against Japan, but against an unpatriotic President who united with aliens to break down the civilization of his own countrymen."[39] The *Examiner,* which hitherto had been the quietest editorially of the four leading dailies, let its views be known: "As for the ninety-three Japanese . . . . they . . . . will be forgotten as soon as President Roosevelt lays aside his pewter sword, sheathes his fire-belching tongue and ceases his tin-soldier yawp about leading the army and navy against our schoolhouses."[40]

The San Franciscans, many of whom had been out of sympathy with the Board of Education, were now thoroughly aroused. The Exclusion League called a mass meeting to enter a protest against the "gross insult and unwarranted attack" upon the people of San Francisco. The Building Trades Council unanimously adopted a resolution condemning Roosevelt's words and denouncing the proposed naturalization of the Japanese.[41] Representative Needham, of California, expressed the belief that the President had unwittingly added fuel to the flames and had made matters worse.[42] The San Francisco *Argonaut* feared that the message was bringing about the very conditions that it was designed to remove, for in other cities steps were being taken, not to segregate the Japanese, but

[38] San Francisco *Chronicle,* Dec. 5, 1906.

[39] *Ibid.,* Dec. 10, 1906. Indeed, such extreme utterances as these were regarded in the East as foreshadowing secession. See *Literary Digest,* Jan. 12, 1907, p. 44.

[40] San Francisco *Examiner,* Dec. 21, 1906.

[41] San Francisco *Chronicle,* Dec. 7, 1906.

[42] *Ibid.,* Dec. 5, 1906; Jan. 31, 1907; London *Times,* Dec. 10, 1906; Jan. 1, 1907.

to shut them out of the public school system altogether.[43]
There is also evidence that the message was directly responsible for an increase of acts of violence against the
Japanese elsewhere in the state.[44] Old Dennis Kearney,
the leader of the sand-lotters in their violent anti-Chinese
campaign of the 'seventies, joined the outcry with dire
predictions as to what would happen if the yellow peril
were not checked.[45] And the San Francisco correspondent
of the London *Times* wrote in evident alarm:

The situation here is certainly graver . . . . Feeling against
the Japanese has become so acute . . . . that it is feared that
nothing that Mr. Roosevelt and the Federal Government can do
will have the slightest effect in improving the situation.[46]

There were a number of reasons why the Californians
should have reacted so unfavorably to Roosevelt's statements. Especially annoying was the intemperateness of
his treatment—a feature of the message which struck not
only the newspapers but also the leaders of San Francisco
as unworthy of a chief executive. Former Congressman
Livernash wrote of Roosevelt's "intemperate, insulting,
and intolerant attitude," and asserted that there was no
need for fuming—the courts could peacefully decide the
question. He concluded that "it was sorry talk for a

[43] Notably Oakland. *Argonaut,* San Francisco, Jan. 5, 1907, p. 355;
San Francisco *Chronicle,* Dec. 14, 1906.

[44] At San Bernardino, an orange-grower was hanged in effigy because
he had erected shacks for his Japanese fruit pickers. *Ibid.,* Dec. 7, 1906.
In Porterville a riot occurred in which a Japanese railroad gang was
reported to have attacked a white man. *Ibid.,* Jan. 5, 1907. This outburst was believed to be related to the school difficulty.

[45] William Inglis, "The Width of a School Bench," *Harper's Weekly,*
Jan. 19, 1907, p. 83.

[46] London *Times,* Dec. 20, 1906.

President and it transformed a very quiet situation into
a roaring Vesuvius."[47] Senator George Perkins, of California, was quoted as remarking that Roosevelt had
"slopped over."[48] It was further noted in San Francisco
that the Japanese would probably become so puffed up
as a result of these encomiums that it would be impossible
to secure an amicable adjustment of outstanding differences.[49]

Moreover, the San Franciscans were especially displeased by evidence that Roosevelt had written his scathing
indictment before he had examined the results of Metcalf's
exhaustive investigation—in other words, that he had
closed his eyes to the facts and had condemned the people
of San Francisco without giving them a hearing.[50] It was
generally known in newspaper circles at the time that the
President had completed his message before leaving for
Panama, a rumor which was confirmed by Congressman
E. A. Hayes and President B. I. Wheeler, of the University of California.[51] In fact, as has just been pointed out,
Roosevelt read certain passages to the Japanese Ambassador some little while before Metcalf had completed his
work in San Francisco. The Secretary of Commerce, it
will be remembered, returned about a week before the

[47] San Francisco *Bulletin,* Feb. 23, 1907.

[48] San Francisco *Chronicle,* Mar. 15, 1907.

[49] *Argonaut,* San Francisco, Feb. 2, 1907, p. 419; Feb. 9, 1907, p.
433.

[50] San Francisco *Chronicle,* Dec. 17, 1906.

[51] Wheeler, who was accused of having provided Roosevelt with misinformation on his recent visit to Washington, cleared his skirts by stating that the message was in the hands of the printer upon his arrival and
that it had been written before Roosevelt had received the Metcalf report. *Ibid.,* Nov. 29, Dec. 6, 1906. See also *ibid.,* Dec. 15, 1906; *Japan
Weekly Mail,* Dec. 29, 1906, p. 820.

submission of the message, and it is possible that Roosevelt may have modified his denunciation as a result of the ensuing conversations; but the nature of Metcalf's report was such that, if anything, it probably confirmed Roosevelt in his determination to castigate the offending city.

As for the contents of the message itself, the San Franciscans particularly resented the recommendation of naturalization and the threat of force. Aside from the possibility of erecting a strong and aggressive voting bloc of Japanese in the state, which in itself was distasteful, the Californians objected to Roosevelt's evident disapproval of their arguments as to the unassimilability of the Japanese.[52] Representative McLachlan of California was reported as saying that the President had "out-Japanned Japan," for to his knowledge the Japanese had never seriously asked that their nationals be made citizens.[53] The *Chronicle* branded the recommendation as "ridiculous," and prophesied that its effect would be to cause the exclusion act to be pressed in Congress.[54]

But it was the reference to force that thoroughly aroused the Californians. Roosevelt was undoubtedly in earnest when he spoke of employing federal troops in behalf of the Japanese, for shortly before his departure for Panama he wrote to Secretary Root: "During my absence . . . . I direct you if necessary to use the armed forces of the United States to protect the Japanese in any portion

[52] See San Francisco *Bulletin,* Feb. 23, 1907.

[53] San Francisco *Chronicle,* Dec. 5, 1906. Aoki was reported as favoring the idea of naturalization on the grounds that the Japanese, like the nationals of other countries, should have the privilege if they wanted it. *Ibid.,* Dec. 10, 1906.

[54] *Ibid.,* Dec. 5, 1906.

of this country if they are menaced by mobs or jeoparded in the rights guaranteed them under our solemn treaty obligations."[55] The passage in the message, however, was unfortunately so phrased as to admit of ambiguity. It read: ". . . . in the matter now before me affecting the Japanese, everything that it is in my power to do will be done, and all the forces, military and civil, of the United States which I may lawfully employ will be so employed."[56]

The press of San Francisco not unnaturally denounced with bitterness what it regarded as a threat of the President to seat Japanese in the schools beside the whites at the point of the bayonet. How could this be done, it was asked, without the call of the governor? How could the federal government constitutionally interfere in this manner with local school affairs? Was not the President laying the ground for impeachment?[57] Roosevelt, however, hastened to assure the California delegation in Congress that what he meant to say was that he was prepared to use federal troops to preserve order, not to force the Japanese into the schools.[58]

It was bad enough, from the standpoint of the Californians, to be verbally lambasted for the purpose of appeasing Japan, but to be misrepresented in so doing was doubly distasteful. The *Chronicle* asserted that the "President has degraded his position by assertions that are not true, assumptions which have no basis in fact, recommendations which can only excite ridicule . . . ."[59] It is true

---

[55] Roosevelt to Root, Oct. 29, 1906, Roosevelt Papers.
[56] *Congressional Record,* 59 Cong., 2 sess., p. 31.
[57] See San Francisco *Chronicle,* Dec. 5, 21, 1906.
[58] *Ibid.,* Dec. 6, 1906.   [59] *Ibid.,* Dec. 5, 1906.

that the President had been inexact in his references to what had actually happened. He had spoken of "shutting them [the Japanese] out from the common schools," and in another passage he had said: "To shut them out from the public schools is a wicked absurdity. . . . ."[60] On the other hand, the San Franciscans repeatedly asserted, what was substantially true, that the Japanese had not been shut out of the public school system at all, but had merely been segregated in a separate public school where the facilities for instruction were as good as those elsewhere in the city. Unfortunately, the President's loose statements probably gave further currency to this misrepresentation. Many San Franciscans also felt that Roosevelt was unwarranted in speaking of the power of the federal government to enforce the treaty rights of the Japanese to enter the public schools, particularly since it was clearly a debatable question, which the courts had not yet decided, whether or not the existing treaty conferred upon Japanese children the privilege of sitting in the *same* schools with the whites.[61]

It is not to be supposed that San Francisco was alone in its condemnation of Roosevelt's message; the entire state voiced its disapproval in no uncertain terms. An analysis which was made of nineteen representative Pacific Coast newspapers, most of them Californian, indicates that the press of the state was virtually united in opposing the President's views. Interference in a local school matter, threats of force, and the use of intemperate language were those features of the message which were most frequently

60 *Congressional Record*, 59 Cong., 2 sess., p. 31.
61 San Francisco *Chronicle*, Dec. 5, 7, 1906.

denounced.[62] Jerome Hart, former editor of the San Francisco *Argonaut,* asserted that rarely had there been such a unanimous outburst of public opinion in the state. He found, however, that condemnation, though universal, was less bitter in southern California, where there was a considerable amount of Middle Western or Eastern influence.[63]

A resolution condemning the outburst of Roosevelt was introduced in the California legislature;[64] and Governor Pardee, in his biennial message of January 10, 1907, defended the state with vigor. "It is safe to say," he asserted, "that the President . . . . was not aware of conditions on this Coast, especially in California." The governor went on to say that the Japanese were neither desirable immigrants nor citizens, and that they were clannish and regarded the Caucasians as inferiors. The people of the East came in contact only with the educated few, and the Easterners, including Roosevelt, did not understand their unassimilability. In these circumstances, continued Governor Pardee, it was not strange that the state should have shown, through a statute of the legislature, its aversion to having the Japanese mingle with the whites in the schools. Until, therefore, "the courts of this country shall have declared that California has no right to do so, this State reserves to itself the prerogative and privilege of conducting, under law, State, National, and treaty, its

[62] For the analysis see *Argonaut,* San Francisco, Dec. 20, 1906, p. 340.

[63] *World's Work,* XIII (Mar., 1907), 8692. The Los Angeles *Times* was the only important California newspaper to show any real sympathy for the Japanese. *Literary Digest,* Jan. 12, 1907, p. 43.

[64] *Senate Journal* (California), 1907, p. 91.

schools in such manner as seems best to us; and this without the slightest disrespect toward the Government of the United States or the subjects of any foreign nation."[65]

The California members of Congress were quick to resent Roosevelt's onslaught upon the metropolis of their state. Six of them were quoted by the press as expressing varying degrees of resentment, some of it extreme. Several were said to have asserted that they would not be surprised if Roosevelt's words provoked mob action in San Francisco. Representative Hayes, denying that there had been any treaty violation, asserted that California "may stand on her strict treaty rights and refuse to permit Japanese to attend the local schools at all."[66] On the floor of the House of Representatives he denied that the treaty with Japan extended school privileges, and asserted that California did not hate Japan or coolies—their ways were simply not our ways. Hayes's remarks were greeted with "prolonged applause," probably from the Democratic side.[67]

It should be noted, moreover, that California received strong support from several of the other trans-Rocky states. The Seattle *News,* however, was unsympathetic and stated that a majority of the thoughtful people of California were not in sympathy with the agitation of the

[65] *Assembly Journal* (California), 1907, pp. 72–73.

[66] San Francisco *Chronicle,* Dec. 5, 1906. See also *Literary Digest,* Dec. 5, 1906, p. 890.

[67] *Congressional Record,* 59 Cong., 2 sess., pp. 1579 ff. Representative Mudd, of Maryland, was said to have remarked that the thing to do was to take all the Japanese out of the schools of California: they had become too cocky after their victorious war; let the United States build up a navy and show them that we were no Russia. San Francisco *Chronicle,* Dec. 7, 1906.

demagogues in the cities against the Japanese, and that in no part of Washington or Oregon, which together exceeded in area and population the state of California, was there any sympathy with the foolish agitation of the people of San Francisco against the Japanese. But the *Literary Digest,* after canvassing fifty leading newspapers of the Coast, concluded that either the Seattle *News* was mistaken or that the press did not represent the thoughtful people, for of the journals examined, only three, the Tacoma *Daily News,* the Los Angeles *Times,* and the Seattle *News,* showed any marked sympathy for the Japanese. Most of the coast newspapers, the *Literary Digest* found, displayed uncompromising antipathy to the Japanese, to the President, and to Secretary Metcalf for his "disloyal" support.[68]

There was, in fact, evidence of a pronounced anti-Roosevelt reaction in the state of Washington.[69] Governor Mead objected vigorously to the message;[70] the Bellingham Central Labor Council went on record as unalterably opposed to the naturalization of Japanese;[71] and the state federation of labor passed resolutions condemnatory of Roosevelt.[72] The anti-Japanese movement in Seattle, which dated from April, 1906, gained momentum, an anti-

[68] *Literary Digest,* Jan. 12, 1907, p. 43. Later, the Seattle *Post-Intelligencer* severely criticized the anti-Japanese policy of California. *Ibid.,* Mar. 2, 1907, p. 320.

[69] On December 4, 1906, in Tacoma, a mob of whites beat a dozen Japanese laborers and threatened them with death if they did not leave. Then followed a mass meeting at which inflammatory speeches were made against the Japanese. San Francisco *Chronicle,* Dec. 5, 1906.

[70] Jerome Hart, "The Oriental Problem, as the Coast Sees It," *World's Work,* XIII (1907), 8693.

[71] San Francisco *Chronicle,* Dec. 15, 1906.

[72] Boston *Evening Transcript,* Jan. 5, 1907.

coolie petition received 10,000 signatures, and the completion of an organization modeled upon the San Francisco Exclusion League was announced.[73] Late in February, 1907, anti-Japanese feeling had advanced to such a point that in a Seattle theatre, after the flags of various nations had been shown amid silence or applause, the Japanese flag was greeted with prolonged hissing.[74]

Evidences of sympathy for California were also forthcoming from other Western states. Senator Gearin, of Oregon, made a powerful speech in the United States Senate on January 7, 1907, in which he stated that the Pacific Coast favored the exclusion of laborers.[75] Senator Newlands, of Nevada, asserted that Roosevelt's arraigning of the local authorities had "created a movement upon the Pacific Coast that will not rest until it ends in Japanese exclusion."[76] And Senator Patterson, of Colorado, citing specific cases of labor troubles with the Orientals in his state, announced that the Japanese question had already "become a burning one" in Colorado.[77] It is evident that a strong movement for exclusion, to which Roosevelt's indictment had contributed powerfully, was now under way on the Pacific Coast. Whatever the views of this region before

[73] San Francisco *Chronicle*, Mar. 3, 1907.

[74] *Ibid.*, Feb. 27, 1907.

[75] *Congressional Record*, 59 Cong., 2 sess., pp. 675 ff. Early in February, 1907, in Woodburn, Oregon, a group of whites drove eight or ten Japanese laborers out of the community. San Francisco *Chronicle*, Feb. 11, 1907. The Portland Chamber of Commerce, however, adopted a resolution in April, 1907, opposing anti-Japanese measures. *Japan Weekly Mail*, Apr. 27, 1907, p. 469.

[76] *Congressional Record*, 59 Cong., 2 sess., p. 3098.

[77] *Ibid.*, p. 3097. Early in February, 1907, it was reported that a number of Japanese pupils in the Denver, Colorado, schools had refused to take part in the flag drill. San Francisco *Chronicle*, Feb. 3, 1907.

the submission of the message, there is no mistaking the fact that opinion, so far as it was expressed publicly, was now preponderantly anti-Japanese.

We have already noted that Roosevelt endeavored to mitigate the severity of his message by explaining to the California representatives that his words, particularly those which suggested force, were not to be construed as they had been. In fact, there are indications that the President, ever sensitive to the workings of public opinion, was alarmed by his loss of popularity and apprehensive of permanent harm to the Republican party in the West. Jerome Hart wrote that, although California had given the largest popular vote to Roosevelt in 1904 that a presidential candidate had ever received in that state, the Chief Executive was now so unpopular that he probably could not equal the Democratic vote of that year.[78] There was even some talk of Roosevelt's having provided Bryan with a golden opportunity in 1908.[79] Representative Knowland, of California, remarked that it was a good thing that the November elections had come before the message, otherwise the Republican ticket would have suffered severely in the state.[80] It is not surprising, then, that Roosevelt should have hastened to make efforts to soften the force of his blow, a development which caused the New York *Nation* to observe, "We dislike to think that the President has shrunk from unpopularity in standing for a principle, but we wish some one would tell us his real reason for running away from it."[81]

[78] Hart, *loc. cit.*, p. 8693.
[79] San Francisco *Chronicle*, Dec. 7, 1906.   [80] *Ibid.*, Dec. 5, 1906.
[81] New York *Nation*, Feb. 21, 1907, p. 168. It is interesting to note that Roosevelt made no mention of this verbal lambasting of San Fran-

The strongest support of Roosevelt's message came from the East, where it was widely applauded for its courage and for its chastisement of a people who seemed bent upon forcing the entire country into war.[82] Nevertheless, considerable uneasiness was voiced by those who observed throughout the entire document, and not merely in Roosevelt's treatment of the San Francisco situation, a tendency to encroach upon the rights of the states and to demand greater centralization of power. The Washington correspondent of the London *Times* noted that conservative statesmen were already declaring that when Roosevelt's recommendations were carried out the last great step would have been taken in making the American government an effective unit in lieu of a federation of states;[83] and the *Saturday Review* believed that "if Mr. Roosevelt intends his threats for anything beyond foreign consumption, we may be at the beginning of a constitutional struggle unequaled in danger to the Union since the Civil War."[84]

Senator Rayner, of Maryland, a distinguished constitutional lawyer, was the ablest spokesman for the states' rights school. On December 4, 1906, immediately following the reading of the President's message, he introduced three resolutions to the effect that the federal government had no right to enter into a controversy with any foreign

cisco in his *Autobiography*. Possibly this was not an incident upon which he could look back with pride.

[82] The San Francisco *Chronicle* quoted with evident disapproval one Bostonian who had said that with the Negro problem one thousand miles to the south and the Oriental problem three thousand miles to the west "we are in a bully position to give disinterested advice." Dec. 12, 1906. See also *ibid.*, Dec. 6, 1906.

[83] London *Times*, Dec. 6, 1906.

[84] Quoted in *Literary Digest*, Dec. 29, 1906, p. 969.

government concerning the public school system of the states; that the treaty with Japan did not confer school privileges; and that it was the duty of the President to notify Japan that the United States had no power to regulate or supervise local schools.[85] On December 12, 1906, Rayner delivered a powerful speech on the floor of the Senate in which he spoke with effect to the resolutions that he had introduced[86]—in fact, his presentation was widely heralded as the ablest statement of the states' rights point of view with respect to treaties that had yet been made. It was not strange, therefore, that several members of the California delegation should have expressed hearty approval of Rayner's arguments.[87]

The views of Roosevelt were particularly distasteful to the traditionally states' rights South. Representative Livingston, of Georgia, asserted that the message sounded to him like the wiping out of state lines, and the South would not stand for that.[88] Representative Garrett, of Tennessee, was applauded on the floor of the House when he criticized the President for having sided with the Japanese against his own country.[89] In the Senate, Senator Carmack, of Tennessee, stated pointedly: "One of the President's favorite aphorisms has been to speak softly and carry a big stick. He seems to have interpreted that in this instance so as to speak softly to foreign nations and carry a big stick for the backs of his own people."[90]

[85] *Congressional Record*, 59 Cong., 2 sess., p. 37.
[86] *Ibid.*, pp. 297 ff.
[87] San Francisco *Chronicle*, Dec. 13, 1906.   [88] *Ibid.*, Dec. 5, 1906.
[89] *Congressional Record*, 59 Cong., 2 sess., p. 3223.
[90] *Ibid.*, p. 3098.

In Europe, however, applause for the President's message was widespread. The French press praised this lesson in international politeness, and in general regarded it as a move in the direction of peace. In England, the ally of Japan, this obvious attempt to lessen the tension of the situation was greeted with approval, and it was felt that the hands of the imperial authorities, who had recently been embarrassed by the anti-Asiatic movement in Australia, would be strengthened by the precedent just established by the federal authority of the United States.[91]

It is difficult, however, to avoid the conclusion that Roosevelt's message did more harm than good. The effect upon the Japanese mind was undeniably soothing; but the President probably could have produced about the same result by a dispassionate statement of his determination to protect the rights of Japan. Furthermore, the acute stage of the crisis had already passed, and the Japanese people were already convinced of Roosevelt's solicitude for their interests. The real danger at this time, however, lay not in Japan, but in San Francisco, where the public mind was already wrought up. A spark among these combustibles might easily have resulted in the lynching of several Japanese—with frightful consequences. Roosevelt's intemperateness and lack of precision in phraseology aroused the San Franciscans mightily, and they were widely supported by public sentiment in the West and South. The resulting uproar worked to the disadvantage of both the federal government and Japan, for passions were now so aroused in California that an amicable solution of the

[91] San Francisco *Chronicle*, Dec. 5, 6, 7, 1906; *Literary Digest*, Dec. 29, 1906, p. 969.

immigration tangle was made immeasurably more difficult. It may have been that Roosevelt had in mind marshaling public opinion in the East against San Francisco, but the obduracy of the Board of Education and the fruits of Metcalf's investigation should have convinced him of the futility of such an effort. There is little doubt, however, that the President recognized his blunder after he had made it, and his subsequent conduct, as we shall see, was in the nature of a retreat from his advanced position.

CHAPTER V

Approaching an Impasse

"I need hardly say I shall do everything that
can honorably be done to preserve the peace."
—Roosevelt to Grey, December 18, 1906

ONE OF THE most important results of Roosevelt's annual
message was to arouse interest in the contents of the Metcalf report, upon the findings of which the passages relating to the Japanese were presumed to have been based.
Accordingly, Senator Flint, of California, introduced a
resolution, which was adopted by unanimous consent, di-
recting the secretary of commerce and labor to provide
the Senate with copies of all official documents filed with
him during his recent examination into the school difficulty.[1] In response to this resolution, Metcalf wrote to the
president of the Senate, under date of December 6, 1906,
stating that his investigation had been undertaken by the
authority and as the representative of the President, and
not in his capacity as secretary of commerce and labor.
Therefore, the report which he had made, together with
the pertinent documents, had been submitted to the President, and was no longer within his custody and control.
It was consequently not within his power to comply with
the request of the Senate.[2]

About the middle of December, 1906, it was reported
in the press that the President was prepared to submit the

[1] *Congressional Record,* 59 Cong., 2 sess., p. 55.
[2] *Senate Documents,* 59 Cong., 2 sess., no. 104.

Metcalf report to Congress, and that he would accompany it with a message which would be even more vigorous in tone than the previous one.[3] The message and report were forthcoming on December 18, 1906, and it was at once noted that Roosevelt's statements were unexpectedly mild. Although the President repeated his determination to use the forces of the government to protect Japanese residents, he conceded that there would be no objection to barring children from the San Francisco schools if they were over a maximum age limit.[4] This brief message was regarded as further evidence that Roosevelt, as a result of the furor in the West, had receded from his original position.[5]

Enough has been said of the Metcalf report to indicate its general nature. It contained but few expressions of opinion, and for the most part tables, maps, charts, newspaper excerpts, letters, and depositions were allowed to speak for themselves. Roosevelt thoroughly approved of the work that Metcalf had done, for in his message on the subject he remarked that the accounts of the assaults were "most admirably put";[6] and in a personal letter to Metcalf he complimented him "upon the painstaking thoroness and admirable temper with which you have been going into the case of the treatment of the Japanese on the coast."[7] Some weeks later the President reiterated his views when he

---

[3] San Francisco *Chronicle*, Dec. 15, 1906.

[4] *Metcalf Report*, p. 1.

[5] San Francisco *Chronicle*, Dec. 19, 1906; London *Times*, Dec. 19, 1906; R. L. Buell, "The Development of the Anti-Japanese Agitation in the United States," *Political Science Quarterly*, XXXVII (1922), 628.

[6] *Metcalf Report*, p. 2.

[7] Roosevelt to Metcalf, Nov. 27, 1906, Roosevelt Papers. It should be observed that Roosevelt promoted Metcalf to the secretaryship of the navy on December 12, 1906, six days before the submission of his report.

wrote to the governor of California of the "careful and eminently impartial report of Secretary Metcalf . . . ."[8]

It is hardly necessary to state that Metcalf's report was received in San Franciso with widespread condemnation. The special correspondent of the London *Times* reported that it had "created more anger . . . . than the President's Message."[9] The Building Trades Council, representing nearly 50,000 members, met and passed a vigorous resolution condemning Metcalf for his treachery.[10] The press of the city was especially bitter, the *Call* remarking that the report bore "the appearance of having been written to bolster up the President's hasty and ill-considered message. It fails lamentably in that purpose, and is a monument of special pleading and one-sided investigation."[11] A resolution denouncing the report was introduced into the legislature of California, and the editor of the *Argonaut* observed: "With a somewhat intimate knowledge of California history, extending over a number of years, we have never known of an instance where a California public man has incurred so much odium in his own State as Secretary Metcalf."[12]

It is readily apparent that Metcalf was placed in a difficult position when he was sent to make the investigation. Since he was a Californian, and presumably a loyal one,

[8] Roosevelt to Gillett, Mar. 11, 1907, Roosevelt Papers.

[9] London *Times*, Dec. 20, 1906. Congressman Hayes, of California, said that the report was not so bad as he had expected it to be. He admitted that the facts may have been as stated, but that they did not warrant the strong language used to conclude the report. San Francisco *Chronicle*, Dec. 19, 1906.

[10] *Ibid.*, Dec. 21, 1906.

[11] San Francisco *Call*, Dec. 20, 1906.

[12] *Argonaut*, San Francisco, Jan. 5, 1907, p. 355.

it was expected on the Coast that his findings would be more or less favorable to San Francisco. No man can serve two masters, and the position of Roosevelt was so thoroughly out of sympathy with that of San Francisco that it was obviously impossible to submit a report, truthful or not, that would receive the approval of both sides. But Metcalf had a duty to perform, not as a Californian, but as a citizen of the United States and an officer of the national government, and in seeking and presenting his facts he was doubtless impressed with this responsibility. Indeed, it is difficult to see how one in his position could have discharged the task with greater fairness.[13] In his effort to be objective he presented a bare statement of facts, rather than his interpretation of them; but the tables and charts that he used were sufficiently damaging in themselves to prove highly distasteful to the people of San Francisco. Accordingly, Metcalf was widely denounced as a renegade, and efforts were made to dig out of his Congressional career incidents illustrative of his former willingness to sacrifice his state for personal considerations.[14] In both Washington and San Francisco it was felt that he had committed political suicide as far as any future elective office was concerned.[15] The *Chronicle* did not

[13] A special correspondent of the London *Times,* then in San Francisco, remarked that Metcalf "had, as an honest man, to report as he did." London *Times,* Dec. 20, 1906.

[14] See San Francisco *Chronicle,* Jan. 3, 1907. The *Argonaut* observed that Metcalf had cast his political fortunes in with those of his chief; that men who went to Washington became intoxicated with the atmosphere there; and that they forgot their states—but their states did not forget them. Jan. 5, 1907, p. 355.

[15] San Francisco *Chronicle,* Dec. 26, 1906. The *Argonaut,* speaking advisedly, stated: "Mr. Metcalf was a Californian." Jan. 5, 1907, p. 355. Metcalf retired from Roosevelt's cabinet in December, 1908, and never

mince words when it said: "The feeling in this State is not now against the Japanese but against an unpatriotic President. From now on Mr. Metcalf will do well to stick by the President who can give him a job. He could get nothing from the people of his own State."[16]

What probably angered the San Franciscans as much as anything else was a feeling that they had been prejudged by Metcalf. Shortly before the close of the investigation, the *Call* hazarded the statement, which it expressed a willingness to retract should events prove it wrong, that "Secretary Metcalf came to California with his conclusion in his pocket. His orders were to find facts to support that conclusion."[17] A few days after the publication of the report the *Argonaut* stated:

The feeling against him [Metcalf] would be less bitter were his report less strained. But it is the almost unanimous belief of the people and press that Secretary Metcalf came here with his mind made up—or perhaps came here with the President's mind made up, and his own made up to reflect his master's mind; also that the Secretary was intent on gathering facts to fit the President's preconceived and prearranged verdict.[18]

The press of San Francisco objected not only to certain alleged errors of fact[19] but also to Metcalf's failure to go out of his way to present the point of view of California.

thereafter emerged from private life. He may not, however, have had any desire to hold future public office.

16 San Francisco *Chronicle*, Dec. 21, 1906.

17 The *Call* professed to have gathered this impression from certain obscure intimations which Metcalf had thrown out during the investigation. San Francisco *Call*, Nov. 15, 1906.

18 *Argonaut*, San Francisco, Jan. 5, 1907, p. 355.

19 The Exclusion League vigorously denied certain charges of Metcalf and offered to show its records as evidence. San Francisco *Chronicle*, Dec. 19, 21, 1906.

The San Franciscans felt that something should have been said of the economic and social problems that were responsible for their attitude toward the Japanese. Metcalf's task, however, was not to explain away conditions but to report conditions as he found them. Nevertheless, so unfairly did many San Franciscans feel they had been represented that the Board of Education was reported as seriously considering the extension of an invitation to Roosevelt to come and look over the situation for himself.[20]

Human nature being what it is, Metcalf doubtless preferred to submit a report pleasing to his superior; but the situation was such that it was not necessary to distort the facts in order to do so. And although Metcalf did not present the alleged grievances of the Californians, it is inconceivable that he could have failed to explain to Roosevelt in private conversations why the San Franciscans felt so keenly about the Japanese problem. These conferences with his secretary of commerce and labor probably had something to do—perhaps a great deal—with Roosevelt's gradual understanding of the California point of view.

In the meantime, the Japanese were patiently waiting for the United States to solve the San Francisco tangle—but it was evident that their patience would not last forever. The atmosphere was uneasy, although perhaps not tense, and there was no telling what untoward incident would cause an eruption. Nor was the situation improved by alarmist reports, most of them utterly without foundation, which persisted in creeping into the press of the United States. These had to do with the alleged designs

[20] San Francisco *Chronicle,* Dec. 21, 1906.

of Japan upon the Philippines, Hawaii, and Alaska; with the activities of Japanese spies in the Philippines and in Monterey Bay, California; with the large number of men with war medals on their chests who were pouring into the Hawaiian Islands; with the fully officered regiments of Japanese that were working on the sugar plantations there; and especially with reports of Japan's feverish preparations for fighting the United States.[21] The San Francisco press, however, was inclined to scoff editorially at these war rumors, pointing to Japan's weakened financial condition and her preoccupation with Manchuria and Korea.[22]

In the midst of these alarms and rumors, a disquieting incident occurred. The American consul general at Yokohama, H. D. Miller, at the time in San Francisco, was reported as having said in an interview that the Japanese were greatly incensed and that they were willing to go to war, if need be, to preserve their national dignity. This statement aroused wide comment, and the administration officials in Washington evidenced uneasiness. But Miller, in a voluntary dispatch to his superiors, which crossed the Department of State's telegram of inquiry, emphatically denied that he had given out any such interview. He asserted that he had spoken to no newspaper representatives, publicly or privately, on the subject, and that the *Examiner*

21 San Francisco *Chronicle,* Dec. 1, 4, 12, 31, 1906; *Japan Weekly Mail,* Nov. 10, 1906, p. 602; San Francisco *Examiner,* Dec. 20, 1906; London *Times,* Dec. 10, 1906.

22 San Francisco *Call,* Dec. 10, 1906. Remarking that the East was much wrought up over comparisons then being made between the navies of the United States and Japan, the *Argonaut* observed: "Oddly enough, California seems quite placid, and the whole affair has aroused but a languid interest here." Nov. 24, 1906, p. 249.

reporter who was responsible for the statement had not even seen him.[23] With this explanation the matter was allowed to drop.

Roosevelt was still watching developments with the keenest interest, and his determination to make ready for any possible contingency was as strong as ever. In a letter to Sir Edward Grey, British secretary of state for foreign affairs, he refused to become alarmed over the alleged warlike preparations of the Japanese and attributed them to a fear that Russia was planning to recover lost ground in the Far East.

But it is also possible that she [Japan] has designs upon some other power—Germany or America, for instance; and again it is quite possible she has no designs on any power, but is simply bent upon achieving and maintaining a commanding position in the Western Pacific and East Asia . . . . It is possible that Japan hopes ultimately to seize the Philippines; altho I should doubt her having any present intention of doing so . . . .

Roosevelt then observed that Japan might not care to enter into an agreement for the reciprocal exclusion of laborers.

If so, there is trouble ahead, altho probably not very serious in my time. We have a formidable navy, as compared with Japan not only in material but in personnel; but in the event of war we should be operating far from our base. I need hardly say I shall do everything that can honorably be done to preserve the peace.[24]

With an eye to maintaining the naval strength of the United States at a high level, Roosevelt wrote to the chairman of the House Committee on Naval Affairs, on De-

[23] San Francisco *Chronicle,* Dec. 1, 4, 1906; *Japan Weekly Mail,* Dec. 29, 1906, p. 807.

[24] Roosevelt to Grey, Dec. 18, 1906, Roosevelt Papers.

cember 19, 1906, just as he had addressed Senator Hale of the Senate Committee on Naval Affairs during the previous October:

I don't want this country to lead the race for big ships, but it seems to me well nigh criminal for us to fall behind. I think the ship provided for last year and the ship to be provided for this year, two in all, should be at least eighteen thousand tons apiece. Japan's new battleship, the Satsuma, is of this size, which is the Dreadnaught size. I do not think we can afford to take any chances with our navy.[25]

An incident which caused no little comment in the press during December, 1906, and early January, 1907, required delicate handling. About December 1 it was announced that a Japanese training squadron of three cruisers, in pursuance of plans laid many months before, would leave Japan on January 5 and arrive at San Francisco about February 18. Certain European newspapers regarded this visit as "a veiled menace"[26]—an interpretation which certainly did not take into account the weakness or the character of the fleet. It was even suggested in the Eastern press that a Japanese naval demonstration at this time in San Francisco Bay would have an irritating effect and would probably provoke ugly disturbances in the city. But Representative Kahn, of California, agreed with the *Chronicle* in stating that the Californians were concerned solely with the coolie-labor problem, and that if the fleet should come it would receive a royal welcome.[27]

As the day set for the departure of the squadron approached, the Japanese Foreign Office grew increasingly

25 Roosevelt to Foss, Dec. 19, 1906, Roosevelt Papers.
26 San Francisco *Chronicle*, Dec. 1, 1906.
27 *Ibid.*, Nov. 30, 1906; Jan. 11, 1907.

apprehensive. The minister for foreign affairs, referring to the revival of anti-Japanese sentiment in San Francisco as described by the press, questioned the American ambassador as to the wisdom of the visit. Wright replied that he could think of no valid reason for avoiding San Francisco, that a sudden change of itinerary "might produce a disagreeable impression both here and in the United States," and that he would ask Root's advice on the matter.[28] Secretary of State Root wired back:

We see no valid reason why the Japanese training ships should not visit the Pacific coast as planned. It may however be suggested that the serious derangements at San Francisco and to the naval depot there might hamper the naval authorities in extending to the visitors the courteous hospitality we would so greatly wish to show, while the prostrated condition of the city itself would tend to restrict shore leave.[29]

Wright hastened to communicate Root's views to Minister Hayashi, and he "did not fail to impress upon him the pleasure with which the visit of the training Squadron would be received" by the government of the United States. The American ambassador reported that "Hayashi appeared to be entirely pleased with the attitude of our Government and to understand the situation, but he stated that he thought it best that the Squadron should not go, as some irresponsible person might cause trouble and further complicate matters." The fleet was consequently ordered to proceed to Australia after leaving Hawaii, a change which caused a certain amount of comment in the Japanese press.[30] The whole episode is illustrative of

[28] Wright to Root (telegram), Jan. 5, 1907, in file 1797.

[29] Root to Wright (telegram), Jan. 9, 1907, in file 1797.

[30] Wright to Root, Jan. 23, 1907, in file 1797. See also Wright to Root (telegram), Jan. 11, 1907, in file 1797.

Japan's deference to the wishes of the United States and a willingness to make every effort to avoid trouble. In later months, when Roosevelt boldly announced the cruise of the American battleship fleet under circumstances which were widely interpreted as lacking in regard for the sensibilities of the Japanese, the training-squadron incident was again discussed, and comparisons were made which reflected unfavorably upon the course of the United States.

In concluding this chapter it may be observed that thus far the brandishing of the big stick had proved more spectacular than effective. Feelings had been soothed that were not in immediate need of soothing; but the danger spot in the situation, San Francisco, was growing more and more ominous. By this time Roosevelt had doubtless come to the realization that if the big stick were to be used at all, it had better be used with more finesse. And when, as we shall see, he began to exert pressure on the San Francisco authorities with less fanfare and flourish, the results were more pleasing from the standpoint of Roosevelt, California, and Japan.

CHAPTER VI

Bludgeoning the Board of Education

"I am having my hands full over the Japanese
business. The San Franciscans are howling
and whooping and embarrassing me in every
way. . . . . We may have serious trouble
ahead."—Roosevelt to Kermit Roosevelt, February 4, 1907

ABOUT the first of January, 1907, it was evident that
affairs had reached an impasse. The test litigation brought
by the federal government on behalf of the Japanese was
dragging through the courts without any prospect of success. The Board of Education was obdurately maintaining its position, and the Japanese children were no nearer
admittance to the public schools of the city than they
had been in October. The San Franciscans, aroused to an
unprecedented degree against both Roosevelt and the Japanese, were in no mood to consider a repeal of the school
order until some means could be found to solve the vastly
more important problem of coolie immigration. And it
was equally clear that the Japanese would entertain no
proposition voluntarily to prohibit coolie emigration until
the irritation caused by the San Francisco affront had been
smoothed over and the objectionable order had been repealed.

The evidence would indicate that Roosevelt was now
convinced that he could accomplish nothing in his dealings
with the Californians by using forceful methods; that
from a political standpoint his message had been unduly

severe; and that it would not be an unwise move, from several points of view, to patch up the difficulty and mollify the Californians. Nor was Roosevelt's evident backing down from the advanced position taken in his annual message purely a matter of expediency. An examination of his correspondence reveals clearly that the President was gradually becoming more sympathetic with the California point of view. Whether as the result of a more careful study of the situation, or of various kinds of pressure from the Coast, or of Metcalf's private analysis of the situation, Roosevelt had at last come around to the point where he perceived that the Californians were in deadly earnest. His correspondence for 1905, as we have seen, reveals an utter inability to understand why the bigoted Californians should create a disturbance over the presence of a few Japanese coolies. But by November, 1906, he was prepared to concede that a mutual exclusion of laborers might prove desirable.[1] And in December, 1906, he confided to Edward Grey: "But most American . . . . working men, will object in the most emphatic way to Japanese laborers coming among them in any number. I think they are right in so objecting."[2]

In January, 1907, Roosevelt wrote to Lyman Abbott, asserting that in his opinion the Japanese should be treated as citizens and that every effort should be made to avoid injuring Japanese self-respect. "Whether we like it or not," he added, "I think we have to face the fact that the people of the Pacific slope . . . . will become steadily more and more hostile to the Japanese if their laborers

[1] Roosevelt to Metcalf, Nov. 27, 1906, Roosevelt Papers.
[2] Roosevelt to Grey, Dec. 18, 1906, Roosevelt Papers.

come here, and I am doing my best to bring about an agreement with Japan by which the laborers of each country shall be kept out of the other country."[3] On February 4, 1907, Roosevelt informed Andrew D. White: ". . . . I am convinced that the people of the Pacific Coast would without a moment's hesitation accept war rather than unrestricted Japanese immigration. I am not speaking about the rights of the attitude, but the attitude, and how we have to deal with it."[4] And to Kermit he wrote on the same day: "I am having my hands full over the Japanese business. The San Franciscans are howling and whooping and embarrassing me in every way, and their manners are simply inexcusable. They have no business to have kept the Japanese out of the schools and their whole attitude is very bad." But, he added, "I have to face facts, and one fact is that . . . . there is a strong and bitter antipathy to the Japanese on the Pacific slope. . . . ." This antipathy was "primarily due to labor competition," but it was "complicated by genuine race feeling." It was imperative to keep the coolies out, "but the Japanese government are loath to admit this. We may have serious trouble ahead."[5]

Roosevelt was not the man, as his record abundantly proves, to drive his head against a stone wall. It is clear that he was now convinced that however reprehensible the attitude of the Californians was to him personally, he was confronted with a condition and not a theory, and that a quieter handling of the problem would doubtless accom-

[3] Roosevelt to Abbott, Jan. 2, 1907, Roosevelt Papers.

[4] Roosevelt to White, Feb. 4, 1907, Roosevelt Papers.

[5] Roosevelt to Kermit Roosevelt, Feb. 4, 1907, Roosevelt Papers; see also Roosevelt, *Autobiography*, pp. 392–93.

plish more satisfactory results. Furthermore, it was now evident that Eastern opinion was becoming more sympathetic with the point of view of the Pacific Coast.[6] The recently published report of the commissioner of immigration, which set forth in graphic detail the remarkable expansion of Japanese influence in Hawaii, was helping powerfully in this direction. The time was evidently ripe for making some decisive move to break the existing deadlock.

On December 22, 1906, the president of the Board of Education was approached with the tentative proposal, believed to have emanated from Roosevelt, that the Japanese be allowed to attend the public schools, providing their ages were the same as those of the whites. The president of the Board refused to consider arbitration along these lines, pointing out that since the Oriental school had already been established, the state law made it mandatory that the Japanese attend no other.[7] About this time Robert Devlin, United States attorney in San Francisco, who was representing the federal government on behalf of the Japanese, was summoned to Washington to confer with officials there. He arrived on December 27, 1906.[8] With remarkable prescience, the *Chronicle* remarked that this move foreshadowed the summoning of the entire Board of Education to Washington, where an attempt would be made to find some common ground for patching up existing differences.[9]

[6] San Francisco *Call*, Jan. 4, 1907.

[7] San Francisco *Chronicle*, Dec. 23, 1906.

[8] *Ibid.*, Dec. 28, 1906. On December 29 he conferred with Attorney-General Bonaparte for two hours on the Japanese case. *Ibid.*, Dec. 30, 1906.   [9] *Ibid.*, Dec. 27, 1906.

On January 5, 1907, the President conferred with Devlin and Senator Perkins, of California, about the school question; and on January 30, 1907, the entire California delegation in Congress met with Roosevelt at the White House. Secretaries Root and Metcalf were also present. At the close of the two-hour discussion, the California members of Congress issued a statement to the effect that the character of the meeting had been such as to lead them to believe that a solution satisfactory to all could be reached.[10] Immediately following this conference, the Congressional delegation dispatched two telegrams to California. The shorter one was addressed to two San Francisco officials, the superintendent of schools and the president of the Board of Education. It read: "At the request of the President and the Secretary of State, we ask you to come here immediately for a conference with them and with the California delegation."[11]

The longer of the two telegrams was addressed to Governor Gillett and was prompted by the recent passing of an anti-Japanese resolution by the state senate and the evident willingness of the California legislature to consider drastic measures against the Orientals. It read:

Delegation has just had important conference with President and Secretary of State. At their request we have wired Superintendent of Schools and President of Board of Education of San Francisco to come here immediately for conference. Entire delegation joins in request that you send for leaders in both houses in Legislature, and ask that all legislative action concerning Japanese matters be deferred for a short time. We consider this most important.

10 *Ibid.*, Jan. 6, 30, 31, 1907.
11 *Ibid.*, Jan. 31, 1907.

On January 31, 1907, Governor Gillett transmitted this telegram to the legislature, accompanying it with a special message in which he urged that "all legislative action concerning Japanese matters be deferred for the present."[12]

The two Board of Education officials, although expressing surprise, immediately told representatives of the press that they were ready and willing to go to Washington, but that they would enter into no compromise which would disregard the mandatory provisions of the state law.[13] This was going too fast, however, for Mayor Schmitz, who evidently had not been consulted. Up to this point he had kept himself conspicuously out of the school imbroglio, but for various reasons he now decided to show his hand. It should be borne in mind that he was then at liberty on a $25,000 cash bail, as a result of five indictments recently returned by the grand jury charging him with extortion, and that the net thrown about him was becoming uncomfortably tight.[14] It should also be remembered that each member of the Board was a personal appointee of the mayor and presumably sympathetic with his methods and point of view.[15]

A meeting of the Board was promptly called, after which it was announced that no decision would be made without consulting the mayor, and shortly thereafter the entire group was closeted with Schmitz in the latter's

12 *Senate Journal* (California), 1907, p. 334.

13 San Francisco *Chronicle,* Jan. 31, Feb. 1, 1907.

14 *Ibid.,* Feb. 2, 1907.

15 Superintendent Roncovieri was an intimate personal friend of Schmitz, having played the trombone in his orchestra at the Columbia Theatre; and former President Altmann was a brother-in-law of Abe Ruef, the political boss of San Francisco and a crony of Schmitz. Thomson, *op. cit.,* pp. 145–46.

office.[16] The immediate outcome of this conference was that President Walsh dispatched a telegram to representatives of the California Congressional delegation in which he stated that if Roosevelt wanted only the superintendent of schools and the president of the Board, they would come; but if any decisive action was to be taken regarding the controversy the entire Board would have to go. Yet it was not definitely decided that the whole body would make the trip even if its presence were desired in Washington.[17]

In response to the telegram of the Board of Education, representatives of the California delegation wired back on February 1: "We hope conference may be decisive of whole matter. President in answer to your telegram instructs us to inform you that he would be glad to have you all come on."[18] Two conferences of the Board of Education with Schmitz followed, after which it was announced in the press that the Board did not feel at liberty to forsake its duties unless the mayor accompanied the party in the capacity of spokesman, mentor, and guide. Whatever may have been the real situation, Schmitz made it appear as if the initiative for this suggestion had come from the Board, and he evidenced a becoming hesitation by pleading that his duties and entanglements in San Francisco would make

16 A reporter for the *Chronicle* wrote: "It is evident that nothing will be done which does not meet with the approval of Mayor Schmitz." San Francisco *Chronicle,* Feb. 1, 1907.

17 Assistant City Attorney Williams advised that the Board had no legal right to accept a compromise in violation of the existing state law. He believed that the entire Board should pass upon any agreement made with the federal government, and for this reason the entire group, if any went, should go. *Ibid.*

18 *Ibid.,* Feb. 2, 1907.

it difficult for him to get away.[19] The upshot of the discussion was that the members of the Board informed
Roosevelt by wire that they would not go unless the mayor
went along.[20] Thereupon Congressman Kahn sent the
following telegram to the Board of Education on the night
of February 2: "At the request of the President and Secretary of State we ask you to come here immediately for
a conference with them and the California delegation."
The next day the *Chronicle* reported that the mayor had
yielded to the personal request of Roosevelt and would go.[21]

This unprecedented invitation calls for more than a
passing word of comment. The unique spectacle of an
entire board of education, accompanied by a city superintendent of schools and a mayor, junketing across the
continent to confer with the representatives of the national
government over a local school ordinance, was provocative
of a considerable amount of sarcastic comment on the
weaknesses of a federal system. The visit of the two originally invited representatives of the San Francisco school
system to Washington would in itself have been unusual,
but the obvious pulling of wires to secure an invitation not
only for the Board but also for the indicted mayor, who
obviously had the entire body under his thumb, was a sorry
exhibition of back-stairs manipulation.[22] It was a curious
combination of circumstances that forced Roosevelt, who

[19] The prosecution was willing to arrange for a postponement of
Schmitz's trial pending his return from Washington. San Francisco
Chronicle, Feb. 2, 1907.

[20] A reporter for the *Chronicle* wrote that the Board frankly admitted that since they held office at Schmitz's pleasure they would do
nothing that he disapproved of. *Ibid.,* Feb. 3, 1907.   [21] *Ibid.*

[22] Members of the California Congressional delegation expressed
disgust with Schmitz's interference. *Ibid.,* Feb. 1, 1907.

in speaking of Schmitz's humble origin was reported to have referred contemptuously to him as "the bassoon player," to extend this invitation to a man about to be convicted of extortion.[23] The New York *Nation* regretted that Roosevelt had backed down from his high-minded position and had "fallen to dickering with an indicted Mayor . . . ."[24] The San Francisco *Chronicle* stated that Roosevelt had abundantly expiated for his scorching annual message by condescending to associate officially with a man whom socially he could not touch with a pair of tongs, and that the President's affront to the city could now be regarded as a closed incident.[25]

There seemed to be an obvious answer to the question as to why Schmitz should have injected himself into the picture. The evidence is purely circumstantial, but intelligent observers in San Francisco and elsewhere quickly arrived at the same conclusion. The indicted mayor, who up to this point had kept astonishingly quiet, appears to have more than welcomed the opportunity for distinction and glory. To bask in the presence of Roosevelt with the eyes of the United States upon him, to avert war with Japan, to save his beloved San Francisco, and to return home a national hero—all this was undoubtedly an alluring prospect to the harassed man. His triumphal progress might conceivably raise him in the estimation of the decent citizens of San Francisco and so obfuscate the charges

---

[23] *Ibid.*, Feb. 9, 1907.

[24] New York *Nation*, Feb. 21, 1907, p. 168.

[25] San Francisco *Chronicle*, Feb. 5, 1907. The *Chronicle* humbly remarked that Roosevelt had been justified in characterizing as wicked and absurd a city that would elect such a man as mayor. *Ibid.* It is evident that both Roosevelt and the *Chronicle* were now backing water.

against him that they might be dropped entirely or at best pressed lightly.[26] His henchmen were openly jubilant at the opportunity, and they were delighted with the possibility of running Schmitz again with added laurels in the November election.[27]

Schmitz's move, however, was not popular among his labor constituents, whatever may have been the jubilation of his cronies. The former group feared, not without reason, that the mayor was preparing to bend the knee on the Japanese issue, and they had no desire to be thrown to the wolves in order to extricate him from his involvements. They further suspected, also not without reason, that Roosevelt would like nothing better than to invite this group of third-rate politicians into his august presence, and then overwhelm them.[28] The *Argonaut,* although not a labor journal, remarked that the President was rejoicing at the opportunity to get these men into the White House and "to daze them with its historic spell, to charm them with his own cordiality, and then, by sheer force of assumption and expectation, to bring them to concede the point."[29] To more than one observer it was evident that when Root and Roosevelt and Bonaparte once began to work on these men the game would be up. In fact, the *Argonaut* insisted that acceptance was surrender, for it was an acknowledgment of national authority where none existed;[30] and the *Chronicle* suggested that since a state

---

26 San Francisco *Chronicle,* Feb. 5, 1907. See also *ibid.,* Feb. 2, 4, 20, 1907; London *Times,* Feb. 19, 1907; *Argonaut,* San Francisco, Feb. 16, 1907, p. 449.   27 San Francisco *Chronicle,* Feb. 4, 25, 1907.

28 *Ibid.,* Feb. 4, 1907.

29 *Argonaut,* San Francisco, Feb. 16, 1907, p. 449.

30 *Ibid.,* Feb. 23, 1907, p. 467.

law was ultimately involved the logical body to invite to Washington was the entire California legislature.[31]

These charges of surrender were not without foundation. On February 2, 1907, the day before his departure for the East, the mayor told a reporter that he was going in a conciliatory spirit, and he hoped that the conference would bring about a satisfactory solution to the controversy.[32] The next day he stated that in case Roosevelt asked him if he would like to persist and make impossible the barring of coolies or give in and make possible their exclusion he would choose the latter course. He further asserted that he would seek a solution that would, if necessary, involve the sacrifice of local interests for the good of the entire country.[33] Several days later he was quoted as saying that it would be good Americanism to take such action as would be for the best interests of the nation.[34] Whether his position was disinterested or not—the man's record would indicate the latter—Schmitz began thus early to prepare the public mind for some kind of surrender on the part of the Board. Perhaps he foresaw the inevitability of the compromise that was ultimately adopted if the exclusion of coolies—one of the major objectives of the labor group—was to be effected.

On February 3, 1907, the entire delegation left San Francisco, arriving at Washington on February 8.[35] Their

[31] San Francisco *Chronicle*, Feb. 18, Mar. 2, 1907.

[32] *Ibid.*, Feb. 3, 1907.

[33] *Ibid.*, Feb. 4, 1907.   [34] *Ibid.*, Feb. 9, 1907.

[35] The entire party consisted of eight men: E. E. Schmitz, mayor; Alfred Roncovieri, superintendent of schools; L. F. Walsh, president of the Board of Education; Aaron Altmann; T. F. Boyle; David Oliver; E. C. Leffingwell, secretary of the Board; and J. T. Williams, assistant city attorney and legal adviser. H. Miyaka, attorney for the Japanese

departure elicited a considerable amount of sarcastic comment, the *Argonaut* referring to them as "those ciphers" and the *Bulletin* as "our ambassadors to Washington."[36] Upon his arrival Schmitz refused to make any formal statement, but he said enough to reveal that he was still disposed to be conciliatory. He remarked that the very fact that they had come so far was evidence that they were open-minded, and that no Californian was going to stand on technicalities when the interests of the nation were involved.[37]

While the Schmitz party was on its way to Washington, there developed what may be regarded as the most serious war scare since the initial flare-up of October, 1906. Enormous headlines appeared in the Eastern newspapers, and the long-deferred conflict with Japan was freely spoken of as inevitable. It is difficult, however, to say with exactness how the scare started. A request for increased military appropriations for Hawaii, which had been decided

Association of America, went on the same train to safeguard as best he could the rights of the Japanese and to confer with the officials of the Japanese Embassy at Washington. San Francisco *Chronicle,* Feb. 4, 1907.

[36] *Argonaut,* San Francisco, Feb. 16, 1907, p. 449; San Francisco *Bulletin,* Feb. 21, 1907. The *Argonaut* regarded the trip as a junket (the federal government paid the bill) with a free ride, free hotel accommodations, and with plenty of pictures in the newspapers. Feb. 16, 1907, p. 449; San Francisco *Chronicle,* Feb. 6, 1907.

[37] The *Bulletin* was thoroughly ashamed of the delegation. San Francisco, it felt, was "ludicrously represented." "For years to come Washington will look upon San Francisco as a city of yahoos . . . . Like a delegation of painted Crow Indians, come to Washington to confer with the Great White Chief, Mayor Schmitz and his retinue of School Directors are wandering up and down Pennsylvania avenue, staring at the sights . . . ." And they were constantly being photographed "but always with Schmitz in the middle . . . ." San Francisco *Bulletin,* Feb. 15, 1907. On the other hand, a special dispatch from Washington reported that the Californians had been well received and had created an excellent impression. San Francisco *Chronicle,* Feb. 10, 1907.

upon some time before the school incident arose, appears to have served as a stimulus to the war mongers.[38] Then, the very fact that Roosevelt had appealed to the California legislature and had invited the school officials to come all the way across the continent indicated that the situation was more serious than it was generally supposed to be.

In San Francisco, however, there was a general belittling of the war rumors. Roosevelt was accused of stirring up the commotion in order to get larger navy appropriations, or of endeavoring to create as critical a situation as possible in order to make concessions more palatable to the San Francisco delegation.[39] The *Literary Digest,* after canvassing the newspaper field, stated flatly that the "consensus of opinion in the American press seems to be that, whatever their source, these sudden war-rumors amount to nothing more than a 'scare'."[40] The *Outlook* advised its readers "not to take too seriously the warnings of certain Washington correspondents of impending war with Japan over the school question. When correspondents

[38] London *Times,* Feb. 4, 1907.

[39] San Francisco *Chronicle,* Feb. 2, 3, 1907; San Francisco *Examiner,* Feb. 5, 1907. In the East the big-navy men were accused of starting the scare. *Independent,* Feb. 7, 1907, p. 342. The *Argonaut* had no sympathy with the war talk. The issue was too trifling; Japan was not prepared; she would not alienate the moral sense of the world by provoking a war over so trivial a matter; and if war came, the United States would wipe Japan out. Feb. 2, 1907, p. 433.

[40] The New York *Tribune* regarded this war talk as ill-founded. The New York *World* suggested that if somebody had to fight Japan, let California bear the burden. That state alone had started all of the trouble, and it might be well for armies of the United States and Japan to co-operate to put her in her proper place. Quoted in *Literary Digest,* Feb. 9, 1907, p. 193. The Minneapolis *Tribune,* observing that about nine-tenths of the war talk was anonymous, guessed that the armament and ship manufacturers were behind it. *Current Literature,* XLII (Mar., 1907), p. 237.

cannot find news, it becomes necessary to make it . . . ."
This weekly then continued with a warning which it would
be well to keep in mind in connection with the problems of
this entire period: "There is no danger of war with Japan
on the school question. The only danger, and that we do
not think is serious, certainly not imminent, is that sensational journalists in America and Japan, unconsciously
co-operating, may fan race prejudices into a wholly irra-
tional race passion."[41]

When it appeared that the scare was in a fair way to
die down, Senator Perkins, of California, made a most
untimely and injudicious speech in which he implied, if
he did not actually predict, that sooner or later war would
come between the United States and Japan for the domi-
nance of the Pacific. Even if Perkins was misquoted—and
he insisted that this was the case—his remarks were certainly inopportune.[42] Richmond P. Hobson, the Spanish
War hero and Japanese baiter *par excellence,* added fuel
to the flames by an inflammatory address.[43] These intemperate outbursts naturally hampered the President in his
efforts to straighten out the tangle, and it was probably
with such remarks as those of Perkins in mind that Roosevelt wrote to Walter Mansfield "in strict confidence" that
he had "been terribly hampered in dealing with Japan by

41 *Outlook,* Feb. 9, 1907, p. 301.

42 San Francisco *Chronicle,* Feb. 4, 1907; the *Argonaut,* San Francisco, Feb. 9, 1907, p. 433. The situation was not improved when a
Reuter dispatch from Honolulu reported that the steamer "Siberia,"
which had left Hong Kong for San Francisco on January 15, 1907, had
arrived with 600 Japanese, many of them wearing uniforms, while two
captains were wearing war medals on their uniforms. London *Times,*
Feb. 6, 1907.

43 *Literary Digest,* Feb. 9, 1907, p. 193.

this extreme radical action in California, and especially by the insulting words used against the Japanese." He observed that the consequence had been "to arouse a corresponding feeling in Japan, which now makes it difficult for the Japanese Government to do in the matter of immigration what they would so gladly have done two months ago."[44]

Fortunately, however, the Japanese press refused to reply in kind to the American outburst. In general, these alarms were regarded as unworthy of comment, and leading men in Japan repeatedly protested that the United States was the last nation in the world with which they wished to go to war.[45] The Tokyo correspondent of the London *Times* noted that the Japanese newspapers had invited the Americans to observe that Japan was perfectly calm. "In this country," he added, "there is absolutely no talk of war. All the excitement, all the bellicose rumors emanate from the American side. Japan from the outset has maintained and still maintains unshaken faith in the American spirit of justice and sentiment of friendship of which she has hitherto had so many practical proofs."[46] The Japanese ambassador to France poured oil on the troubled waters when he issued a statement ridiculing the possibility of war and reasserting the confidence of Japan in the justice of the United States government. Similar assurances were also forthcoming from the Japanese minister to Austria and the ambassador to Rome.[47]

---

[44] Roosevelt to Walter D. Mansfield, Feb. 7, 1907, Roosevelt Papers.
[45] *Japan Weekly Mail*, Feb. 16, 1907, p. 168; London *Times*, Feb. 5, 1907; San Francisco *Chronicle*, Feb. 4, 1907.
[46] London *Times*, Feb. 6, 1907.   [47] *Ibid.*

.One salutary effect of this war scare was to jar certain elements in San Francisco out of their attitude of complacency. The *Argonaut,* which hitherto had looked upon the international aspects of the dispute with mild amusement and had scoffed at any suggestion of hostilities, stated frankly that the time had come to look the matter in the face and seek its solution on the basis of common sense and expediency. California must adopt a spirit of compromise and consider the matter in the light of international obligations. "Regarded from any point of view," this journal concluded, "the situation grows more serious —so serious, in fact, that a time has come when the President, our school authorities, and everybody else concerned owes it to common sense and to patriotism to abandon all petty motives of contention."[48] Roosevelt, too, seems to have been more impressed than ever with the gravity of the situation, for in writing to Kermit of the arrival of the school authorities in Washington he remarked that "we are now doing our best to come to an agreement with them by which we shall be able to bring to an end the condition of things which threatens so much trouble between us and Japan." He then discussed the necessity of checking coolie immigration in order to quiet the Californians, adding, "I earnestly hope we can do it without hurting Japan's feelings. The Japanese, however, are pretty cocky and unreasonable and we may have trouble with them any time."[49]

In the midst of all these rumors of war, Roosevelt received a reassuring letter from Sir Edward Grey, British

48 *Argonaut,* San Francisco, Feb. 9, 1907, p. 433.
49 Roosevelt to Kermit Roosevelt, Feb. 9, 1907, Roosevelt Papers.

secretary of state for foreign affairs. The President's hands must have been strengthened by this statement from the representative of a power which, as Japan's ally, would have become vitally concerned in any outburst of hostilities.

> I cannot think that you are likely to have serious trouble with Japan. The Californian difficulty must be trying for them as well as for America; but I am sure the Japanese want to pursue a quiet policy for some time to come and the strong line you have taken must have made matters easier by enabling the Japanese Govt. to show their people that they are not being met with a blank denial of any grievance.[50]

On February 9, 1907, the day after the arrival of the Schmitz party, there began a series of conferences between the San Franciscans on the one hand and Roosevelt and Root on the other. The conferees were pledged to secrecy, and the California Congressional delegation was not invited to participate, partly, it was believed, as punishment for Senator Perkins' part in the war scare.[51] After an interchange of views, which doubtless opened the eyes of both sides, Roosevelt presented his case. He explained that the duty of the national government was twofold: to look after the legitimate needs of the states and to deal exclusively with foreign powers. He then hastened to add that he was "in entire sympathy with the people of California as to the subject of immigration of the Japanese in mass" but that he wanted to secure exclusion with the least possible offense to the Japanese. The action of the

---

[50] Grey to Roosevelt, Feb. 12, 1907, Roosevelt Papers.

[51] London *Times,* Feb. 11, 1907; San Francisco *Chronicle,* Feb. 10, 14, 1907. Schmitz, however, did confer privately with members of the California delegation.

Board of Education, however, "could only have bad effects, and would in no shape or way achieve the purpose that the Californians had in mind." Roosevelt further asserted that he would use "every resource of the National Government to protect the Japanese in their treaty rights." And he promised that "the Nation would at once, and in efficient and satisfactory manner, take action that would meet the needs of California."[52] From later statements of Schmitz or members of the party it seems that Roosevelt played upon the fears of the San Franciscans by stressing the dangers of war with Japan, and that he constantly emphasized the point that the school ordinance was the greatest obstacle in the way of securing what the Californians most wanted—the exclusion of coolies.[53]

After the preliminary discussions, the conviction spread in San Francisco, particularly among the labor leaders, that Schmitz was prepared to surrender after making a feeble show of resistance. Accordingly, on February 10 and 11, 1907, more than four hundred telegrams poured in upon the mayor and the Board urging them to stand firm.[54] In reply Schmitz wired the Exclusion League that under no circumstances would he and his associates yield on the point of Japanese coolie exclusion, and that nothing could be accomplished unless the Californians quieted down.[55] This evidence of disapproval at home, however,

[52] Roosevelt, *Autobiography*, p. 394.

[53] San Francisco *Chronicle*, Feb. 19, 1907; see also statement of a surviving member of the Board in March, 1928, quoted in Butzbach, *op. cit.*, p. 39.

[54] The Exclusion League insisted that under no circumstances should Japanese be permitted to attend school with the whites. It wired: "California is the white man's country and not the Caucasian graveyard." San Francisco *Chronicle*, Feb. 11, 12, 1907.   [55] *Ibid.*, Feb. 13, 1907.

appears to have temporarily stiffened the mayor's resistance, and the conferences were prolonged for several days in what was regarded as a deadlock resulting from the unreasonable demands of the San Franciscans. The New York *Times* was led to remark sarcastically a short time later on the difficulties "in endeavoring to negotiate upon delicate affairs with the official products of hoodlum rule."[56] And on February 16, 1907, when the clouds seemed to be breaking, Roosevelt wrote to Kermit:

> Slowly and with infinite difficulty and frequent setbacks, I am getting both the Californians and Japan into an attitude that will permit of a solution of our troubles in that quarter—altho of course the whole business may be upset before I am able to achieve the result I have in mind.[57]

One factor that doubtless hastened the capitulation of the San Francisco delegation was the rise in the tide of Japanese immigrants entering the Golden Gate. Coolies were pouring into California at the rate of a thousand a month even while the conferences in Washington were being held.[58] This influx, alarming to the Californians, was undoubtedly the strongest card that the federal government held. And the administration realized this, for Secretary Root had cabled Wright a few weeks earlier: "If we can represent to California labor leaders that their action stands in the way of international agreement to relieve them from pressure of labor competition, I think we can get settlement of school question."[59]

[56] New York *Times,* Mar. 14, 1907.
[57] Roosevelt to Kermit Roosevelt, Feb. 16, 1906, Roosevelt Papers.
[58] San Francisco *Chronicle,* Feb. 11, 1907.
[59] Root to Wright (telegram), Jan. 16, 1907, in file 1797.

How, it may well be asked, was it possible for thousands of coolies to be entering the United States while the first Gentlemen's Agreement, that of 1900, was presumably in operation? The answer is that practically all of these Japanese laborers were coming by way of the Hawaiian Islands, to which the agreement was not applicable. After remaining there for a period of time which varied with the individual, many of these coolies were lured away by the higher wages and more desirable laboring conditions of the Pacific Coast states.[60] Anticipating trouble from this movement, the Japanese consul general at Honolulu, acting under orders from his government, had tried to dissuade his countrymen from going in such numbers to the mainland, but to no avail.[61] The problem was made all the more vexatious by the fact that hundreds of those arriving at San Francisco were contract laborers who were openly violating the spirit, if not the letter, of the federal law. They should have been stopped in Hawaii, if at all; but once they had established residence there they could not be prevented from traveling from one American port to another, even though admittedly under contract.

A few statistics will convey a more adequate understanding of the magnitude of the problem. In January, 1907, the immigration authorities in San Francisco temporarily detained two ships transporting about 700 Japanese from Hawaii; but the landing of these coolies could not legally be stopped.[62] On February 10, 1907, another steamer brought in 250 more; and again the authorities

---

[60] *Argonaut,* San Francisco, Feb. 2, 1907, p. 419.
[61] San Francisco *Chronicle,* Nov. 11, 1906.
[62] *Ibid.,* Jan. 23, 24, 26, 1907.

were powerless to act because the newcomers had arrived from Hawaii.[63] Fearful of further difficulties, the Japanese government acted on the advice of its consul general at Honolulu and cut down the number of emigrants leaving Japan from 2,000 to 1,500 each month.[64] But on February 25, 1907, another steamer arrived at San Francisco with 600 coolies from Hawaii.[65] Distasteful as any concession on the school question may have been to the exclusionists, the wisdom of sacrificing smaller things to gain the more important objective was becoming increasingly evident.

The deadlock between the representatives of the national government and those of the San Francisco school system was finally broken by a compromise. The Californians got what they most wanted, assurance that the influx of coolies would be stopped;[66] the federal administration got what it most wanted—a promised repeal of the school order. The San Francisco delegation, fully aware that a surrender on the school issue would cause a storm of protest in their city, were reluctantly brought around to Roosevelt's point of view, and they were finally persuaded only after prolonged discussions. In fact, it was not until February 15, 1907, that the agreement was concluded.[67] As a final gesture, however, Schmitz issued

[63] *Ibid.*, Feb. 11, 1907.   [64] *Ibid.*   [65] *Ibid.*, Feb. 27, 1907.

[66] The *Bulletin* stated: "There is no desire in California to insult or humiliate the Japanese. All we want is exclusion, and whether we get it from Washington or Tokio, from Congress or the Mikado, by statute or by treaty, does not matter as long as we really get it." Jan. 17, 1907.

[67] San Francisco *Chronicle*, Feb. 16, 1907. In a statement, said to have been approved by the White House, Schmitz stated that this was merely a temporary agreement, and that Roosevelt had given direct and positive assurances that he would begin negotiations at once to secure the exclusion of all Japanese laborers from the mainland of the United States. *Ibid.*

a statement in which he asserted that the Board did not concede, nor did it intend to concede, that its action had been in violation of the existing treaty with Japan; and that if any part of the treaty conflicted with the local school law that part of the treaty was null and void.[68]

In return for assurances that coolie immigration would be stopped and that legal proceedings would be abandoned, the school authorities agreed to rescind their order and permit certain qualified non-adult Japanese to enter the public schools. These restrictions, however, applied to all alien children alike, and in this way the Japanese complaint of discrimination was met—at least to the extent of saving face.[69] It was agreed that the prospective pupil would have to demonstrate a satisfactory familiarity with English; that he would have to be sixteen years of age or under; and that he would have to be within the age limits set for a given grade. For example, no alien child over ten could enter the first grade, over eleven the second, and so on. If the child proved unable to satisfy any one of these requirements, he would be segregated in special classes or sent to a separate school.[70]

So much, then, for the concessions made by San Francisco. The federal government, on its part, was obligated to stop the influx of Japanese laborers. Fortunately, this

[68] The first agreement was reached only after Schmitz had visited the Department of State and had received an answer to certain inquiries from Aoki. Boston *Evening Transcript*, Feb. 14, 1907.

[69] It was obvious, however, that these provisions were aimed at the Japanese, and in certain quarters in Japan it was objected that the arrangement was still discriminatory because the Japanese, unlike most other aliens, could not become naturalized. *Japan Weekly Mail*, Mar. 9, 1907, p. 252.

[70] San Francisco *Chronicle*, Feb. 19, 1907.

restriction was made immediately possible by the immigration bill which had recently passed both houses of Congress and which was then in the hands of the conference committee. In order to avoid the delay necessarily involved in the introduction of a new measure—Congress was about to adjourn—the administration agreed to tack on to the pending immigration bill an amendment covering Japanese coolie immigration. Accordingly, on February 13, 1907, the conference committee reported back the following:

. . . . whenever the President shall be satisfied that passports issued by any foreign government to its citizens to go to any country other than the United States or to any insular possession of the United States or to the Canal Zone are being used for the purpose of enabling holders to come to the continental territory of the United States to the detriment of labor conditions therein, the President may refuse to permit such citizens of the country issuing such passports to enter the continental territory of the United States from such other country or from such insular possessions or from the Canal Zone.[71]

Several features of this amendment are deserving of comment. In the first place, there was no mention of Japan—an omission consciously made in deference to the susceptibilities of that nation—although the purpose of the arrangement was perfectly clear.[72] In the second place, the amendment covered only those Japanese who had secured passports for destinations other than the mainland of the United States. No provision was made for the exclusion of coolies coming directly to the United States, because it was assumed that Japan would follow the un-

[71] *Congressional Record,* 59 Cong., 2 sess., p. 2809.

[72] The Japanese regarded this feature of the amendment with satisfaction. *Japan Weekly Mail,* Feb. 23, 1907, p. 190.

derstanding embodied in the first Gentlemen's Agreement of 1900 and continue to withhold passports from such emigrants. In the third place, the amendment made provision for stopping the flow from Mexico ("any country other than the United States") and from Hawaii ("any insular possession"), although these two places, the principal halfway houses, were not specifically mentioned. And in the fourth place, the authority to check this coolie influx was conferred solely upon the President of the United States and was to be exercised at his discretion.

The immigration bill, with its hastily added amendment, encountered a flurry of opposition in the Senate. Senator Tillman, of South Carolina, was disposed to put up a fight, but he capitulated upon discovering that he would receive no support. In the course of his remarks, however, he asserted that if the Pacific Coast was threatened with a Mongolian invasion, he was willing to try to stop it even "if it brings on war."[73] What little protest there was in the Senate collapsed when the President used the Rivers and Harbors bill to force certain members into line, and threatened to call an extra session in case the bill was not passed before March 4, 1907.[74]

In the House of Representatives, however, the immigration bill, particularly the amendment, was strongly attacked. Representative Burnett, of Alabama, objected that under the rules of the House the conference committee was obliged to confine itself strictly to the matters

[73] At this point Senator Lodge, of Massachusetts, arose and suggested that if that phase of the question was going to be discussed the Senate had better go behind closed doors. *Congressional Record,* 59 Cong., 2 sess., p. 2951.

[74] San Francisco *Chronicle,* Feb. 16, 1907. There was no record vote in the Senate.

committed to it and not to bring in new amendments.[75] A warm debate ensued, at the close of which Speaker Cannon, in a vigorous decision which elicited applause from the Republican side, ruled that the amendment was in order. An appeal was then taken from the decision of the chair, but the Speaker was sustained, 198 to 104, the opposition being almost solidly Democratic.[76] It was evident that, rules or no rules, the Republican Congress was determined to help the administration out of a disagreeable situation by passing the amendment.

Other objections were voiced during the debate on the conference report. Representative Underwood, of Alabama, thought it unfortunate that no provision had been made to exclude coolie immigration direct from Japan.[77] Moreover, the Democrats, who had been viewing with increasing disquietude the centralizing tendencies of the Roosevelt administration, were alarmed at the prospect of a further extension of executive power, and they frequently applauded attacks on this feature of the amendment.[78] Representative McCall, of Massachusetts, noted that the bill conferred "on the President of the United States what I think is high legislative discretion."[79] Southern members, in particular, were alarmed at the prospect of authorizing the President to flourish the big stick over the people of California and dictate to them what they should do in their school systems. Such au-

[75] *Congressional Record,* 59 Cong., 2 sess., pp. 3216–17.

[76] *Ibid.,* p. 3220.   [77] *Ibid.,* p. 3228.   [78] *Ibid.,* pp. 3223 ff.

[79] *Ibid.,* p. 3226. The New York *Nation* felt that too much power was being lodged in Roosevelt. Under the provisions of the amendment he might keep out Italians and others not coming directly to the United States. Feb. 21, 1907, p. 168.

thority, thought Representative Burnett, of Alabama, would enable Roosevelt to assert, "You do what I say regarding the schools, or I'll let hordes of Japanese in."[80] Representative Williams, of Mississippi, felt that it would be unwise to interfere in this manner with the local affairs of California, in that such a step might lead ultimately to an attempt to prevent segregation of Negro children in the Southern schools.[81] Representative Burnett developed this point with frankness:

Any man who believes in the right of local self-government and in the autonomy of the States . . . . is in duty bound . . . . to vote against the report. The big stick which it permits the President to hold over the States may sometime be wielded to the overthrow of the most sacred institutions of the South. This constant trenching on the reserved rights of the States is becoming more dangerous with every Republican Administration [Applause on the Democratic side].[82]

Some of the opposition to the amendment in the House was expressed in inflammatory terms. Ridiculing Roosevelt's compromising attitude and contrasting it with the high ground that he had taken in his annual message, Representative Michalek, of Illinois, asserted "that the big stick has dwindled, sir, to the magnificent dimensions of a toothpick. [Laughter.]" He continued:

Now, I ask you, Mr. Speaker, and you gentlemen of this House, by what law of human reasoning based upon the logic of the situation can we, the greatest nation of the West, kowtow to the little pampered bully of the East [applause on the Democratic side], whose self-asserted greatness lies solely in his highly developed sense of imitation, and in his recent success in the art of glorified murder . . . .[83]

80 *Congressional Record,* 59 Cong., 2 sess., pp. 3216–17.
81 *Ibid.,* pp. 3222–23.   82 *Ibid.,* p. 3227.   83 *Ibid.,* p. 3229.

An important factor in making possible the compromise was the approval of the California members of Congress. Although the amendment did not go so far as they liked, they were willing to accept it because it was a substantial move in the right direction.[84] Finally, on February 18, 1907, the bill passed the House, 193 to 101, the opposition being almost solidly Democratic,[85] and was signed by Roosevelt on February 20. Two days later the President could write that only with "infinite labor and against every kind of opposition" had he been able to work out this solution, which was "the most satisfactory . . . . of which the Japanese business was capable."[86]

[84] San Francisco *Chronicle*, Feb. 14, 1907.

[85] *Congressional Record*, 59 Cong., 2 sess., p. 3232.

[86] Roosevelt also testified that the Japanese government had "behaved very well, and Aoki . . . . is most intelligent, and appreciates thoroly the wide difference . . . . between coolie and non-coolie immigration." Roosevelt to Strachey, Feb. 22, 1907, Roosevelt Papers.

CHAPTER VII

Behind the Diplomatic Curtain

"We have made good progress toward settlement of the Japanese difficulty; but of course are not quite out of the woods yet . . . . I am much pleased at the way in which we have met the acute phase of the question."—Roosevelt to Grey, February 28, 1907

CONFERENCES with the school authorities were carried on more or less before the public eye. Although the injunction to secrecy was observed during the discussions, the details of what had occurred were freely given to the press upon adjournment. The public, however, was completely at a loss to know what was going on behind the diplomatic curtain, although it was surmised, and correctly so, that negotiations had been begun shortly after the school outburst looking to a treaty that would control coolie immigration. These diplomatic interchanges were of such importance and delicacy that they were necessarily enshrouded with secrecy, and this circumstance accounts for the large amount of guesswork, much of it wide of the mark, surrounding the Gentlemen's Agreement of 1907. It is therefore fortunate that the documents have been made available for the reconstruction of an authentic picture.

It will doubtless be remembered that under the first Gentlemen's Agreement of 1900, Japanese coolies were no longer permitted to come directly from their country to the United States. This prohibition, however, applied only to the mainland. Once the Japanese laborers were in the Hawaiian Islands, which are an integral part of the United States, nothing could legally prevent them from moving on to California, any more than the national government could keep aliens in Oregon from crossing the state line into Washington. Secretary Root turned the problem over in his mind and came to the conclusion that in these circumstances the only way to cut down the influx into Hawaii, and from there into California, was strictly to enforce the federal contract labor statutes, which coolies arriving in Hawaii to work on the sugar plantations were apparently violating. Observing that this open disregard of the laws of the United States appeared "to be one of the real causes of the difficulty in San Francisco," Root wired Wright several weeks after the school outburst to discover if the Japanese government would be willing to withhold passports from coolies intending to go to Hawaii pending an investigation of their status with regard to the contract labor laws.[1]

Wright took the matter up with the Japanese Foreign Office, and in response to his overtures finally secured a memorandum from the minister for foreign affairs setting forth the official Japanese view. This communication, the text of which follows, the American ambassador wired to Root on December 15, 1906:

Japanese Government have always exercised especial supervision in case of Japanese proposing to proceed to the United States, and no breach of contract labor law by these is within their knowledge. Passports for Hawaii are always inscribed to Hawaii only, therefore it would seem these facts not responsible

[1] Root to Wright (telegram), Nov. 19, 1906, in file 1797.

for San Francisco troubles. The Japanese Government anxious to respond so far as practicable to the suggestion of the Government of the United States, but cannot overlook difficulties which would result from absolute refusal of passports to Hawaii. Japanese who have disposed of their effects and made arrangements for proceeding thither would suffer loss which the Japanese Government would be obliged to make good. It is impossible also to refuse passports to those called on to join relatives in Hawaii sick or otherwise circumstanced. But with the exception of these and other similar cases, the Japanese Government will as far as it is possible discourage and restrict emigration in question till facts can be ascertained. They desire to be informed as to the time when the Government of the United States expects such facts will be ascertained.[2]

It would appear from this memorandum, which Wright described as "unsatisfactory,"[3] that the Japanese government was unwilling to recognize the fact that great numbers of coolies were using Hawaii merely as a stepping-stone to the mainland. No further attempt appears to have been made by Root to secure exclusion by invoking the contract labor laws.

Roosevelt enthusiastically co-operated with the Department of State in helping to prepare the ground for the mutual exclusion of laborers. On November 27, 1906, he wrote to Metcalf describing an interview which he had recently had with Ambassador Aoki. During this conversation Roosevelt had suggested that the only way to prevent friction between the United States and Japan was to restrict the movement of citizens from one country to the other to the non-laboring classes. Since no American

[2] Wright to Root (telegram), Dec. 15, 1906, in file 1797.

[3] Wright wired that "this unsatisfactory communication" materially modified the formal verbal assurance. *Ibid.*

workingmen were going to Japan, Roosevelt "earnestly hoped" that the Japanese government would stop the emigration of coolies to the United States. According to Roosevelt's account, Aoki "assented cordially to this view and said that he had always been against permitting Japanese coolies to go to America or to Hawaii." But, concluded Roosevelt in his letter to Metcalf, "the great difficulty in getting the Japanese to take this view is the irritation caused by the San Francisco action."[4]

Almost a month later, and two weeks after the spectacular annual message, Roosevelt wrote to Sir Edward Grey and stated that the "immediate source of danger to the relations between us and Japan" was in the labor question, which was but one phase of the race question. He observed that Americans and Australians and Canadians would object to coolie immigration *en masse,* and added, "I think they are right in so objecting." Furthermore, he was convinced that if the "influx of Japanese laborers to the United States goes on it is certain to be stopt by law within a few years; and very possibly the stoppage will be accomplished by acts of international bad breeding which will make trouble." Roosevelt concluded:

If it is possible I shall try to arrange some agreement, either by treaty or otherwise, by which both Japan and the United States shall agree to keep out one another's laborers. I think such an agreement is the only way by which permanently to remove what as far as I can see is the only radical cause of friction between the two countries. The Japanese may be reluctant to enter into such an agreement. If so, there is trouble ahead . . . .[5]

[4] Roosevelt to Metcalf, Nov. 27, 1906, Roosevelt Papers.
[5] Roosevelt to Grey, Dec. 18, 1906, Roosevelt Papers.

It is evident, then, that Roosevelt was convinced of the desirability of coolie exclusion; the difficulties lay in bringing the Japanese around to this point of view and in deciding on a method. Whatever the solution, Roosevelt hoped that it would be one that would "leave Japan our friend instead of an enemy eager and perhaps able to do us frightful damage whenever the opportunity arises."[6]

Further correspondence during this period reveals that Roosevelt was doing some serious thinking on the problem. Writing to J. St. Loe Strachey, on December 21, 1906, he observed that under the treaty with Japan the United States had specifically reserved the right to exclude Japanese coolies by act of Congress, but "to do it would mean to arouse very bitter feelings in Japan, unless I can have it done on Japan's initiative, so to speak. That it must be done, I am sure." Roosevelt confessed that he had hoped to accomplish this result through a non-discriminatory general immigration bill, but it was evident that he could get no such measures through Congress. He had to face the fact that there were differences in race and consequent antipathies, but if he could secure some agreement whereby laborers were mutually excluded "it will remove what is a growing, and probably otherwise permanent, cause of irritation. Moreover, the Japanese are coming in increasing numbers on the western coast, and if they begin to come by the hundred thousand it would be a very, very bad thing indeed, and it would then be too late to have a peaceful, or at least a non-irritating, solution."[7]

6 Roosevelt to Wheeler, Dec. 20, 1906, Roosevelt Papers.
7 Roosevelt to Strachey, Dec. 21, 1906, Roosevelt Papers.

For some time the method of straightening out the tangle that appeared most feasible was to persuade Japan to extend to Hawaii the passport restrictions which she had already adopted for the mainland of the United States in the first Gentlemen's Agreement of 1900.[8] Ambassador Wright took this matter up with Minister Hayashi, and out of these discussions came what appears to have been the first suggestion of the plan finally adopted. In his telegram of December 26, 1906, Wright reported that the Japanese minister, after having looked with some favor on the suggestion that the passport restrictions be extended to Hawaii, had finally concluded that this step could not then be taken without embarrassment. Hayashi's position was that Japan issued passports only to Hawaii, not to the mainland, and that she could not be expected to control the movements of her subjects after they had reached the territory of the United States. The Japanese minister had observed, however, that the United States could prevent their leaving Hawaii. This led Wright to suggest—and here we see the essence of the immigration bill amendment—

Would it not be possible to amend our Emigration Laws so as to provide that when foreign governments issue limited passports, our government should or might restrict emigrants accordingly? I see difficulties in the way, but perhaps at the present time some unobjectionable amendment might be drawn which would largely relieve the situation.[9]

[8] David Starr Jordan wrote to Roosevelt that if the United States, in a diplomatic manner, asked Japan to extend the passport agreement to Hawaii, she would readily do so. Dr. Jordan had received assurances from friends in Japan that Japan had but two interests in the matter: to do what the United States wanted her to do, and at the same time to save her face. Jordan to Roosevelt, Jan. 3, 1907, Roosevelt Papers.

[9] Wright to Root (telegram), Dec. 26, 1906, in file 1797.

Roosevelt, however, was convinced that in the interests of amicable relations the proposal for any restrictive agreement should come, not from the United States, but from Japan. Writing to Dr. David Starr Jordan on January 9, 1907, he earnestly hoped "that Japan of her own accord and of her own initiative will propose a reciprocal arrangement by which American laborers will be kept out of Japanese possessions and Japanese laborers out of American possessions." Roosevelt was certain, given the rising tide of antipathy on the Coast, that "sooner or later an explosion of feeling on the subject is certain unless some such agreement as I have outlined above is adopted. Therefore I earnestly hope I can persuade the Japanese Government to see this and to take action accordingly."[10]

The initiative for the immigration bill solution finally came, as the Roosevelt administration had been hoping, from the Japanese government about the middle of January, 1907. In a letter to Viscount Aoki, confirming a conversation of that day, Root wrote that "we have been unwilling to propose any measure to restrict the labor competition which lies at the basis of the whole difficulty lest the proposal should be misunderstood by the people of Japan and should be erroneously ascribed by them to the same attitude on our part which they resented in the action of the . . . . school board. . . . . A suggestion by your Government would not however be liable to any such

---

10 Roosevelt to Jordan, Jan. 9, 1907, Roosevelt Papers. On the previous day Roosevelt had written: "In strict confidence, I am endeavoring to secure what I am sure we must in the end have; that is, preferably by mutual agreement, the exclusion of Japanese laborers from the United States just as we should not object to the Japanese excluding our laborers from Japan." Roosevelt to Harrison G. Otis, Jan. 8, 1907, Roosevelt Papers.

misconstructions or lead to any such feeling, and I was very glad to take up the subject upon your initiative." In response, however, to Aoki's question as to whether the United States could prevent the passing of Japanese from Hawaii to the mainland without the intervention of the Japanese government, Root replied that he was having a careful examination of that point made, but "my impression is that additional legislation by Congress will be necessary to empower our Government officers to prevent persons passing from one part of our territory to another and I hesitate to ask for such legislation lest it should be misinterpreted by the people of Japan."

Nevertheless, Root believed that "the result desired could probably be accomplished by a formal agreement between the Governments which under our Constitution would have the force of law," and he thought "that the result would be accomplished if the two Governments were to agree formally that neither Government should admit to its territories citizens of the other country except upon passports issued by the Government of that other country and that neither Government should issue such passports to laborers." Root assured Aoki, in answer to the latter's question, that such an arrangement need not apply to the Hawaiian Islands. The American secretary of state also explained in some detail, to reinforce his arguments regarding the necessity for action, that the root of the Pacific Coast difficulty was labor competition, not race antipathy, and that the only way to remove the basic irritation was to remove Asiatic competition.[11] Root

11 Root rather cleverly suggested that the Japanese laborer was offensive to the white because of his superiority, not his inferiority. His

regarded this letter to Aoki of such importance that he cabled it *in toto* to Wright.

Ambassador Wright, in Japan, was still actively working for a solution of the difficulty. He had learned from Minister Hayashi that the Japanese did not want their laborers to go where their presence was not desired, and that with the rescinding of the offensive school order the Japanese government would continue its refusal of passports to coolies desiring to emigrate to the mainland of the United States. Those going to Hawaii would be limited by their passports, as before, to that destination. Wright had suggested to Hayashi that a treaty forbidding the immigration of laborers from Japan to the United States and from the United States to Japan might prove desirable, with the understanding, of course, that the school order would be rescinded before negotiations were begun. The Japanese minister had replied that since no American laborers desired to go to Japan such an arrangement would be so obviously one-sided as to subject his administration to severe criticism—an argument which the American ambassador had difficulty in meeting.[12]

On February 1, 1907, Wright informed Root by cable of certain definite developments. The American ambassador had just seen Minister Hayashi, who had stated that the Cabinet was agreed that when the San Francisco Board could be induced to rescind their order a way might be found to prevent the emigration of Japanese coolies to

superior industry, skill, and initiative enabled him to crowd the white man out. Root to Wright (telegram), Jan. 16, 1907, in file 1797. The letter to Aoki, contained in this cablegram, is undated but appears to have been written about January 15, 1907.

[12] Wright to Root, Jan. 23, 1907, in file 1797.

the United States; but time was needed to consider certain details. Hayashi had then authorized Wright to tell Root that with the repeal of the school resolution Japan would be willing to agree to some arrangement to prevent coolie labor from coming to the United States, Hawaii excepted, provided that the stipulations were such as not to hurt the *amour propre* of Japan. When Wright pointed to the necessity of cutting off the Hawaii flow, Hayashi stated that the Japanese government would not object to legislation on the part of the United States to that end if it would allay the existing irritation. The Japanese minister suggested, however, that it might be better to await the results of the pending suits to determine if, under the treaty, the Japanese were entitled to enter the schools. But Wright, speaking frankly, feared that the decision might not be favorable to the federal government, and even if it were, the effect would be to increase rather than to allay the feeling of irritation on the Pacific Coast and elsewhere.[13]

On the next day, February 2, 1907, Root sent Wright a cablegram in which he described the situation with more apprehension than he had evidenced in his instructions for some time. He stated flatly, presumably with the recent outburst of the California legislature in mind, that the situation on the Coast was growing worse; that there was no practical chance of settling the school question independently and in advance of the immigration question; and that Roosevelt had brought pressure to bear on the California legislature to suspend anti-Japanese

[13] Wright to Root (telegram, copy), Feb. 1, 1907, inclosure in Wright to Root, Feb. 8, 1907, in file 1797.

activity. Root added that with the concurrence of the California Congressional delegation he had suggested to Ambassador Aoki a new treaty providing for the exclusion of laborers and for the most-favored-nation treatment in the schools. Aoki had reacted favorably to this proposal, and had immediately telegraphed it to his government. Root thought it desirable, however, that this suggestion should come from the Japanese, but, if they preferred, the United States was willing to make it. Without some such arrangement, continued Root, "we can see no escape from increased excitement and conditions growing worse rather than better, to an extent making position of all Japanese on Pacific Coast quite intolerable in ways that no Government can control directly." He feared particularly that this agitation would result in exclusion legislation by Congress, which was permissible under the treaty of 1894 with Japan but which would be much less satisfactory from the standpoint of Japanese national pride than exclusion by mutual consent. Root again revealed his apprehension in his closing statement: "Important that prompt action be taken both because conditions growing worse on Pacific Coast and because this Congress ends fourth of March."[14]

On February 4, 1907, Wright cabled further developments. He reported that Minister Hayashi was somewhat disturbed by the newspaper attacks being made on him by the opposition party, which had heard that a settlement of the San Francisco difficulty was about to be made on the basis of an exclusion of Japanese laborers. Wright had

[14] Root to Wright (telegram, copy), Feb. 2, 1907, inclosure in Wright to Root, Feb. 8, 1907, in file 1797.

pointed out to Hayashi the necessity for haste, and the latter had stated that if the school order were repealed the Japanese government would probably agree to a treaty excluding laborers reciprocally, providing that those of the non-laboring group who entered the United States were entitled to naturalization on the same basis as other aliens. Wright had urged the minister to see his cabinet as soon as possible and return a definite answer. This Hayashi had promised to do.[15]

Hayashi's answer to these overtures was forthcoming on February 6, 1907, and was immediately telegraphed to Root by Wright. It read:

. . . . I hasten to inform you that I have referred the matter to the Cabinet meeting held yesterday and that I am now able to state that this Government sharing the desire of your Government to remove the feeling of irritation arising from the immigration of Japanese cooly labor in the Pacific coasts will be prepared to enter into some agreement on the subject. Such an arrangement however can only be concluded after the San Francisco school question has been satisfactorily solved and it is proposed that the restriction of Japanese cooly laborers (as distinguished from the settled agriculturist) should be made conditional upon the most favored nation treatment to be accorded to Japanese subjects in the United States in the matter of naturalization.

Wright was satisfied that the cabinet was anxious to settle the matter to meet the wishes of the United States, but they feared an "outcry here against a one-sided treaty and hence desire rights of most favored nation in the matter of naturalization." Since, however, few Japanese would avail themselves of such a privilege, it was evident

15 Wright to Root, Feb. 4, 1907 (telegram, copy), inclosure in Wright to Root, Feb. 8, 1907, in file 1797.

that this move was a sop to public opinion. Wright himself testified, "I do not think they regard the right of naturalization as intrinsically important . . . ."[16]

Root immediately wired further instructions in which he discouraged the naturalization proposal. He was unequivocal:

> It is wholly useless to discuss the subject of naturalization at the present time. If right exists under act of June twenty-ninth nineteen hundred six discussion unnecessary. If not it is clear that no statute could be passed or treaty ratified now extending Japanese rights beyond the limits of their contention regarding the schools.

Furthermore, Root made it clear that all newspaper reports about the conferences which were then being held with the San Francisco officials in Washington were unauthorized. Although he believed that under the treaty Japanese children were entitled to the same educational advantages in California as other aliens, he doubted if the treaty were being violated by giving them those advantages in separate schools. In Root's opinion it was at least an even chance that the courts would decide that the San Francisco school order violated no treaty. The United States, however, was willing to settle the question of doubt in favor of Japan if the latter should prove willing to join in a plan for labor exclusion, which under the treaty of 1894 the United States had the express right to secure by statute. Root concluded:

Such a treaty would give the United States nothing whatever it has not now, but it would be in accordance with Japanese

---

16 Wright to Root, Feb. 6, 1907 (telegram, copy), inclosure in Wright to Root, Feb. 8, 1907, in file 1797.

policy regarding her laborers and would make it possible for us to put an end to school question in accordance with Japan's wishes and to put an end to the whole cause of disagreeable conditions on the Pacific coast. We have the power to put a stop to labor competition on the coast by statute and unless some such treaty arrangement is made Congress will undoubtedly exercise that power. We are however exceedingly unwilling that this should be done except avowedly in accordance with the wishes of Japan and in such way as to dispose of school question at the same time.[17]

Wright promptly communicated Root's instructions to Hayashi, emphasizing particularly the impossibility of naturalization. In the ensuing conversation, the Japanese minister for foreign affairs conceded that it was probably true that under the letter of the existing treaty the school order could not be objected to, but the Japanese believed that the spirit of the treaty guaranteed them equal school rights in the United States. Hayashi further noted that the Japanese felt that to accede to the Root proposal was simply to exclude their laborers without a corresponding concession, and he again stated that as far as the administration was concerned the difficulty was largely a matter of preserving the *amour propre* of the Japanese.[18]

The San Francisco delegation had now been in Washington for some time and there was obviously a pressing need for a prompt solution of the difficulty. Root's proposal for a treaty mutually excluding laborers was making little progress because of the one-sided nature of such an agreement, and the Japanese cabinet was striving des-

---

[17] Root to Wright (telegram, copy), Feb. 6, 1907, inclosure in Wright to Root, Feb. 8, 1907, in file 1797.

[18] Wright to Root (telegram, copy), Feb. 9, 1907, inclosure in Wright to Root, Feb. 20, 1907, in file 1797.

perately, as was evidenced by the naturalization proposal, to secure some substantial concession from the United States that would act as a salve for the national pride of Japan.[19]   It was evident to Root that if any immediate solution of the San Francisco difficulty were to be had it would have to be a temporary arrangement, and that the negotiation of a treaty, on which agreement seemed impossible for some time to come, would have to be deferred. He therefore fell back upon Hayashi's assurance, conveyed in Wright's telegram of February 1, 1907, that the Japanese government would not object to legislation by the United States to stop the flow from Hawaii;[20] and the immigration bill amendment was consequently pushed through Congress.

In transmitting to Wright the terms of the agreement with the school authorities, Secretary Root hoped that the solution would be regarded with satisfaction by the Japanese. He specifically instructed Wright to express to Hayashi informally the hope that Japan would continue to withhold passports from laborers wishing to go directly to the mainland of the United States, and of the desire of the United States to proceed with the negotiation of a

---

[19] Wright learned from an indirect source that the Japanese would probably agree to a mutual exclusion treaty with most-favored-nation school privileges, provided the United States would agree that the Japanese might make a customs union with Korea by which there would be free trade between Korea and Japan. Such an agreement would also have to be made with the other powers, and the United States would have the same tariff rights as any other power. Wright to Root (telegram, copy), Feb. 13, 1907, inclosure in Wright to Root, Feb. 20, 1907, in file 1797. Roosevelt was favorably impressed with the Korea proposal, but it was not found feasible to work out an exclusion treaty on that basis. Root to Wright (telegram, copy), Feb. 15, 1907, inclosure in Wright to Root, Feb. 20, 1907, in file 1797.

[20] *Ibid.*

treaty.[21] Wright conveyed these instructions to Hayashi, and reported that "he seemed pleased with the solution and will write me a note giving assurance that the Japanese Government will not issue passports to the mainland of the United States but to Hawaii only."[22]

On February 24, 1907, Wright received the note that Minister Hayashi had promised him. It was of the first importance because it provided definite, written assurance that the existing passport arrangements upon which the recent immigration legislation was based would be continued. This note, then, may properly be considered the basis of the second Gentlemen's Agreement, or the Gentlemen's Agreement of 1907. The press was kept in ignorance of the arrangement, although it gradually became evident that some kind of understanding had been reached, and in view of the resultant speculation it is refreshing to be able to point so definitely to the genesis of the agreement. Minister Hayashi's statement reads as follows:

The Imperial Government . . . . beg to state that they have no intention of canceling or modifying the order now in force under which no passports are granted to either skilled or unskilled Japanese laborers for the mainland of the United States other than settled agriculturists, farmers owning or having an interest or share in their produce or crops. The Imperial Government confidently believe that a strict adhesion on their part to the foregoing order coupled with the continuation of the existing practice of inserting in all labor passports the destination of the laborers will be sufficient to make the new legislation of

[21] Root to Wright (telegram, copy), Feb. 20, 1907, inclosure in Wright to Root, Feb. 20, 1907, in file 1797.

[22] Wright to Root (telegram, copy), Feb. 21, 1907, inclosure in Wright to Root, Mar. 3, 1907, in file 1797.

the United States more satisfactory and obviate the necessity of adopting additional measures.[23]

How the details of the Gentlemen's Agreement of 1907 were worked out between Japan and the United States is not altogether clear. The files of the Department of State which were consulted for this period shed no further light on the problem.[24] For such information as is available on this point we are beholden to the commissioner-general of immigration, who in his annual report for 1908 referred to the understanding that had just been reached with Japan, under the terms of which passports to the mainland of the United States would be issued only to those of the laboring class who were former residents of the United States, close relatives of Japanese already here, or settled agriculturists. The commissioner-general also reported that the Japanese government had by that time voluntarily limited Japanese emigration to Hawaii to former residents and to the parents, wives, and children of residents.[25]

Roosevelt's plans for a new treaty, although not entirely abandoned,[26] were pushed into the background, and thus ended the efforts of diplomacy to effect a solution of the San Francisco tangle. The most pressing question that remained was whether or not the San Francisco authorities would carry out their end of the bargain. The

[23] Wright to Root (telegram, copy), Feb. 24, 1907, inclosure in Wright to Root, Mar. 3, 1907, in file 1797.

[24] See Oscar Straus, *Under Four Administrations* (Boston, 1922), p. 227.

[25] *Annual Report of the United States Commissioner-General of Immigration, 1908*, in *Annual Report of the Secretary of Commerce and Labor, 1908* (Washington, 1908), pp. 221–22.

[26] Roosevelt to Root, Feb. 15, 1907, Roosevelt Papers.

prospect of a last-minute backdown caused Roosevelt some uneasiness. He wrote to Sir Edward Grey that although they had "made good progress toward settlement of the Japanese difficulty" they were "not quite out of the woods yet." Nevertheless, he felt that "we have established the main lines of the solution; and have done it in a way that satisfies California without bringing a break with Japan. . . . . I am much pleased at the way in which we have met the acute phase of the Japanese question."[27]

[27] Roosevelt to Grey, Feb. 28, 1907, Roosevelt Papers.

CHAPTER VIII

Final Settlement of the School Imbroglio

"As for the San Francisco incident, it caused
me more concern than you can imagine . . . ."
—Roosevelt to Takahira, April 28, 1907

THE ROOSEVELT administration now appeared to be almost "out of the woods." All that remained to complete the agreement was for the Board to return to San Francisco and repeal the school order and for the President to drop the test litigation and issue an executive order putting into effect the immigration bill amendment. The Washington correspondent of the London *Times* wrote that "unless the sensation-mongers and mischief makers further complicate matters, it is reasonable to suppose that the incident is closed."[1] Unfortunately, however, "mischief makers" put in an appearance, and there developed a situation which caused Roosevelt no little disquietude. The Schmitz party returned to San Francisco, there to be greeted by certain elements with unmistakable evidences of displeasure,[2] as a consequence of which the school officials showed no haste to fulfill their promise and repeal the order. But the most serious development was a growing disposition on the part of the California legislature, which had been reasonably quiet since Roosevelt's appeal late in January, 1907, to complicate the situation by enacting several discriminatory anti-Japanese measures.

[1] London *Times*, Feb. 20, 1907.
[2] See San Francisco *Chronicle*, Feb. 18, 1907.

After some preliminary rumblings early in the month,[3] the assembly of the California legislature passed a bill on February 28, 1907, designed to limit the ownership of land by Japanese and Chinese to a period of five years.[4] The New York correspondent of the London *Times* reported that the "Californians seem bent on creating a serious international situation," and that one San Francisco newspaper had already openly hinted that if the Japanese children were allowed to return to the white schools they would be mobbed.[5] The Tokyo *Nichi Nichi* protested against this proposed legislation as discriminatory,[6] and the Tokyo correspondent of the London *Times* wrote: "The new phase of the California question is deeply resented in Japan as far more radical than any labor agitation, but the Press maintains the same calm tone which it has observed throughout. The idea of any real rupture of friendship between America and Japan seems wholly untenable to the Japanese nation."[7]

The situation in the legislature grew steadily more ominous. On March 6, 1907, the Keane Bill, which was designed to prevent Japanese over ten years of age from entering the same primary grades with the whites, was reported in the senate.[8] President Roosevelt was alarmed. He wrote to Secretary Root and directed him to come in and discuss the situation in California, adding: "I am convinced that it has been a mistake on our part not to take open action before this." Roosevelt then suggested

[3] San Francisco *Chronicle*, Feb. 5, 7, 8, 1907.
[4] *Ibid.*, Mar. 1, 1907.   [5] London *Times*, Mar. 2, 1907.
[6] San Francisco *Chronicle*, Mar. 5, 1907.
[7] London *Times*, Mar. 7, 1907.
[8] San Francisco *Chronicle*, Mar. 7, 1907.

that a letter or a telegraphic communication to Governor Gillett might "accomplish the result." "If we let things drift," he concluded, "we may get into a very bad situation. Of course we can always refuse to restrain the Japanese immigration; but while this will treat the San Franciscans just as they deserve, it will not solve the situation but on the contrary will make it worse. We should not longer delay."[9]

With characteristic vigor and utter disregard of state lines, Roosevelt intervened openly to prevent further complications. On March 10, 1907, he sent the following telegram to Governor Gillett:

> The action of the Legislature, reported in this morning's papers, is most unfortunate in its effects upon my efforts to secure the exclusion of Japanese laborers by friendly agreement, and if continued will probably render the recent legislation by Congress for that purpose ineffective. Please secure a suspension of further action until the receipt of a letter from me.[10]

Gillett forwarded this telegram to the assembly and in an accompanying letter urged compliance with the President's wishes. This request was favorably received by the majority, but one member who raised objections was applauded by the San Francisco delegation.[11]

On March 9, 1907, Roosevelt wrote the first of a series of four remarkable letters to Governor Gillett.[12] At the outset he stated flatly that the whole difficulty "in secur-

9 Roosevelt to Root, Mar. 10, 1907, Roosevelt Papers.

10 San Francisco *Chronicle,* Mar. 12, 1907.   11 *Ibid.*

12 The other three were written on March 11, March 12, and March 14. It may be observed that Gillett was indebted to Roosevelt for support in the gubernatorial campaign of 1906. See San Francisco *Chronicle,* Oct. 25, 1906.

ing the exclusion of Japanese laborers had come from the attitude of the violent extremists in San Francisco who profess to have this very object in view." This was so obvious that Roosevelt was inclined to think that many of them did not desire exclusion at all because it would deprive them of a source of agitation and consequently of "notoriety and temporary influence." The President then pointed out that he had the power under the recently enacted immigration law to exclude laborers coming indirectly, but not directly, from Japan. Moreover, the Japanese government had voluntarily promised to prohibit coolie emigration to the mainland of the United States, but this agreement had been based upon an understanding that the Japanese in America would not be discriminated against. The anti-Japanese measures before the legislature might therefore "just as well be called a proposal to prevent the exclusion of Japanese laborers; for every man introducing or favoring such a proposal is simply doing all that he can to prevent the accomplishment of what is profest to be the purpose of the labor unions and other bodies . . . ." Roosevelt then asserted that he would not issue the executive order preventing indirect immigration, particularly that from Hawaii, until the Board had fulfilled its part of the agreement. And he closed with the further threat that the order would not "be issued or enforced if other measures are taken of petty persecution toward the Japanese. . . . ."[13]

The President's second letter to Gillett, that of March 11, 1907, presented the administration's point of view with even greater force. First of all Roosevelt noted that

[13] Roosevelt to Gillett, Mar. 9, 1907, Roosevelt Papers.

he had written his previous letter before he had learned that one house of the California legislature had passed a bill including the Japanese with other Mongolians for whom separate schools were to be established. If this legislation, he continued, "is meant to be ineffective and simply an expression of opinion or assertion of an abstract right . . . . then it is merely a foolish and wanton insult to Japan, and may have little effect save to make it more difficult on the part of the national Government to secure for California what California desires, and to keep on terms of cordial friendship . . . . with a great and friendly nation." But if the legislation were intended to be effective and to destroy the agreement arrived at with such difficulty, "then it is exceedingly mischievous." Roosevelt further asserted that

it is most unwise for the people of California to insist upon something which is absolutely useless, which works no possible benefit, and which can not but be taken as insulting to a people with whom we have ancestral ties of friendship and with whom we wish to remain at peace. Moreover, any such insistence in a course of hectoring and insulting the Japanese renders nugatory what we have accomplished in providing for excluding Japanese laborers, skilled and unskilled.

The likelihood of the Californians defeating their own purposes, which Roosevelt had referred to in his previous letter, was then fully elaborated. The President pointed out that under the arrangement just consummated "we now have absolute power to exclude all Japanese laborers from this country . . . ." If the proposed anti-Japanese legislation should "become effective, so as to bring to naught what has been done, all solution of the matter will be indefinitely delayed." Then, as if to soften the sting of his blunt words, Roosevelt asserted that he was "earnestly and eagerly desirous of standing for California's need"; that the "interests and honor of the men of the Pacific Slope" were dear to him; and that he would like to meet consistently with his duty to the rest of the country "every one of their desires." Roosevelt thereupon concluded:

I have been able to bring about a solution of this question which secures every particle of what the Californians wish, and which secures it in a way which commands the hearty assent of the rest of the nation; and this in a manner honorable to the United States and honorable to the proud nation of Japan, with whom it must ever be one of our prime objects to remain on terms of self-respecting peace.[14]

On March 11, 1907, Governor Gillett wired Roosevelt to ascertain if a bill then before the legislature would hamper the President in his efforts to straighten out the Japanese tangle. This measure provided that after two years the question of whether or not the Californians wanted Japanese exclusion would be submitted to the voters of the state for their decision.[15] Roosevelt promptly replied, in his third letter, of March 12, 1907, which appears to have supplemented a telegram, that the proposed legislation would not only be futile but would needlessly complicate the progress of negotiations with Japan. He further pointed out that such a proposal was a step in the direction of usurping the treaty powers of the national government, which alone had the authority to deal with coolie exclusion.[16]

The last letter of the series, that of March 14, 1907, was

14 Roosevelt to Gillett, Mar. 11, 1907, Roosevelt Papers.
15 San Francisco *Chronicle,* Mar. 13, 1907.
16 Roosevelt to Gillett, Mar. 12, 1907, Roosevelt Papers.

one of congratulation and assurance. The President was pleased with what Gillett had been able to do in stopping adverse legislation, and he was relieved by the belated action of the Board, which, on the previous day, had finally rescinded the now famous order. "I have no question," Roosevelt wrote, "that we shall now be able to accomplish by direct negotiation with Japan just what we desire. But . . . . now that California has clearly put herself in the right, the national Government is able to stand straight for California's interest; and if it should prove necessary I would myself immediately advocate the passage of an exclusion law." While California was in the wrong and violating the spirit if not the letter of the treaty with Japan, Roosevelt was not able to support her cause with conviction; but now "I am in the position of being able wholeheartedly to champion California's interest . . . ." It must have been with a feeling of relief that Roosevelt was able to conclude: "Therefore, my dear Governor, I congratulate not only the United States but especially California upon the wisdom of her Legislature and her Governor in this matter; and I congratulate the City of San Francisco upon the wisdom of her School Board."[17]

Roosevelt's vigorous methods of dealing with the governor and legislature of California elicited varying comments. The country had been treated to an unusual sight when the San Francisco School Board, led by an indicted mayor, had journeyed across the continent to confer with the President; and the direct application of pressure to the California officials caused many to wonder what step

[17] Roosevelt to Gillett, Mar. 14, 1907, Roosevelt Papers.

would be taken next in the direction of obliterating state boundaries. The New York *Times* asserted that the tactics of Roosevelt "would have made George Washington stare and gasp . . . . It is a startling novelty. But in this case it seems to have worked."[18] And although a number of newspapers in California held that it was highly improper for Roosevelt to try to coerce a state legislature,[19] there was surprising agreement throughout the press of the nation that Roosevelt's course had been the wise one.[20]

In the meantime the school officials had tardily and unenthusiastically fulfilled their promise. On March 12, 1907, Schmitz wired Roosevelt that the Board would rescind the order the next day, and he suggested that the President give notice of the dismissal of the test litigation at the same time.[21] The President was doubtless relieved at the immediate prospect of final action, for he wired in reply: "I thank you and congratulate the people of the United States and especially the people of California on the outcome. I have directed dismissal of suit to take place immediately upon the adoption of resolution by the Board of Education as you request."[22] The President then sent a copy of the mayor's telegram to Root, adding: "Schmitz is a game man and has acted like a trump."[23]

18 New York *Times,* Mar. 14, 1907.

19 See San Francisco *Chronicle,* Mar. 13, 1907.

20 See *Literary Digest,* Mar. 23, 1907, p. 451.

21 San Francisco *Chronicle,* Mar. 13, 1907.

22 Roosevelt to Schmitz (telegram), Mar. 12, 1907.

23 Roosevelt to Root, Mar. 12, 1907, Roosevelt Papers. Roosevelt seems to have been favorably impressed by Schmitz. Several weeks later, in referring to the "grizzly situation" in San Francisco which resulted in Schmitz's conviction, the President wrote: "I am genuinely sorry that Schmitz should have been involved in it." Roosevelt to Wheeler, Apr. 6, 1907, Roosevelt Papers.

On March 13, 1907, the Board met and rescinded the order, although its members freely admitted that they were acting in violation of the state law which they had tried so valiantly to uphold.[24] The next day, March 14, Roosevelt issued an executive order putting into effect the passport arrangement and at the same time ordering the dismissal of legal action.[25] The school incident was at last closed.

This question cannot properly be left, however, without some reference to the reaction of public opinion, at home and abroad, to the settlement. Early in February, 1907, when it was rumored that the two governments were discussing a convention for the mutual exclusion of laborers, the leading journals of Japan expressed pronounced dissatisfaction, two of them attacking Minister Hayashi "viciously."[26] Ambassador Wright confirmed this reaction in a telegram to Root under date of February 8, 1907. "Leading independent and opposition newspapers," he stated, "strongly criticize reported settlement on the basis of reciprocal exclusion of laborers as one-sided and, inasmuch as the Government of the United States has acknowledged injustice of school discrimina-

[24] San Francisco *Chronicle*, Mar. 14, 1907. In an interview President Walsh said that if Roosevelt did not keep faith, the Board could rescind its action and cause all Japanese children to attend the Oriental school. London *Times*, Mar. 15, 1907.

[25] San Francisco *Chronicle*, Mar. 15, 1907. See also Roosevelt to Bonaparte, Mar. 12, 1907, Roosevelt Papers.

[26] *Japan Weekly Mail*, Feb. 9, 1907, p. 136. On February 3, 1907, the *Hochi Shimbun,* which was inclined to be sensational, regretted that the Japanese were being discriminated against because of color, and observed that Roosevelt himself had said that it was wrong to seek peace at the cost of one's conscience. "Our nation is getting tired of sluggish diplomacy," this journal concluded. Translation in Wright to Root, Feb. 8, 1907, in file 1797.

tion, a reflection on Japanese compared with European laborers."[27] And the *Japan Weekly Mail,* discussing the possibility of Congressional action against Japanese immigration, was certain that the "nation would be profoundly offended did such legislation form a condition of the settlement of the San Francisco problem."[28]

When the first rumors of the immigration bill settlement came to Japan, they were greeted with evidences of displeasure. There were many who were unable to understand why the school matter could not be settled solely on its merits and entirely apart from the larger question of labor. Why, it was asked, did Japan have to offer a *quid pro quo* to the United States when the San Franciscans had been wholly in the wrong? Besides, this group argued, the alleged non-discriminatory features of the immigration bill were but a thin subterfuge. On the other hand, there was a general feeling in the best-informed circles that under the existing circumstances Japan could find no grounds for complaint against the action of the United States government. Indeed, the Council of Elder Statesmen and the cabinet ministers betrayed no concern whatever over the diplomatic situation.[29] But when news of the final settlement reached Tokyo certain financially interested groups expressed profound dissatisfaction and the sensational journals censured the government for its alleged diplomatic surrender.[30] Yet, after examining the

[27] Wright to Root, Feb. 8, 1907 (telegram, copy), inclosure in Wright to Root, Feb. 8, 1907, in file 1797.

[28] *Japan Weekly Mail,* Feb. 9, 1907, p. 136.

[29] London *Times,* Feb. 18, 1907 ; San Francisco *Chronicle,* Feb. 17, 20, 1907.

[30] *Ibid.*

comments of the more substantial and influential newspapers, Wright was able to report: "It will be noted that
the general tone . . . . is one of satisfaction and of conviction that, while the settlement reached leaves, perhaps,
much to be desired on the part of Japan, it was the best
one possible under existing circumstances." Moreover,
the situation was eased somewhat by an interview given
out by Viscount Hayashi, in which he praised the earnest
efforts of Roosevelt and pointed out that the settlement,
so unobjectionable to Japan, would make the negotiation
of a supplementary convention unnecessary. Ambassador
Wright believed that the timely publication of this statement would go far to correct Japanese public opinion on
the subject.[31]

The next day, February 21, 1907, Wright wired that
the Japanese newspapers were generally accepting the immigration legislation "without bitterness and as the best
obtainable solution."[32] Yet two journals in particular,
the *Mainichi Dempo* and the *Kokumin Shimbun*, did not
attempt to conceal their dissatisfaction with an arrangement which they regarded as a great concession on the
part of Japan without adequate compensation.[33] The reaction of most of the influential newspapers, however,

[31] Wright to Root, Feb. 20, 1907, in file 1797. Hayashi also pointed
out that Japanese emigrants were not forbidden to enter Hawaii, and
that Mexico, South America, and Manchuria would doubtless prove desirable outlets for Japan's surplus population. *Japan Weekly Mail*, Feb. 23,
1907, p. 192.

[32] Wright to Root (telegram), Feb. 21, 1907, inclosure in Wright to
Root, Mar. 3, 1907, in file 1797.

[33] *Japan Weekly Mail*, Feb. 23, 1907, p. 190. This weekly reported
that the "Japanese press . . . . shows signs of considerable dissatisfaction."

was summarized by the *Japan Daily Mail,* of Yokohama, in the following words:

> On the whole the Japanese press seems to be content though not satisfied with the settlement of the San Francisco question. There appears to be a feeling that more has been surrendered than has been acquired. Admission to San Francisco schools for a mere handful of Japanese children is a small matter compared with the exclusion of thousands of Japanese labourers from the United States, which offers a splendid field for their employment. But we do not detect any signs of a disposition to blame Japanese diplomacy. The truth is that Japanese diplomacy is in no sense responsible.[34]

The Japanese mind gradually accustomed itself to the terms of the settlement, and on March 3, 1907, Wright could report that the *Jiji Shimpo,* an independent newspaper which was perhaps the most influential in Japan, had given its powerful support to the solution and had expressed the conviction that the relations between Japan and America would become all the more intimate because of this slight controversy.[35] It may further be noted that Roosevelt's evident fairness to and respect for Japan made the pill a less bitter one to swallow, for Minister Hayashi, in defending his position in response to an interpellation in the lower house of the Diet, pointed to the indisputable good will of Roosevelt and his government toward Japan.[36] And the President's friend, Baron Kaneko, wrote from Tokyo that Roosevelt had done all that he could "do under such circumstances" and that "they all regard you the *greatest* friend for Japan . . . ."[37]

[34] *Japan Daily Mail,* Feb. 22, 1907.

[35] Wright to Root, Mar. 3, 1907, in file 1797.

[36] London *Times,* Mar. 11, 1907.

[37] Kaneko to Roosevelt, Apr. 15, 1907, Roosevelt Papers. Several months later Kaneko wrote that the President's attitude toward Japan

Reference has been made to the opposition of certain financially interested groups. The most influential of these were concerns engaged in the shipping of coolies to the United States by way of Hawaii. Five large emigration companies and some smaller ones had been making large profits in this business, but now that the Hawaiian labor market was almost glutted, they were deeply disturbed by the ban on mainland immigration. Furthermore, a number of the directors of these companies were men prominent in public life, and they succeeded in making themselves heard. They were clever enough, however, not to base their objections on personal considerations, but rather on the pride and self-interest of the Japanese people. These officials complained, therefore, that the Japanese had been discriminated against and had been put in the same class with the Chinese; that since the Japanese in Hawaii could not go to the mainland the Hawaiian sugar barons would immediately lower their wages;[38] and that the arrangement was not final but would merely whet the appetite of the exclusionists in America.[39] Thus it was that Wright could report on March 3, 1907:

What open dissatisfaction there is with the basis of settlement has centered in the manifesto and public meeting of the "Tabei Doshikwai," a society that has been organized for the purpose of

and his friendly views toward the Japanese were well understood in the remotest parts of the empire. Kaneko to Roosevelt, July 7, 1907, Roosevelt Papers.

38 The thirty Japanese agencies and companies interested complained bitterly, and some of them accused the Hawaiian planters of starting the exclusion agitation so that they could beat down the wages of their coolie laborers. When the official quota for Hawaii was prorated among the companies, some of them could send only five immigrants to Hawaii, and five only nine. *Japan Weekly Mail*, Feb. 23, 1907, p. 191.

39 *Ibid.*, Mar. 2, 1907, p. 219.

opposing any restriction on Japanese laborers entering the United States. The Society is composed chiefly of persons interested in emigration companies (among which are a number of members of the Diet), small journalists and chronic agitators. It is not supported by any newspaper or politician of the first rank.[40]

That passage in the immigration bill amendment which permitted continued coolie immigration to the Hawaiian Islands was to some extent a concession to the labor needs of the sugar planters. The Japanese in Hawaii, however, were vehement in their protests against the erection of a barrier on the mainland. Honolulu representatives of the Japanese emigration companies, the owners of Japanese hotels in Hawaii, and coolie laborers generally, who felt that their wages would be beaten down, were responsible for a considerable amount of the agitation that followed. The new law became operative on February 19, 1907, and a large number of coolies who had purchased tickets for the mainland were not allowed to depart. A mass meeting of Japanese was consequently held in Honolulu on the evening of February 18. Many speeches were made but there was no war talk, and resolutions were passed to the effect that the enactment of such an arbitrary, oppressive, and discriminatory law was incompatible with the dignity of Japan and destructive of Japanese interests in Hawaii, and that it threatened in the near future a complete obliteration of Japan's influence, rights, and interests there.[41] To the Japanese Foreign Office the following cablegram was sent: "The Hawaiian Japanese are unanimous in firm opposition to the action of the American Congress

40 Wright to Root, Mar. 3, 1907, in file 1797.

41 London *Times,* Mar. 16, 1907 (Report of Honolulu correspondent, Feb. 19).

in prohibiting them from emigrating to America, which is incompatible with the empire's dignity and ruinous to Japanese interests in Hawaii. Energetic diplomatic opposition is requested."[42] The telegram to Roosevelt was less emphatic: "Hawaiian Japanese respectfully protest in the name of humanity and civilization, and also in the name of liberty, against the prohibition of their emigration to the United States. It enslaves them permanently to Hawaiian capitalists."[43]

The white people of California viewed the settlement with mixed emotions. Although hundreds of telegrams poured into Washington congratulating the members of the school delegation on the results of their work, few of these were from San Francisco.[44] The Exclusion League was particularly bitter over what it regarded as a betrayal at the hands of Schmitz, for it looked upon the arrangement for permitting whites and Orientals to attend the same schools as offensive to a high degree. The president of this organization wired Schmitz that what California needed was an exclusion act and not an arrangement dependent upon the whims of the President.[45] The *Chronicle* observed that never before in the history of the city had the labor union agitators been so greatly disturbed or so thoroughly disgusted.[46] It was the current belief in San Francisco that Schmitz had ruined himself po-

[42] San Francisco *Chronicle*, Feb. 20, 1907.

[43] *Ibid.* It may also be observed that the San Francisco Japanese cabled a strong appeal to Tokyo in which they asked the government to support their cause and pointed out that the restrictions would eventually result in the extinction of their group in San Francisco. *Ibid.*, Feb. 22, 1907.

[44] *Ibid.*, Feb. 15, 19, 1907.

[45] *Ibid.*, Feb. 15, 1907.   [46] *Ibid.*, Feb. 18, 1907.

litically, and one spokesman for the Exclusion League remarked that if the agreement was as reported the mayor had better not come back.[47] The New York correspondent of the London *Times* concluded that Schmitz was now so unpopular that it was doubtful if he could carry out the agreement he had made with Roosevelt.[48] In its stand against Schmitz the Exclusion League received the support of many labor organizations and patriotic bodies throughout the state. A movement was even started to form anti-Japanese clubs in every assembly district—an answer to the Japanese claim that the agitation was solely the work of labor leaders. These clubs were to be composed of small business men, farmers, laborers, and others who were not eligible to membership in the Exclusion League, and the promoters promised even more direct methods than had yet been used.[49]

The San Francisco *Chronicle,* however, was to be found in the unaccustomed rôle of moderation. It felt that the workingmen were a trifle premature in condemning Schmitz, and that it would be wise to wait and see what had been accomplished. This newspaper, furthermore, pointed to several tangible gains. As a result of the recent agitation, the exclusion movement, which had got under way only two years before, had been pushed to a point that its most ardent advocates could not have dreamed of a short time before. The *Chronicle* viewed with satisfaction the acceptance of the principle, both by the United States and by Japan, that the coolies must be kept out. "It makes no difference to us," continued this

47 *Ibid.,* Feb. 17, 1907.   48 London *Times,* Feb. 19, 1907.
49 San Francisco *Chronicle,* Feb. 18, 1907.

journal, "who keeps them out, so long as they do not come, and if the Mikado can and will do it, that will be entirely satisfactory so far as the Japanese are concerned." But the arrangement was merely a *modus vivendi,* and was bound in time to give way to something more permanent. A few Japanese children would do no harm, and they would remain few in number if the coolie influx was stopped. "What we get," concluded the *Chronicle,* "is worth what we give, provided we get it." But, it warned, "If there is failure, the whole trade is off" and drastic steps would be taken to secure exclusion.[50]

Other journals in San Francisco, however, were severe in their denunciation of Schmitz. The *Call* demanded exclusion that excluded—not merely a polite request to the Japanese to stay away.[51] The *Bulletin* referred sarcastically to the "Battle of Washington," and one of its special writers took the mayor to task for his "unseemly obsequiousness."[52] The *Argonaut* was especially bitter. It lamented the surrender of the just powers of a state; predicted that this infatuated solution would result in an anti-Japanese campaign that would match the one against the Chinese in former years; and bemoaned the fact that Japan's wishes, not those of San Francisco, were to determine the domestic affairs of the municipality. Not since the days of the Algerian pirates, the *Argonaut* asseverated, had the diplomacy of the United States sunk to such a low level. This journal had nothing but scorn for the men who had bent the knee when they came into

50 San Francisco *Chronicle,* Feb. 19, 20, 1907.
51 San Francisco *Call,* Feb. 20, 1907.
52 San Francisco *Bulletin,* Feb. 21, 23, 1907.

the presence of Roosevelt, remarking, "All the bold talk about demanding reciprocal concessions came to nothing when once this little coterie of cheap men got under the shadow of the big stick."[53]

As the day for the return of Schmitz drew near,[54] these denunciations increased in violence. Intelligent observers doubted if it would be possible to carry out the agreement with the President in the face of such disapprobation; and this circumstance does much to explain Roosevelt's disquietude and his subsequent pressure on the California legislature. Even so responsible a man as the Catholic Archbishop of San Francisco joined in the outcry against the mayor, while his former friends among the labor unions were described as being "incoherently profane" when Schmitz's name was mentioned.[55] A few days after the mayor's return, the *Bulletin* printed a full-page editorial denouncing the settlement chiefly on the grounds that it placed Japanese on a footing with all other aliens. This newspaper emphatically stated that all that had been done was "to deprive Japanese steerage passengers of their stopover privilege [in Hawaii]."[56] Even the *Chronicle* was now disposed to forsake moderation, for it remarked that Roosevelt had got much the better of the mayor; that he had forced Schmitz to make the first move; and that he had compelled the Board of Education to ignore a state law.[57]

[53] *Argonaut*, San Francisco, Feb. 23, 1907, p. 468.
[54] He arrived on Mar. 6, 1907.
[55] London *Times*, Mar. 2, 1907.
[56] San Francisco *Bulletin*, Mar. 11, 1907.
[57] San Francisco *Chronicle*, Mar. 14, 1907.

Elsewhere in California the settlement received a less stormy reception. The Sacramento *Bee* probably represented moderate sentiment when it remarked that what was needed was outright exclusion but since Congress and Roosevelt were not ready for it the immigration-bill solution was a step in the right direction.[58] Public opinion elsewhere in the United States appears to have been somewhat wearied of the prolonged discussion and to have greeted the settlement more or less apathetically. In general, it may be observed that few groups, either in America or in Japan, were thoroughly satisfied with the solution; and this fact in itself would indicate that the compromise was about as fair as was possible at that time. The labor union groups in California felt that they had been sold out; the exclusionists considered the agreement but a halfway measure; the anti-exclusionists regarded the settlement as a step in the wrong direction; the states' rights advocates, on the Coast as well as farther east, deplored the unprecedented extension of the federal arm; the Southern whites feared a dangerous precedent that might later be used against Negro segregation; the legalists regretted that the courts had not had an opportunity to interpret the treaty once and for all; the Japanese coolies in Hawaii anticipated a lowering of wages; the Japanese emigration companies bemoaned a loss of profits; and the Japanese masses were disgruntled because a *quid pro quo* had not been obtained and because of the veiled discrimination involved.

The courts never decided whether or not the action of the Board was in violation of the treaty of 1894 with

[58] Quoted in *Literary Digest*, Mar. 2, 1907, p. 320.

Japan. From the standpoint of the student of constitutional and international law it is unfortunate that this question was not passed upon by the highest tribunals. But from the standpoint of diplomacy it was fortunate that the matter was dropped, for a decision in favor of one party doubtless would have caused a most unfavorable reaction on the part of the other. The historian is concerned with what happened, and conjecture as to how the courts would have voted had they voted must be left to the legal authorities.[59] For the purposes of this study, however, it is of the greatest importance to observe what the principals in the drama thought about the legal points involved, because their views led to the decision to settle out of court.

The diplomats were concerned with three questions:[60] (1) Did the treaty of 1894 with Japan contain the most-

[59] See Simeon E. Baldwin, "Schooling Rights under Our Treaty with Japan," *Columbia Law Review*, VII (Feb., 1907), 85–92; Amos Hershey, "The Japanese School Question and the Treaty-Making Power," *American Political Science Review*, I (May, 1907), 393–409; Charles C. Hyde, "The Segregation of Japanese Students by the School Authorities of San Francisco," *The Green Bag*, XIX (Jan., 1907), 38–49; Theodore P. Ion, "The Japanese School Incident at San Francisco from the Point of View of International and Constitutional Law," *Michigan Law Review*, V (Mar., 1907), 326–43; Arthur K. Kuhn, "The Treaty-Making Power and the Reserved Sovereignty of the States," *Columbia Law Review*, VII (Mar., 1907), 172–85; William D. Lewis, "Can the United States by Treaty Confer on Japanese Residents in California the Right to Attend the Public Schools?" *American Law Register*, LV (Feb., 1907), 73–90.

[60] A fourth point, which did not affect the diplomatic negotiations, was developed by the constitutionalists and states' rights advocates. This group argued with plausibility that if the national government had negotiated a treaty forcing colored children into the public schools of a state in defiance of local ordinances, then the treaty-making power under the Constitution had been exceeded and the resulting treaty was consequently void. Senator Rayner, of Maryland, gave an able exposition of this view in the Senate, and introduced supporting resolutions. *Congressional Record*, 59 Cong., 2 sess., pp. 298 ff.

favored-nation clause? If it did not, then the Japanese had no legal grievance. The segregation of American citizens (Negroes) in the schools of the South had been upheld by the courts, and surely the Japanese could not claim for their subjects, in the absence of a treaty guaranty, rights which the United States did not confer upon its own citizens. But if the treaty of 1894 could be construed to contain the most-favored-nation clause, then the Japanese were entitled to public school privileges just as were the citizens or subjects of the great European powers. (2) If the treaty did entitle the Japanese to public school privileges through the most-favored-nation clause, would not a separate public school (Oriental school) satisfy the letter of the treaty? (3) Even if the letter of the treaty did not permit the Japanese to attend the same public schools as the whites, did not the spirit in which the treaty was conceived protect the Japanese against any such discrimination?

Upon arriving in California to begin his investigation, Metcalf met in a conference with the justices of the state supreme court, who assured him that if the treaty did contain the most-favored-nation clause they would rule unanimously that the action of the Board was invalid. Metcalf then proceeded to study the text of the treaty, and he discovered that such a clause was to be found in Article II with reference to "matters of commerce and navigation" but not with reference to education. Article I did provide, however, that "In whatever relates to rights of residence . . . . the citizens or subjects of each Contracting Party shall enjoy in the territories of the other the same privileges, liberties, and rights . . . ." Did "rights of residence" embrace education in the *same public schools* with the whites? Metcalf and Robert Devlin, United States attorney in San Francisco, thought not; hence in their opinion the Japanese did not have a sound legal position.[61]

Secretary Root, however, wrote a letter to Attorney General Bonaparte in which he took exception to Metcalf's interpretation. He held that the reference to "rights of residence" was so sweeping as to entitle the Japanese to most-favored-nation school privileges. But the question as to whether or not public school privileges *in a separate school* fulfilled the letter of the treaty seemed to him "to present more difficulty." The segregation of the Japanese was admittedly humiliating, and Root pointed out that the treaty had been drawn up primarily to remove consular jurisdiction and other offensive discriminations against the Japanese. "The whole purpose and end of the treaty of 1894," he concluded, "was to do away with and prevent just such exclusions as are now provided by the San Francisco School Board. The particular language of the treaty must be read with reference to this general purpose. . . . . [The school order] is completely subversive of the purpose and spirit of the treaty, and is, in my judgment, a violation of its terms."[62]

The question dragged through the courts until February, 1907, when the necessity for an agreement became evident. On February 6 Root wired Wright that,

[61] For text of treaty of 1894 see W. M. Malloy, comp., *Treaties, Conventions, International Acts, Protocols and Agreements between the United States of America and Other Powers, 1776–1909* (Washington, 1910), I, 1028–36.

[62] Root to Bonaparte, Nov. 13, 1906, in file 1797.

although in his opinion the Japanese were entitled to the educational privileges of the most favored nation, it was doubtful if that right was being violated by the establishment of a separate school. In fact, Root believed that it was at least an even chance that the courts would decide that the existing arrangement was violative of no treaty.[63] A day or so later, in a conversation with Wright, Hayashi was disposed to concede that under a literal construction of the treaty San Francisco was probably within its rights, but he argued that the spirit of the treaty would require that Japanese attend the same schools as the whites.[64] Finally, on February 24, 1907, Hayashi wrote the note that prepared the ground for the Gentlemen's Agreement, and in doing this he was no doubt influenced by Wright, who told him frankly that the decision of the courts might not be favorable to Japan and that even if it were the effect might be to increase rather than allay irritation on the Pacific Coast and elsewhere.[65]

To summarize the legal situation, then, it may be said that the treaty of 1894 did not contain the most-favored-nation clause and there was considerable doubt as to whether it could have been construed to contain such a clause. Root thought that it could have been so construed; Devlin and Metcalf thought otherwise. But even if this hurdle could have been cleared, the courts would have had to decide whether or not sending Japanese children to the Oriental school, a public school with

[63] Root to Wright (telegram), Feb. 6, 1907, in file 1797.

[64] Wright to Root (telegram), Feb. 9, 1907, inclosure in Wright to Root, Feb. 20, 1907, in file 1797.

[65] Wright to Root (telegram), Feb. 1, 1907, inclosure in Wright to Root, Feb. 8, 1907, in file 1797.

standard equipment and facilities, was violative of the treaty.[66] Even Root doubted if the courts would uphold Japan on this point. The school order, however, was clearly at variance with the spirit which had motivated the treaty of 1894. Minister Hayashi and the Japanese ambassador to France, Shinichiro Kurino, the negotiator of the treaty, both emphasized this argument; and the contemporary correspondence in the Department of State on the subject supports their position.[67] But courts are wont to look at the letter rather than the spirit of the law; and Root's prediction that the Japanese contention had legally an even chance was probably a bit optimistic.

In the last analysis it seems as if the Japanese Foreign Office was willing to drop the test litigation and accept the rather distasteful Gentlemen's Agreement because no matter how the courts decided the Japanese were bound to lose. If the order of the Board of Education had been declared invalid, the people of California, then in no amiable mood toward Oriental labor, would doubtless through their local bodies and their state legislature have entered upon a period of petty persecution of all Japanese that would have invited even more serious trouble. An adverse decision, furthermore, would undoubtedly have spurred the Californians on to militant support of a

[66] The San Franciscans argued that the Japanese would learn more rapidly if they were all thrown together in the same school. See, however, Reginald Bell, *Status of Public School Education of Second-Generation Japanese in California*, University Series, Stanford University, 1934.

[67] See Payson J. Treat, *Diplomatic Relations between the United States and Japan, 1853–1895* (Stanford University, 1932), II, 418–22; also earlier chapters. See also San Francisco *Chronicle*, Dec. 6, 1906; London *Times*, Feb. 21, 1907.

sweeping coolie-exclusion law, which not only was permissible under the treaty but which would have been a more serious affront to Japan than the school order. If the position of the Board had been upheld by the courts, then the Japanese would thereafter have been excluded from those San Francisco public schools to which whites were admitted, as well as from the schools of all those other cities that cared to follow this precedent. It is reasonable to conclude, therefore, that the Japanese accepted the school compromise because under it they were sure of getting their children of proper age into the public schools and at the same time of doing a great deal to prevent further harmful agitation. It would also seem as if they agreed to a voluntary restriction of coolies because they saw clearly, what with the rising temper of the Pacific Coast, that exclusion by act of Congress was inevitable within a few years. Hence Japan chose the easier way out.

CHAPTER IX

Riots and Discrimination in San Francisco

"Apparently nothing will disturb the smug satisfaction with which San Francisco officials
pursue a policy of insult and irritation sure to
land us in war . . . ."—Root to Roosevelt,
July 21, 1907

DURING the three months following the repeal of the
school order Japanese-American relations were comparatively tranquil. The California hoodlums were kept
within bounds, and the excitement that had been aroused
on both sides of the Pacific gradually quieted down. In
May, 1907, a Japanese delegation, headed by General
Kuroki, visited the Jamestown Exposition. On the Pacific Coast, as well as in the East, these distinguished
guests were greeted with manifestations of extreme
cordiality, and throughout the United States the press
rejoiced that the American people had been given an
opportunity to demonstrate to the Japanese that the attitude of San Francisco was thoroughly unrepresentative
of feeling elsewhere in the United States. One of the
many fortunate results of this visit was the organization
of the Japan Society of New York, which had for its
purpose the promotion of friendly relations between the
two nations.[1] But the love feast was soon ended. Late

[1] New York *Nation*, May 23, 1907, p. 466; *Outlook*, June 1, 1907,
p. 231; *Literary Digest*, May 25, 1907, p. 822. Oscar Straus wrote that
General Kuroki received "ovations . . . . all the way across the continent from the time he landed at San Francisco." Straus, *op. cit.*, p. 219.

in May, 1907, the San Francisco mob broke out of control, and the fat was once more in the fire.[2]

The evidence as to what happened is conflicting, but the following facts are undisputed. On the evening of May 20, 1907, a mob of about fifty San Franciscans, none of whom was afterward identified, attacked a Japanese restaurant, assaulted and drove off the customers, broke all the windows, and rendered the place unfit for business. Then the assailants crossed the street and damaged in like fashion a bath house operated by a Japanese. Repeated calls were sent in for the police, who did not respond in time to prevent the outrage. For more than a week following the outburst, mobs gathered and menaced various Japanese places of business, most of them restaurants, but the authorities were by this time sufficiently forewarned to prevent further damage.[3]

Representatives of the Japanese in San Francisco, chief among whom was the acting consul, K. Matsubara, investigated the situation and came to the conclusion that the attacks were simply the result of race hatred—that the places had been assaulted solely because the proprietors were Japanese. In support of this contention, Matsubara pointed out that only Japanese establishments had been molested. He further claimed that the police had been purposely negligent and that if they had taken even ordinary precautions after his warnings to them of

---

[2] The New York correspondent of the London *Times* remarked that nobody who knew anything about the San Francisco situation believed that "the settlement of the Japanese trouble at San Francisco recently arranged would settle it long." London *Times*, May 27, 1907.

[3] See Root to Gillett (telegram), May 25, 1907, in file 1797.

impending disturbances these outrages would not have occurred.[4]

The San Francisco authorities, however, gave an entirely different version of the affair. They maintained that the large number of lawless and unemployed men in the city made it impossible for them to prevent disturbances, and they insisted that the assaults were merely another outgrowth of the labor difficulties from which the city had been suffering for some months. The testimony, in fact, is rather convincing that the trouble began when some union men approached several white customers who were eating in a non-union Japanese restaurant. The whites claimed that the resulting damage was incidental to the fight; the Japanese claimed that the fight had been started to provide an excuse for demolishing the establishment. The municipal authorities asserted that the police force, which was admittedly inadequate for the needs of the city, had on this occasion been occupied elsewhere with a strike, but that after the initial disturbance Japanese property had been adequately protected. As for the charge of discrimination, an officer of the United States army, who was detailed by Governor Gillett to make an investigation, testified that similar attacks had occurred on non-union white places of business.[5]

The truth probably lies somewhere between these two accounts. It seems clear that labor union difficulties were

[4] Matsubara to Devlin, May 28, 1907; Matsubara to J. F. Dinan (chief of police), May 28, 1907, inclosures in Aoki to Bacon, June 4, 1907, all in file 1797.

[5] For a summary of the testimony, see Bonaparte to Root, June 11, 1907; Devlin to Bonaparte, May 27, 1907, in file 1797.

in some way involved in the incident; but it is equally clear that the prevailing anti-Japanese sentiment in the city had much to do with the form that the riots took. The fight between the union and the non-union men might have occurred in any event; but the places probably would not have been so thoroughly wrecked had not race hatred flared up during the struggle. Secretary Root expressed a similar conclusion in a letter to Attorney General Bonaparte:

While the recent attacks and threats of attack upon Japanese business establishments, chiefly restaurants, in San Francisco, have doubtless been incident to the disorder prevailing in that city because of the street car strike, they appear nevertheless to be a renewal of the attacks upon Japanese restaurants which occurred in the autumn of 1906. No business establishments except those kept by Japanese appear to have been attacked. There is no suggestion of any provocation or specific occasion for attack except in one instance, and I think we are bound to recognize the fact that the attacks are violations of the treaty rights of the Japanese.[6]

Although Acting Consul Matsubara protested to the San Francisco police authorities and to the mayor, and although he appealed to Governor Gillett, the San Francisco newspapers, as in the case of the school incident, remained profoundly indifferent to the attacks. It was not until May 25, 1907, five days after the affair, that the *Chronicle* mentioned the matter. This brief account appeared on the third page, and was given to explain a Washington dispatch which alluded to anti-Japanese riots in the city. On this same day, May 25, 1907, Wright wired from Tokyo: "Japanese newspapers publish sen-

[6] Root to Bonaparte, June 5, 1907, in file 1797.

sational cables from San Francisco reporting repeated attacks on Japanese stores and their customers. So far no comment or apparent excitement. Have you any advices as to the facts?"[7] Root's reply indicates that the incident had not yet been reported in the East, for he wired: "We have heard nothing here of any attacks on Japanese store or customers in San Francisco. There is, however, very serious street railroad strike in San Francisco and much disturbance. All business probably interfered with, but have no reason to believe Japanese more than others. Will investigate immediately."[8]

Secretary Root thereupon bestirred himself. He asked the attorney general to secure a telegraphic report of the incident from the United States attorney and also from the United States marshal in San Francisco.[9] At the request of Roosevelt he wired Governor Gillett asking him to undertake an immediate investigation of the situation and to call upon the state for a prompt and effective enforcement of the treaty obligations of the United States in case they were being disregarded.[10] In his reply, two days later, Gillett promised to refer Root's telegram to the attention of the San Francisco chief of police and to request him to use every effort to protect the Japanese.[11] The San Francisco police authorities, however, had already assured the acting consul that they would look out for the Japanese, and even Matsubara himself admitted

[7] Wright to Root (telegram), May 25, 1907, in file 1797.
[8] Root to Wright (telegram), May 25, 1907, in file 1797.
[9] See Acting Attorney General to Root, May 25, 1907, in file 1797.
[10] Root to Gillett (telegram), May 25, 1907, in file 1797.
[11] Gillett to Root (telegram), May 27, 1907, in file 1797.

that after the first outburst the municipal authorities had the situation well under control.[12]

Ambassador Aoki naturally brought the state of affairs in San Francisco to the attention of Root. His communications to the secretary of state on this subject bulk larger than those on the school incident, but this does not necessarily mean that he was greatly disturbed. He submitted no formal notes of protest and for the most part contented himself with forwarding to Root, with the significant passages heavily underscored, the voluminous reports that Matsubara was sending him from San Francisco. Secretary Root did not hesitate to assure Aoki that the "Government of the United States shares in the expression of regret of the authorities of San Francisco at this unfortunate incident which evidently was the result of temporary relaxation of vigilance on the part of the police, owing to the existence of the disturbances incident to the street car strike." Moreover, Root was careful to send to Aoki copies of all correspondence and reports indicative of the solicitude of the federal government, and it must have been clear to the Japanese ambassador that every possible kind of pressure was being applied to federal, state, and local authorities to secure justice for the Japanese. The consequence was that the communications between the secretary of state and the ambassador took on a tone of extreme cordiality, especially so when Root promised the aid of federal officials in California in pressing a damage suit against the

[12] Dinan to Matsubara (acting consul), May 23, 1907, copy, in file 1797; Matsubara to Dinan, May 28, 1907 (copy), inclosure in Aoki to Bacon, June 4, 1907, in file 1797.

city of San Francisco. Thus it was that on June 7, 1907, Root could write to Roosevelt that "so far as the two Governments go this San Francisco affair is getting on all right as an ordinary diplomatic affair about which there is no occasion to get excited. All the trouble is being made by the leprous vampires who are eager to involve their country in war in order to sell a few more newspapers."[13]

It is probable that Ambassador Aoki was informed of Roosevelt's views on the outburst, for the President was vigorous in his condemnation of what had occurred. On June 15, 1907, he wrote to Henry White:

I am concerned about the Japanese-California situation and I see no prospect of its growing better. The San Francisco mob has behaved atrociously; and as, in my judgment, there will be much suffering in that city in the near future and great multitudes of men out of work, I fear a recurrence of trouble at any time. Between ourselves, I have arranged to have plenty of troops in the neighborhood. One trouble, of course, is that I must be very certain that the provocation completely justifies my sending troops, or else the action will merely do harm; in a democracy like ours a public servant must continually keep in mind not only what the letter of the law permits, but how far he can arouse and guide public sentiment so that it will justify him.[14]

Since the federal government had expressed its regrets and the San Francisco authorities had admitted their liability under the state law, the affair soon ceased to be a diplomatic incident, and it was left to the courts to decide the exact amount of damages. The matter

[13] Root to Roosevelt, June 7, 1907, Roosevelt Papers. See also Aoki to Bacon (acting secretary of state), June 4, 1907; Root to Aoki, June 5, 1907; Aoki to Root, June 6, 1907, in file 1797.

[14] Roosevelt to White, June 15, 1907, Roosevelt Papers.

dragged along until March, 1908, when, as a result of the good offices of United States Attorney Devlin, the case was settled out of court to the satisfaction of all parties concerned by the payment of $450.[15]

It was as a problem in public opinion, however, rather than in diplomacy, that the San Francisco outburst assumed an alarming aspect. A number of the more moderate Japanese newspapers were inclined to view the situation calmly, pointing to the uniform friendliness of the federal government and to the unfairness of regarding the action of an irresponsible mob in one corner of the great republic as representative of the entire nation.[16] Nevertheless, there were some alarmist newspapers that quickly warmed to their task, and in a few days telegrams began to arrive from Tokyo in which the outbreaks were referred to as "the second San Francisco incident."[17] Although Roosevelt felt that the Japanese were "absolutely right in contending for their treaty rights and for the proper treatment of the Japanese who are here," he felt that the "utterances of the extremists in Japan have begun to make an unpleasant feeling in this country."[18] And on June 12, 1907, Wright wrote from Tokyo:

It will be observed that, in spite of the statements and explanations given out by the embassy . . . . and by the Japanese Foreign Office, the agitation has continued to grow until of all the newspapers of the capital the "Jiji" is the only one that has retained an attitude of entire moderation. All the other leading

[15] Devlin to Attorney General, Mar. 11, 1908 (copy), in file 1797.

[16] *Japan Weekly Mail*, June 15, 1907, p. 647. This journal regretted particularly that there should have been a tendency to depart from the level-headedness evidenced during the San Francisco school incident.

[17] London *Times*, June 4, 1907.

[18] Roosevelt to White, June 15, 1907, Roosevelt Papers.

papers have expressed surprise, dissatisfaction, annoyance or apprehension, while journals of the second and lower ranks have gone to absurd extremes . . . . There are certain things, however, that must be considered in connection with this apparently unreasonable display of public temper. The first is that the recent incidents have been regarded as a continuation of the school question in spite of all official assurances to the contrary. The people of Japan as a whole are undoubtedly dissatisfied with the solution of that question.[19]

Within two weeks after the riots the opposition leaders in Japan were speaking openly of war, and the press of the United States and of Europe was reporting that the affair had become so serious that France had extended her good offices to promote an understanding. This last rumor appears to have been without foundation, for the diplomatic situation was in no way disquieting, but it contributed to the growing feeling that affairs were nearing a crisis.[20] In fact, the Japanese government became so concerned over the attitude of the alarmist press that it officially advised the newspapers to abstain from the publication of inflammatory material on the American question. This action was deemed necessary because photographs of the wrecked Japanese places of business appeared in several journals, together with highly colored descriptions of the outrage.[21]

The San Francisco riots of May, 1907, were so much less serious than the school incident of 1906 that observers in the United States were at a loss to understand why such an unfriendly attitude should have been assumed by

19 Wright to Root, June 12, 1907, in file 1797.
20 San Francisco *Chronicle*, June 9, 1907; London *Times*, June 8, 10, 11, 1907.
21 London *Times*, June 14, 1907.

the press of Japan. The action of the Board of Education was a deliberate act of discrimination, carefully planned and long persisted in by a body of presumably responsible officials. The San Francisco riots, on the other hand, were merely a temporary flare-up which was immediately disavowed by local, state, and federal officials; and there was every indication that the Japanese would secure speedy redress for the damage done. As a matter of fact, the destruction of American property by mobs in Japan was not unknown, yet the people of the United States had passed these incidents off without great concern. Indeed, the influential *Japan Times* stated flatly that the new San Francisco affair was no more worthy of diplomatic cognizance than the burning of the American mission buildings in Tokyo during the course of the riots of 1905, when extreme dissatisfaction was being expressed over the terms of the Peace of Portsmouth.[22] It is probably true that the national pride of the Japanese and the desire of the emigration companies to keep alive the issue account for some of the agitation over the San Francisco riots of 1907. But the real explanation must be sought elsewhere.

Party politics was undoubtedly responsible for most of the uproar in Japan that followed the San Francisco riots. It was quickly noted that the *Hochi Shimbun*, regarded as the organ of Count Okuma, the head of the opposition (Progressist) party, took the lead in attacking both the United States for its racial hostility and the Japanese ministry for its pusillanimity.[23] These denun-

[22] *Japan Times*, June 16, 1907.
[23] *Japan Weekly Mail*, June 15, 1907, pp. 647–48; *Japan Times*, June 14, 1907.

ciations alarmed the press of the United States, and the
Literary Digest of June 22, 1907, devoted its leading
article to the subject, "What the Japanese War Rumors
Mean." From the numerous newspaper excerpts reproduced in this article it is evident that the American press
correctly diagnosed the furor as a political phenomenon.
It was baldly observed that Count Okuma, the mouthpiece of the jingoes, was out of a job.[24] Wright's observations in Tokyo confirm this interpretation. On
June 12, 1907, he wrote that there could be no doubt
that a strong effort was being made to discredit Minister
Hayashi and Ambassador Aoki as a part of a larger
scheme to unseat the Cabinet. This opposition was evidenced in the House of Peers as well as in the press.
Referring to the agitation of the emigration companies,
the American ambassador concluded that "the motives
of party politics and self interest play so large a part in
the present popular agitation that it might well be ignored
were it not for the unpleasant effect that it may have upon
the friendly sentiments now entertained by the two
peoples." In fact, Hayashi told Wright that "about 70
per cent of the feeling displayed by the newspapers and
public men was for political effect and that the remainder
was probably genuine resentment on the part of the
people who did not understand why such a prolonged
state of disorder should be permitted by the authorities in
San Francisco."[25]

Fortunately, by the latter part of June, 1907, public
opinion in Japan was showing an increasing disposition to

[24] *Literary Digest*, June 22, 1907, pp. 977–78.
[25] Wright to Root, June 12, 1907, in file 1797.

view the difficulty with moderation. The leading newspapers and public men asserted that they were relying upon
diplomacy to settle the matter and that they were anticipating no impairment of the traditional friendship.[26] The
Foreign Office gave out another official statement pointing out that there was no ground for diplomatic action—
as indeed there never is until the ordinary means of
settlement fail.[27] The *Jiji Shimpo* asked how the Japanese would like to have their riots against the Americans
in 1905 regarded as representative of the entire nation;[28]
and the *Chuwo Shimbun,* noting that the United States
government had expressed regrets and had made proper
assurances to the Japanese, inquired: "What kind of
strong measures can we adopt against one who says, 'I
have been in the wrong and will adopt measures of protection'?" This journal was disposed to let the courts
settle the matter without further agitation.[29] So, on
June 27, 1907, Wright could inform Root:

I am pleased to report that the extravagant utterances indulged in
by a large section of the press of Japan at the first reports of
the so-called outrages against the Japanese has brought about a
strong reaction, as a result of which practically all of the responsible newspapers have begun to counsel moderation in speech
as well as in action. The "Hochi" [Okuma's mouthpiece] and
other opposition papers alone continue the discussion.[30]

Nevertheless, Ambassador Wright was careful to
point out that there was still a strong undercurrent of

[26] *Japan Weekly Mail,* June 29, 1907, p. 701.
[27] Wright to Root, June 27, 1907, in file 1797.
[28] Cited in *Japan Weekly Mail,* June 22, 1907, p. 670.
[29] Translation inclosed in Wright to Root, June 27, 1907, in file 1797.
[30] Wright to Root, June 27, 1907, in file 1797.

resentment which did not augur well for the future. The Tokyo *Puck* had devoted an entire issue to a most inflammatory treatment of recent anti-Japanese agitation in America. The *Hochi Shimbun,* Count Okuma's organ, was advocating a boycott of the port of San Francisco and the transfer of Japanese trade to Seattle. There was good reason to believe that at the joint meeting of the Chambers of Commerce of Japan some such proposal was considered, but no action was taken in this direction, probably because of the obviously suicidal nature of such a move. In fact, the Chamber of Commerce of Yokohama replied to Consul General Miller's inquiry that they had no intention of boycotting American goods. Nevertheless, the continued concern of the leading political parties of Japan over the situation showed that it was still prominently before the entire country. Wright added:

In fact, even the opposition seems to have largely abandoned the idea that the reported acts of violence constitute a valid reason for diplomatic interference and to have fallen back upon the more general ground of undue discrimination by the United States against the Japanese in matters of immigration and naturalization. They would insist upon being granted equal treatment in these respects with white races and attribute the objections of America to race prejudice and the inactivity of their own officials to incompetence.[31]

When the agitation over the riots seemed in a fair way to be dying down, the Board of Police Commissioners of San Francisco met, late in June, 1907, and refused to license six Japanese to conduct employment bureaus. Four of these applications were for renewals,

[31] *Ibid.;* Wright to Root, July 10, 1907, in file 1797.

and two were new.[32] This was clearly a case of racial discrimination, and Roosevelt was disgusted. He wrote: "I see that a new San Francisco fool has cropped up to add to our difficulties with the Japanese. What will be the outcome, I do not know. I have called upon Bonaparte to investigate the matter."[33] Attorney General Bonaparte immediately wired Devlin to look into the situation, and the latter confirmed the newspaper reports. He stated that licenses had been granted by the Board to Japanese up until the recent action; that the Board was carrying out a policy of giving preference to American citizens; and that the commissioners would welcome a test case to determine whether or not they were wrong.[34] Roosevelt sent this report from Devlin to Root, who was then at Clinton, New York. The secretary of state returned it with this comment:

What I feel and think about it is not fit to write. Apparently nothing will disturb the smug satisfaction with which San Francisco officials pursue a policy of insult and irritation sure to land us in war, except some explicit official statement pointing out the inevitable result of their conduct. Probably that would not and I do not yet see that it is admissible for us officially to impute warlike intentions to Japan.[35]

Roosevelt was greatly concerned over these recent developments in San Francisco. On July 23, 1907, he wrote to Secretary Root: "As for the San Francisco

32 *Promemoria* handed to A. A. Adee by Aoki, July 31, 1907, in file 1797; San Francisco *Chronicle,* June 28, 1907.

33 Roosevelt to Root, July 2, 1907, Roosevelt Papers.

34 Devlin to Bonaparte, July 8, 1907 (copy), in file 1797.

35 Root to Roosevelt, July 21, 1907, Roosevelt Papers.

business, I am quite prepared to issue the most solemn possible warning to our people as to the effect of such a fatuous policy of insult and injury." Roosevelt then remarked that he had been thinking of putting such a statement in his annual message where it would serve the added purpose of making more pointed his recommendation for a stronger army and navy.[36] Later in the month he wrote again to Secretary Root complaining that "our people wantonly and foolishly insult the Japanese in San Francisco," and that everything "we can do must be done to remedy the wrongs complained of." Roosevelt then added that he was only waiting to hear more about the employment agency matter before taking action. "As you know," he concluded, "we now have plenty of troops in the neighborhood of San Francisco, so that in the event of riot we can interfere effectively should the State and municipal authorities be unable or unwilling to afford the protection which we are bound to give the Japanese."[37]

It is surprising how little comment the license refusals elicited in Japan. Although a number of newspapers did point out the discriminatory and other disagreeable features of the affair, their tone was mild when compared with their reaction to the riots of the previous month. The Foreign Office gave out a statement to the effect that the reports so far received did not warrant the Japanese government in regarding the matter as a diplomatic

[36] Roosevelt to Root, July 23, 1907, Roosevelt Papers.

[37] Roosevelt to Root, July 26, 1907, Roosevelt Papers. In a letter to the German ambassador Roosevelt remarked that he had troops near San Francisco and was watching the situation warily. Roosevelt to von Sternberg, July 16, 1907, Roosevelt Papers.

question.[38] Most surprising of all, the *Hochi Shimbun,* which had tried desperately to make political capital out of the San Francisco riots, wrote of the affair with "noteworthy restraint."[39] It is difficult, aside from the less spectacular nature of the incident, to account definitely for this moderation of tone. One possible explanation is that at this particular time the people of Japan were deeply preoccupied with developments in Korea. Another explanation is that the announcement of the cruise of the battleship fleet, which came almost a week after the license refusals and which will be considered shortly, appears to have had a sobering effect on Japanese public opinion.

The diplomatic representations of the Japanese government on the license matter were neither prompt nor vigorous. Perhaps the fleet announcement had something to do with this; but more fundamental was the fact that the Japanese, for reasons that will be pointed out, did not have a good legal case. The riots were admittedly a violation of the treaty; the school segregation at least admitted of argument on that point; but in the case of the license refusals the San Francisco authorities appear to have been within their rights. In any event, it was not until July 31, 1907, more than a month after the event, that Aoki presented a *promemoria* to A. A. Adee at the Department of State outlining the Japanese case. The Japanese ambassador explained that he was making his representations in this form because he considered a *pro-*

---

[38] Wright to Root, July 10, 1907, in file 1797; *Japan Times,* July 3, 1907; *Japan Weekly Mail,* July 6, 1907, p. 4; *ibid.,* July 13, 1907, pp. 31, 33; London *Times,* July 5, 1907.

[39] *Japan Weekly Mail,* July 13, 1907, p. 33.

memoria, which was merely an aid to the memory, less formal than a note. In this statement Aoki emphasized the arbitrary exercise of power by the commissioners and their apparent violation of the treaty of 1894. He hoped that the United States would take appropriate action.[40]

Although it soon became clear that no licenses were being denied to any persons other than Japanese, A. A. Adee and Huntington Wilson, second and third assistant secretaries of state respectively, were of the opinion that the action of the San Francisco commissioners was not in violation of the treaty of 1894, which in its second article provided specifically that the right to restrict trade might be exercised reciprocally.[41] Nevertheless, Secretary Root suggested to Attorney General Bonaparte that he have United States Attorney Devlin, then in San Francisco, explain to the Board of Police Commissioners the importance of the affair "as bearing upon the peaceful relations between Japan and the United States and the peaceable execution of provisions for the exclusion of Japanese laborers." Secretary Root further suggested that Devlin point out that "by discriminating against the Japanese now here, in this matter of comparatively trifling importance, they [the commissioners] would seriously hinder the action of the United States in the vastly more important matter of labor exclusion."[42]

[40] Aoki to Adee (*promemoria*), July 31, 1907; Adee to Roosevelt, July 31, 1907, in file 1797.

[41] Wilson to Root (memorandum), Aug. 5, 1907; Adee to Roosevelt, July 31, 1907; G. W. Russell (acting attorney general) to Root, Aug. 7, 1907, in file 1797.

[42] Root to Bonaparte, Sept. 23, 1907, in file 1797.

Bonaparte carried out these instructions, and Aoki was greatly pleased with Root's intervention.[43] The Japanese consulate in San Francisco was also convinced that everything was being done that could reasonably be expected. The matter dragged along, however, until December, when under pressure skilfully applied by Devlin, the Board of Police Commissioners met and granted licenses to those Japanese applying for them.[44]

It is against the background of the San Francisco riots and the license refusals that the announcement of Roosevelt's intention to send the fleet to Pacific waters must be considered. The warlike utterances of the opposition group in Japan, although designed primarily for political effect, had created an unpleasant impression in the United States. The more excitable of the American journals, which were in no great need of encouragement, were becoming dangerously sensational in their interpretation of events. Roosevelt was now convinced that the time had come to act with vigor. And the most significant result of this conviction was the announcement that the entire American battleship fleet would be transferred to the Pacific.

43 Bonaparte to Root, Sept. 23, 1907, in file 1797; Root to Roosevelt, Sept. 25, 1907, Roosevelt Papers.
44 Devlin to Bonaparte, Dec. 11, 1907 (copy), in file 1797.

CHAPTER X

Announcement of the Battleship Cruise

> "I am more concerned over the Japanese situation than almost any other. Thank Heaven we have the navy in good shape. It is high time, however, that it should go on a cruise around the world . . . ."—Roosevelt to Root, July 13, 1907

ROOSEVELT gives the impression in his *Autobiography* that the sending of the fleet to the Pacific was a sudden development.[1] As a matter of fact, for about two years prior to the announcement of the cruise the naval authorities had seriously considered and had several times recommended a voyage to the Pacific as a needed substitute for the customary short cruising and harbor work.[2] In October, 1906, these plans were complicated by the crisis resulting from the San Francisco school incident, and Roosevelt was believed to have postponed the trip in order to avoid further misunderstanding.[3] At this time, however, there was considerable agitation in the United States in favor of moving a part of the fleet to the Pacific, and the well-known naval authority, Captain A. T. Mahan,

[1] Roosevelt wrote: "I determined on the move without consulting the Cabinet, precisely as I took Panama without consulting the Cabinet. A council of war never fights, and in a crisis the duty of a leader is to lead and not to take refuge behind the generally timid wisdom of a multitude of councillors." Roosevelt, *Autobiography*, p. 563.

[2] *Annual Report of the Secretary of the Navy, 1907*, p. 7; Boston *Evening Transcript*, July 5, 1907; New York *Times*, July 6, 1907; San Francisco *Chronicle*, July 6, 1907.

[3] Boston *Evening Transcript*, July 1, 1907.

alarmed by rumors that four of the best battleships were to be detached for that purpose, wrote to Roosevelt on January 10, 1907, regarding the danger of dividing the fleet.[4] The President immediately reproved Mahan for thinking him capable of an act of such "utter folly" and asserted that he had no more intention of taking such a step while there was the least friction with Japan than he had of "going thither in a rowboat myself." On the contrary, should war become in the slightest degree possible he would "withdraw every fighting craft from the Pacific until our whole navy could be gathered and sent there in a body." As a matter of fact, he had already called home all battleships from the Asiatic squadron, leaving only cruisers there. Thus early Roosevelt expressed his conviction that if a fleet were to go it should be the most formidable that the United States could muster; yet he gave no indication of favoring such a cruise.[5]

The tension was greatly relieved when the San Francisco authorities repealed the objectionable school order in March, 1907, but in May there occurred the riots which, as we have seen, aroused to new bitterness the opposition press of Japan. While affairs were in this critical posture, the usually well-informed Washington correspondent of the Boston *Evening Transcript* wrote on June 11, 1907, that the administration had decided that it would be highly injudicious to send the Atlantic fleet of sixteen battleships to the Pacific.[6] A number of newspapers, however, notably the New York *Herald* in

4 Mahan to Roosevelt, Jan. 10, 1907, Roosevelt Papers.
5 Roosevelt to Mahan, Jan. 12, 1907, Roosevelt Papers.
6 Boston *Evening Transcript,* June 11, 1907.

the East and the San Francisco *Call* in the West, began a belligerent campaign to secure the transfer of sufficient naval strength to the Pacific to make American sea-power there superior to that of Japan.[7] Whatever the results of this agitation may have been, the same correspondent of the Boston *Evening Transcript* made the startling revelation on July 1, 1907, that the administration had just adopted the policy of concentrating the entire battleship fleet in the Pacific, and it was hoped that this movement could soon be made without offense to Japan. When the truth of this announcement was officially denied several days later, the correspondent flatly asserted that he had spoken "by authority," and that he had purposely refrained from being embarrassingly specific.[8] Subsequent events tended to support his claims.

On the next day, July 2, 1907, the same information was reported by a large number of reliable correspondents, and it was evident to discerning observers that the news had come, directly or indirectly, from an official source.[9] Nevertheless, Truman H. Newberry, assistant secretary of the navy, and William Loeb, secretary to the President, immediately denied that any such movement of the battleships was in contemplation.[10] Two days later, on July 4, 1907, Loeb issued the following supplementary statement:

[7] For a convenient summary of a few of these expressions see London *Times*, June 21, 29, 1907.

[8] Boston *Evening Transcript*, July 1, 5, 1907.

[9] London *Times*, July 3, 1907; San Francisco *Chronicle*, July 2, 1907; Pringle, *Roosevelt*, p. 410.

[10] New York *Times*, July 3, 1907.

There is no intention of sending a fleet at once to the Pacific. For the last two years the Administration has been perfecting its plans to arrange for a long ocean cruise. . . . . This cruise may possibly be to the Pacific, but might possibly be only to the Mediterranean, or the South Atlantic. It may possibly take place next Winter, but, on the other hand, it may not be convenient to arrange it until later . . . . The relations between the United States and all the other powers never were more peaceful and friendly than at the present time, and if the fleet were sent to the Pacific the fact would possess no more significance than the further fact that three or four months later it would be withdrawn from the Pacific. Both would merely be part of the ordinary routine of the naval administration.[11]

Later on the same day and obviously without the knowledge of Loeb, the new secretary of the navy, Victor H. Metcalf, who was then visiting friends in California, stated in an interview that a fleet of eighteen or twenty battleships would definitely come to San Francisco during the approaching winter on a practice cruise. He further observed that he might have made this announcement before leaving Washington, but, being a Californian, he wanted to bring the good news in person to the people of the Coast.[12] This unequivocal statement, which flatly contradicted the official denial issued two days previously, indicated a lack of co-operation in high places. It would appear, however, from the official leaks and Loeb's tergiversating explanation, that Roosevelt had made up his mind to send the fleet to the Pacific, but in

[11] New York *Times,* July 5, 1907.

[12] *Ibid.* It will be remembered that Metcalf had been promoted to the secretaryship of the navy. There were many who believed that, with political ends in view, he had a great deal to do with persuading Roosevelt to send the fleet. It may well have been that Metcalf seized this opportunity to restore some of the popularity he had lost as a result of his report on conditions in San Francisco.

order to avoid stirring up the jingoes at home and abroad he had thrown out the general suggestion of a long cruise, which, when the excitement had died down, would be followed with an announcement of the specific destination. Metcalf's statement appears to have ruined this strategy.[13]

Further denials were now out of the question, and the various battleships were soon ordered to make ready.[14] On July 9, 1907, Metcalf gave out another statement, which, in the light of his previous experience, may be considered official. He asserted that the fleet would definitely move to the Pacific during the coming winter on a practice cruise.[15] This declaration was confirmed by Loeb on August 1, 1907; and on August 23, 1907, following a conference of high naval officials with Roosevelt, it was officially announced that the battleship fleet of sixteen vessels would sail for San Francisco in December through the Straits of Magellan and would return by a route not yet decided.[16] As yet, however, the administration had made no public mention of a world cruise, although this was undoubtedly what Roosevelt had in mind,[17] and the

---

13 See *ibid.*, July 6, 1907. For some time after this interview rumors were current that Metcalf would resign. The Roosevelt correspondence, however, contains no mention of this apparent indiscretion, and there is good evidence that the relations between the President and his secretary of the navy were particularly cordial for some time thereafter. See Roosevelt to Metcalf, Nov. 13, 1908, Roosevelt Papers.

14 Boston *Evening Transcript,* July 6, 1907.

15 *Ibid.*, July 9, 1907.   16 New York *Times,* Aug. 2, 24, 1907.

17 Within a few days after the Pacific voyage had been announced, Roosevelt was making repeated references in his correspondence to the "world cruise." Roosevelt to Lodge, July 10, 1907; Roosevelt to Root, July 13, 23, 1907; Roosevelt to Speck von Sternberg, July 16, 1907; Roosevelt to Newberry, Aug. 6, 10, 1907; Roosevelt to Senator Jonathan Bourne, Aug. 13, 1907, Roosevelt Papers.

movement was spoken of merely as a practice cruise from one coast of the United States to the other.

The question naturally arises as to when Roosevelt definitely decided to send the fleet to the Pacific. Although the project had been discussed for some time by the naval authorities, there is no evidence in the voluminous Roosevelt correspondence that the President seriously entertained this idea until late in June, 1907. At that time, in response to an inquiry from Roosevelt as to what steps should be taken in the event that war should become imminent between the United States and Japan, the joint board of army and navy experts recommended, among other things, that the "battle fleet should be assembled and despatched for the Orient as soon as practicable."[18] About this time, and apparently before the submission of the report, Roosevelt talked the matter over with Henry Cabot Lodge, and he appears to have given the latter to understand that he favored sending the fleet but that he was not then prepared to make a definite decision. Upon reading Metcalf's announcement, Lodge wrote to Roosevelt in some perturbation, hoping that there had been no new developments which implied danger.[19] Roosevelt replied that there had been "no change save that the naval board decided sooner than I had expected."[20]

In view of the delicate international situation and the suspicious manner with which the announcement was

[18] Dewey to Taft, June 18, 1907, inclosure in Taft to Roosevelt, June 22, 1907, Roosevelt Papers.

[19] Lodge to Roosevelt, July 8, 1907, Roosevelt Papers.

[20] Roosevelt to Lodge, July 10, 1907, Roosevelt Papers.

made, the Japanese might well have been expected to show resentment. Yet Ambassador Aoki came forward with assurances that the contemplated dispatch of ships from one American port to another would not be regarded as an unfriendly act, even if the fleet were to be sent on to the Philippines.[21] Japanese naval officials remained unmoved and expressed surprise that the news should have been sensationally reported.[22] The Japanese press, in the words of the Tokyo correspondent of the London *Times,* "showed absolute *sang-froid.*"[23] The general view was that since the United States had definitely launched out upon an imperialistic policy it was only natural that her naval strength in the Pacific should be increased to a point more nearly commensurate with her interests there.[24] It was also felt that a great naval power should be permitted to engage in extensive maneuvers, as did other nations, without having its motives called in question. A majority of the leading Japanese newspapers refused to consider the movement a demonstration against Japan, for there was a feeling among them that if any demonstration were in order it should be undertaken by Japan, which was the aggrieved nation.[25] Indeed, the hope was widely expressed that the

21 New York *Times,* July 3, 1907.

22 *North China Herald,* July 19, 1907, p. 118.

23 London *Times,* July 9, 1907. It must be remembered that the Japanese mind was much more concerned with Korea at this time than with America.

24 The Kaiser rejoiced that the arrival of the American fleet would shift the balance of naval power in the Pacific and upset the calculations of the British and their allies, the Japanese. *Die Grosse Politik der Europäischen Kabinette,* XXV, 87, 88, 89.

25 For a useful symposium of the views of the leading Japanese newspapers see *Japan Weekly Mail,* July 13, 1907, pp. 30–31. See also New York *Times,* July 8, 1907 ; London *Times,* July 11, 1907.

fleet would continue on to the Orient and give the Japanese an opportunity to show the sincerity of their friendship and hospitality.[26] As a further indication of the improved state of feeling, it was noted that the Tokyo share market, which had been depressed for months, was showing considerable improvement.[27] Roosevelt naturally viewed these developments with satisfaction, and on July 10, 1907, wrote to Lodge:

> I think that before matters become more strained we had better make it evident that when it comes to visiting our own coasts on the Pacific or Atlantic and assembling the fleet in our own waters, we can not submit to any outside protests or interference. Curiously enough, the Japs have seen this more quickly than our own people.[28]

There was, however, an occasional disapproving voice among the Japanese statesmen, and the jingo press evidenced some displeasure.[29] Ambassador Wright, although observing that the newspapers were "uniformly calm," feared that the proposed demonstration might have "an unfavorable effect upon the mind of the average Japanese."[30] Of the leading newspapers, the *Hochi Shimbun*, regarded as the mouthpiece of Count Okuma, alone ques-

[26] *Japan Weekly Mail*, July 13, 1907, pp. 30–31; Dec. 21, 1907, p. 690; *North China Herald*, July 12, 1907, p. 63; New York *Times*, Dec. 20, 1907; London *Times*, July 9, Nov. 6, 1907.

[27] *Ibid.*, July 16, 1907.   [28] *Lodge Letters*, II, 274–75.

[29] London *Times*, July 12, 13, 1907; October 3, 1907; New York *Times*, July 12, 1907; *North China Herald*, July 12, 1907; Allan Nevins, *Henry White* (New York, 1930), pp. 292–93; D. S. Jordan, *The Days of a Man* (Yonkers-on-Hudson, 1922), II, 423. The New York correspondent of the London *Times* learned from a private source that Aoki's public statements were made simply for publication and that Japan resented this inopportune and tactless waving of the big stick in her face. London *Times*, July 13, 1907.

[30] Wright to Root, July 10, 1907, in file 1797.

tioned the timeliness of the cruise. The fear was expressed by a few Japanese that the San Francisco hoodlums would see in the fleet transfer official approval of their conduct and that the jingoes on both sides would be spurred to renewed outbursts. In some quarters it was even suggested that the United States would have done well to follow the example of the Japanese government, which, a few months before, had not permitted the Japanese training squadron to call at San Francisco lest some untoward incident result.[31]

The question has frequently been asked why Roosevelt should have chosen this critical time to take a step which could easily have resulted in the gravest misunderstanding. Some observers professed to see in the projected cruise an object lesson that would hasten the completion of the Panama Canal; others interpreted it as an attempt to follow up the extraordinarily happy results of Secretary Root's recent South American good-will trip.[32] There was also some feeling, particularly abroad, that for the first time the United States had come to recognize its obligations as a world power in the Pacific and was making a belated attempt to wrest from the Japanese their naval supremacy in those waters and to restore the proper balance.[33] Roosevelt himself later confessed in

[31] *Japan Weekly Mail,* July 13, 1907, p. 31.

[32] London *Times,* Oct. 3, 1907; San Francisco *Chronicle,* May 8, 1908; *Fortnightly Review,* Feb., 1908, p. 211. It was also suggested that the cruise was designed to stimulate recruiting, and Roosevelt testified that for the first time since the Spanish War the battleships put to sea overmanned. *Autobiography,* p. 566; *Harper's Weekly,* Feb. 29, 1908, p. 16.

[33] London *Times,* Dec. 18, 1907; June 24, 1908; *Argonaut,* San Francisco, Oct. 5, 1907, p. 212; *Fortnightly Review,* Feb., 1908, p. 211.

his *Autobiography* that his "prime purpose was to impress the American people," and he quoted with approval a statement from the London *Spectator* to the effect that he was seeking to arouse popular support for a more ambitious battleship program.[34] This was probably why Roosevelt devoted so much attention to the problem of securing acceptable newspaper correspondents for the trip.[35]

The reason most frequently given at the time, at least in official quarters, was that the proposed voyage was merely a necessary practice cruise. In his private correspondence Roosevelt referred repeatedly to "the practice cruise," and on July 24, 1907, he informed Truman H. Newberry, acting secretary of the navy, that the "fleet is not now going to the Pacific as a war measure. . . . ."[36] Moreover, at that time considerable doubt existed as to whether the fleet, in case of necessity, could make the trip around South America and arrive in fighting trim. Roosevelt was aware of this uncertainty, and

---

The article in this journal by Sydney Brooks developed at some length the relation of the cruise to the Pacific rôle of the United States. It struck Roosevelt as being "so sympathetic and appreciative" that he sent a personal letter of congratulation to the writer. Roosevelt to Brooks, Mar. 21, 1908, Roosevelt Papers.

[34] Roosevelt, *Autobiography*, pp. 564–65.

[35] Roosevelt to Newberry, Aug. 10, 17, 1907; Admiral W. H. Brownson to Roosevelt, Aug. 17, 1907, Roosevelt Papers.

[36] See Roosevelt to Newberry, July 24, 1907; Roosevelt to von Sternberg, July 16, 1907; Roosevelt to Albert Shaw, Sept. 3, 1907, Roosevelt Papers. Captain A. T. Mahan stated that such a practice cruise was imperative, particularly since "the navy has only now reached the numbers, sufficiently homogeneous, to make the movement exhaustively instructive." A. T. Mahan, "The True Significance of the Pacific Cruise," in *Scientific American*, Dec. 7, 1907, p. 407. This consideration may also have appealed to Roosevelt. See Roosevelt to Lodge, July 10, 1907, Roosevelt Papers.

he was insistent that the experiment, with its inevitable mistakes, should be made in time of peace, and not in time of war. If the voyage could not be completed successfully, he concluded, it "was much better to know it and be able to shape our policy in view of the knowledge."[37] Furthermore, Roosevelt was convinced that only by showing the difficulties involved would it be possible to force opponents of a big navy in the Senate "into providing what the navy actually needs."[38]

It is probably true that all of the reasons thus far mentioned were taken into consideration when the final decision was made. But none of them, not even the practice cruise, explains why this movement was deemed necessary at the very time when deference to the already injured sensibilities of Japan would have suggested further postponement. It was frequently observed that if a long cruise was highly imperative a trip to the Cape of Good Hope would serve the purpose admirably and would not be interpreted as a threat against Japan. In fact, a number of naval experts of high repute were prepared to argue that short, intensive cruises were more beneficial than long, tedious ones, and that the departure of the fleet at that time would seriously interrupt the perfection of certain technical details. Furthermore, it was noted that this was a peace-time voyage during which the ships could cruise along at the most economical speed and put into various ports. Such an experience would obviously be of little value in time of war, when the vessels would

[37] Roosevelt, *Autobiography*, p. 564. See also Roosevelt to Lodge, July 10, 1907; Roosevelt to Root, July 13, 23, 1907, Roosevelt Papers.
[38] Roosevelt to Taft, Aug. 21, 1907, Roosevelt Papers.

have to steam under pressure and depend on themselves, instead of upon neutrals, for all their needs.[39]

What appears to have been an important factor—perhaps the most important factor—in the sending of the fleet to the Pacific was a desire on the part of the administration to handle the Japanese situation with greater firmness. Such a motive could obviously not be mentioned publicly in official quarters, but the press, quick to sense the logic of the situation, generally held that this otherwise untimely maneuver could not possibly be dissociated from the tension between the United States and Japan.[40]

The private letters and statements of Roosevelt provide a further key to the situation. The President, as we have seen, was greatly worried over developments on the Pacific Coast, and he wrote to Henry White on June 15, 1907, that "the utterances of the extremists in Japan have begun to make an unpleasant feeling in this country."[41] On July 13, 1907, shortly after the fleet announcement, Roosevelt confided to Root: "I am more concerned over the Japanese situation than almost any

[39] See *Independent*, Dec. 26, 1907, pp. 1546, 1548; *Harper's Weekly*, Nov. 30, 1907, p. 1755; *Literary Digest*, July 13, 1907, p. 41; *Current Literature*, Nov., 1907, p. 480.

[40] The Washington correspondent of the New York *Times* wrote that "no grown man in Washington will believe that if the whole navy goes at once to the Pacific coast it can be for any other reason than because trouble is expected with Japan." New York *Times*, July 5, 1907. The New York correspondent of the London *Times* wrote: "All of which deceives nobody. America is not going to remove the best part of her fleet from the Atlantic for the purpose of seeing how successfully it can make a long and trying voyage." London *Times*, July 6, 1907. For similar expressions see *Fortnightly Review*, Feb., 1908, pp. 211, 215; *Living Age*, Jan. 11, 1908, p. 121.

[41] Nevins, *Henry White*, p. 292.

other. Thank Heaven we have the navy in good shape. It is high time, however, that it should go on a cruise around the world. . . . . I think it will have a pacific effect to show that it can be done. . . . ."[42] And in a conversation with the British ambassador at Washington, James Bryce, Roosevelt stated that his principal reason for sending the American fleet to the Pacific was to "impress Japan with the seriousness of the situation."[43]

One other aspect of this problem remains to be considered. Roosevelt had become convinced, probably as a result of the tone of the Japanese press, that his sympathetic handling of the San Francisco difficulties and the immigration problem was being interpreted as fear of Japan. A man of Roosevelt's temperament was unable to permit such a challenge to remain unanswered. On July 30, 1907, the President wrote to Henry White substantially the same thing that he later told J. B. Bishop: "I am exceedingly anxious to impress upon the Japanese that I have nothing but the friendliest possible intentions toward them, but I am none the less anxious that they should realize that I am not afraid of them and that the United States will no more submit to bullying than it will bully."[44] In October, 1911, with perhaps an uncon-

[42] J. B. Bishop, *Theodore Roosevelt and His Time* (New York, 1920), II, 64.

[43] G. P. Gooch and Harold Temperley, eds., *British Documents on the Origins of the War, 1898–1914* (London, 1932), VIII, 457.

[44] Nevins, *Henry White*, pp. 292–93. Bishop quotes Roosevelt as having said that "the Japanese people should not think that his action had been taken in fear of Japan, and he accordingly decided to send the battle fleet into the Pacific and around the world to show that the United States earnestly desired peace, but was not in the least afraid of war." Bishop, *Roosevelt*, II, 65. The Washington correspondent of the London *Times* reported that it was rumored in Washington that Roosevelt

scious coloring of the events that had occurred four years before, Roosevelt wrote more positively:

> I had been doing my best to be polite to the Japanese, and had finally become uncomfortably conscious of a very, very slight undertone of veiled truculence in their communications in connection with things that happened on the Pacific Slope; and I finally made up my mind that they thought I was afraid of them. . . . . I found that the Japanese war party firmly believed that they could beat us, and, unlike the Elder Statesmen, thought I also believed this. . . . . I definitely came to the conclusion that . . . . it was time for a show down.[45]

In short, Roosevelt appears to have been convinced that the time had come for an impressive naval demonstration, not against Japan, but for the benefit of Japan. The yellow journals of both countries had worked themselves into a veritable frenzy, and Roosevelt was of the opinion that the appearance of a mighty armada in the Pacific, a grim reminder of the fact that the United States was the second naval power of the world and Japan the fifth, would have a quieting effect upon the jingoes of Japan. And that was why Roosevelt wanted "every battleship and armored cruiser that can be sent to go."[46] The President believed "that the only thing that will prevent war is the Japanese feeling that we shall not be beaten,"[47] and that

---

wanted to send the fleet just to show that he was not afraid of trouble. London *Times,* Oct. 3, 1907.

[45] Bishop, *Roosevelt,* II, 249–50.

[46] Roosevelt wanted all twenty battleships to go, if possible. Roosevelt to Newberry, Aug. 6, 1907, Roosevelt Papers. It is significant that only four battleships remained in the Atlantic, and they were all undergoing repairs. Roosevelt to L. F. Abbott, Sept. 13, 1907, Roosevelt Papers.

[47] Roosevelt to Root, July 23, 1907, Roosevelt Papers. German high naval officials agreed that the sending of the fleet was the right thing to do. Charlemagne Tower (American ambassador to Germany) to Roose-

if the most powerful fleet ever sent on a long cruise would not serve this purpose nothing would. So it was that Roosevelt wrote that "far from its being a war measure," the dispatch of the fleet was "really a peace measure."[48]

There is some ground for believing that the fleet announcement helped to produce the anticipated quieting effect. It was widely observed in the East, with or without reason, that this step was followed by a sudden cessation of the "pin-pricks" and the constant "hectoring" directed at the United States.[49] Roosevelt himself wrote that his action had proved useful in silencing the clamor "for hostilities against us by the Japanese yellow press,"[50] and from Tokyo Ambassador O'Brien, who had succeeded Wright, reported that the disposition of the United States "to make ready for contingencies" had had a salutary effect on public sentiment.[51] Unquestionably, improved relations with Japan followed the fleet announcement; but so many different factors were involved that care must be taken not to overestimate the influence of Roosevelt's flourish.

The first reaction of many Eastern editors to the an-

velt, Nov. 2, 1907, Roosevelt Papers. The Kaiser remarked that the dispatch of the battleships had greatly strengthened the position of the United States, perhaps "even to the extent of preventing an immediate attack upon us by the Japanese." Tower to Roosevelt, Jan. 28, 1908, Roosevelt Papers.

[48] Roosevelt to Newberry, Aug. 6, 1907, Roosevelt Papers.

[49] New York *Times,* Sept. 27, 29, 1907.

[50] Roosevelt to Albert Shaw, Sept. 3, 1907, Roosevelt Papers. Four years later, in October, 1911, Roosevelt wrote that "every particle of trouble with the Japanese Government and the Japanese press stopped like magic as soon as they found that our fleet had actually sailed, and was obviously in good trim." Bishop, *Roosevelt,* II, 250.

[51] O'Brien to Root, Oct. 25, 1907, in file 1797.

nouncement was to cry out against stripping the Atlantic Coast of its defenses. Stressing the cost of the voyage, the likelihood of destruction from natural phenomena or sudden attack, the wear and tear on machinery, and the danger of precipitating war, the more militant of these journals issued "frantic appeals to Congress to stop the fleet from going."[52] Others urged, without response, a Congressional investigation of the cost;[53] and one Southern newspaper suggested impeaching the President to prevent the fatal step.[54] Eugene Hale, chairman of the Senate committee on naval affairs, himself from the Eastern seaboard state of Maine, announced that the fleet would not go because Congress would refuse to appropriate money. Roosevelt, more determined than ever now that his will was being opposed, silenced the attack from this quarter by replying that he had enough money on hand to send the fleet to the Pacific, and that if Congress did not care to vote the money to bring it back it could stay there.[55] In private, the President wrote caustically of the "hysterical violence of the attacks of the Wall Street crowd" and the "campaign on behalf of

[52] Roosevelt, *Autobiography*, p. 568. See also *Annual Report of the Secretary of the Navy, 1908*, pp. 5–6.

[53] The cost of the voyage was $1,619,843.32 above the normal cost of maintaining the fleet in home waters. *Information Relative to the Voyage of the United States Atlantic Fleet Around the World* (Washington, 1910), p. 16.

[54] See London *Times*, Dec. 16, 1907; *Current Literature*, Nov., 1907, p. 480.

[55] Roosevelt, *Autobiography*, p. 568. See also Roosevelt to von Sternberg, July 16, 1907; Roosevelt to Newberry, July 30, 1907, Roosevelt Papers. To Congressman E. A. Hayes Roosevelt wrote on Sept. 18, 1907: ". . . . I am Commander-in-Chief, and my decision is absolute in the matter." See also Roosevelt to Taft, Sept. 5, 1907, Roosevelt Papers.

the wealthy malefactor class . . . . to prevent the fleet from going to the Pacific."[56] Striking back at his critics in a speech at Cairo, Illinois, on October 3, 1907, Roosevelt remarked that "some excellent people in my own section of the country need to be reminded that the Pacific coast is exactly as much a part of this nation as the Atlantic coast."[57] Yet, in spite of the uproar, the President was of the opinion that "the people as a whole have been extremely well pleased at my sending the fleet to the Pacific. . . . ."[58]

During the ensuing weeks the naval authorities settled down to the task of preparing the battleships for their long cruise. But in the meantime, the American press, stimulated by the announcement of the voyage, had whipped up what was probably the most serious war scare throughout the entire period under consideration. This jingo campaign was the most unfortunate aspect of the newspaper opposition to the departure of the battleships from the East coast; and it was fraught with more danger than appeared at the time on the surface.

[56] Roosevelt to Albert Shaw, Sept. 3, 1907, in Bishop, *Roosevelt*, II, 66–67.

[57] New York *Times,* Oct. 4, 1907. In a similar vein the *Argonaut,* San Francisco, criticized "Easterners who regard the United States as a country bounded on the east by the Atlantic and on the west by the Alleghenies." Sept. 28, 1907, p. 196.

[58] Roosevelt to Lodge, Sept. 2, 1907, *Lodge Letters,* II, 279.

CHAPTER XI

The War Scare of 1907

> "I do not believe we shall have war; but it is
> no fault of the yellow press if we do not
> have it. The Japanese seem to have about the
> same proportion of prize jingo fools that we
> have."—Roosevelt to Lodge, July 10, 1907

IT WILL BE remembered that when the Japanese press
flared up in 1906 immediately following the school incident, the American public remained calm, scarcely understanding what the commotion was about. In February,
1907, on the other hand, when the sensational newspapers
of the United States staged their intemperate outburst,
the Japanese press expressed mild surprise at this apparently uncalled-for demonstration. And in June, 1907,
when the yellow journals of Japan indulged in inflammatory language as a result of the San Francisco riots,
public sentiment in America did not evidence resentment.
We are now entering upon a troubled period, however,
when the jingo press of both countries synchronized in
its incendiary interpretation of events. This was a unique
and dangerous development, all the more so because the
belligerent pronouncements of the newspapers of one
nation aroused to new heights of intemperance those of
the other. This was obviously a process that could not
go on indefinitely without an explosion.

It was more than fortunate that the newspapers at
this time did not have access to the correspondence that
was coming to the Department of State and to the Presi-

dent. Some of these communications, written as they were by responsible persons apparently in a position to know what they were saying, may well have caused a less self-assured executive than Roosevelt to lose his head. In this connection it is well to bear in mind the President's background. Prior to his accession to office, it would have been difficult to find an intelligent and responsible man in the United States who more sincerely believed in or enthusiastically preached the virtues of war. It is, therefore, a tribute to Roosevelt's balance that he kept his head and steered a straight course while the air was surcharged with war rumors, while the jingo press of both countries was rising to new levels of sensationalism, while foreign friends were predicting not only war but the defeat of the United States, and while Roosevelt's official advisers were succumbing to the hysteria. It is remarkable that in this situation the disciple of Mars should have won new laurels in the cause of peace.

On April 1, 1907, before the war scare had really got under way but while there was some conjecture as to the possibility of hostilities with Japan, the German ambassador to the United States and a warm friend of Roosevelt, Speck von Sternberg, sent certain information to the President which had come from a German military attaché in Japan whom the ambassador considered thoroughly reliable. This observer noted at the outset that there was "absolutely nothing noticeable here of those feverish war preparations which some countries seem to be believing in." The Japanese were reorganizing their army, but this was in consequence of their new position as a world power. That this reorganization was but a normal development was indicated by the careful planning and lack of haste that were in evidence, and by the state of the military budget. There were no additions to the army that could be considered alarming, and it was quite impossible to detect the slightest signs of a warlike feeling among the people toward America and Russia. There was nothing to be feared so far as the immediate future was concerned.[1]

One other development at this time remains to be noted. General Kuroki, who as we have seen visited the United States in May, 1907, made a strong impression on Roosevelt. This was not remarkable, the President wrote to Kermit, for "indeed all Japanese military and naval officers do. They are a formidable outfit." Then Roosevelt went on to preach his favorite doctrine: "I want to try to keep on the best possible terms with Japan and never do her any wrong; but I want still more to see our navy maintained at the highest point of efficiency, for it is the real keeper of peace."[2]

It was not until May, however, that the jingo campaign began to take shape. Much impetus was given to it by the observations of European military and naval experts, who for a number of reasons would not have been displeased to see the United States involved in hostilities with Japan. In this month the New York *Times* printed long translated passages from a volume recently published in Berlin by an officer of the German navy, who wrote with confidence that the next great war would be fought between the United States and Japan over the

---

[1] Von Sternberg to Roosevelt, Apr. 1, 1907, Roosevelt Papers.

[2] Roosevelt to Kermit Roosevelt, May 12, 1907, Roosevelt Papers.

Philippines. Shortly thereafter *Collier's Weekly,* an American magazine, printed an article by a French writer in which an outbreak between the United States and Japan was freely predicted. The American mind was being prepared for the jingoistic efforts that were to follow.[3]

Throughout this period Roosevelt was not regarding the possibilities of war with Japan lightly. On June 22, 1907, probably in response to the President's request, Secretary of War Taft submitted a detailed report on the proper steps for defending the Philippine Islands, Hawaii, Guam, and the Pacific Coast in the event of hostilities with Japan.[4] A few days later Roosevelt sent a code message to General Wood, who was in command of the Philippines, outlining instructions for holding the islands should the Japanese attack them.[5] During July, 1907, particularly as a result of the manifestations of race hostility in San Francisco, Roosevelt's concern over the situation increased measurably. On July 1, 1907, he wrote to Cecil Spring Rice:

The San Francisco mob bids fair, if not to embroil us with Japan, at any rate to arouse in Japan a feeling of rankling anger toward us that may at any time bear evil result, and the Japanese jingoes are in their turn about as bad as ours. I am doing everything I can to meet the just grievances of the Japanese, to atone for and remedy any wrong. But I am also doing everything I can to keep our navy at the highest point of efficiency.[6]

[3] For war feeling at this time see *Literary Digest,* May 18, 1907, p. 790; *ibid.,* May 25, 1907, p. 822.

[4] Pringle, *Roosevelt,* p. 408. The succeeding pages in this book give a good account of some of the alarming letters that Roosevelt received from abroad.

[5] This was on July 6, 1907. *Ibid.*

[6] Roosevelt to Spring Rice, July 1, 1907, Roosevelt Papers.

At this time reassuring information came to Roosevelt through Taft. The latter, on July 2, 1907, forwarded to the President a preliminary report of Major Reber of the General Staff, who had been detailed to tour Japan with a view to observing conditions there. This officer, whose report was dated May 23, 1907, remarked that he had not found a spirit of hostility toward the Americans anywhere in Japan, and although he had traveled incognito he had neither been interfered with nor had he been an object of suspicion. He was of the opinion that Japan was ready for war at any time with any power, yet could not afford to fight because of the economic state of the empire and because hostilities would sever important financial arteries. Major Reber's significant conclusions appeared in two sentences: "The Japanese are making no immediate preparation for war with the United States, and I do not believe that anything is farther from their thoughts at the present time. The whole future of the empire depends upon the success of its commercial expansion and hostilities with the United States would absolutely stop this." To Major Reber's report Taft appended the statement: "It only confirms my view of the situation."[7]

Roosevelt's growing concern over the situation is clearly evident in a letter that he wrote to Lodge from Oyster Bay on July 10, 1907:

I have the Japanese Ambassador and a Cabinet Minister out here the day after tomorrow. I shall continue to do everything I can by politeness and consideration to the Japs to offset the worse than criminal stupidity of the San Francisco mob, the San Fran-

[7] Taft to Roosevelt, July 2, 1907, Roosevelt Papers.

cisco press, and such papers as the New York *Herald*. I do not believe we shall have war; but it is no fault of the yellow press if we do not have it. The Japanese seem to have about the same proportion of prize jingo fools that we have.[8]

The President's disquietude was further increased by official figures which seemed to indicate that the Gentlemen's Agreement was not being faithfully observed by Japan. His secretary, William Loeb, informed Huntington Wilson, of the Department of State, that the President was "much disappointed in the showing of the failure to reduce Japanese immigration . . . ."[9] On the next day, July 13, 1907, Roosevelt wrote to the acting secretary of commerce and labor:

The admission of Japanese during May and June, instead of showing a falling off, shows an increase over those admitted in May and June of last year. I am more concerned over this Japanese question than over any other, including that of the trusts.

He then suggested to the acting secretary that steps be taken to find out with exactitude how many Japanese had formerly come through Hawaii, Canada, or Mexico, in order that there might be some basis for comparison, and what occupations those then coming in as "petty traders" eventually took up. The President concluded, "There is no one matter where we want to be armed with so full a statement of the facts."[10]

On the same day, July 13, 1907, Roosevelt sent to Root the "disquieting statistics," which he had just re-

[8] Roosevelt to Lodge, July 10, 1907, *Lodge Letters,* II, 275.

[9] Loeb to Wilson, July 12, 1907, in file 1797.

[10] Roosevelt to the acting secretary of commerce and labor, July 13, 1907, Roosevelt Papers.

ceived, "of the Japanese arrivals in the United States for the fiscal year just closed as compared with the fiscal year preceding." In general, there had been "a great increase in these arrivals; and for the last two months, during which the new policy [Gentlemen's Agreement] has been in effect, while the increase is less marked, it still exists. More Japanese came here during May and June than during the preceding May and June, or than during March and April." Roosevelt was inclined to believe that many of these immigrants who entered as petty traders were really laborers. He continued:

In any event I believe we shall have to urge most strongly upon the Japanese Government the need of restricting the total number of passports if we are not to have trouble. If there is not a falling off in the number of Japanese arrivals, I think we can safely count upon at least a very dangerous agitation in Congress next year for their total exclusion by a law modeled after our Chinese exclusion act.

Referring to recent difficulties with England, Roosevelt concluded significantly: "The Newfoundland business and similar matters are mere child's play compared with this Japanese business from the standpoint of its ultimate importance."[11]

Although greatly annoyed by these apparent infractions of the Gentlemen's Agreement, Roosevelt was keeping his head in the midst of the increasingly ominous war rumors. An interesting bit of evidence may be offered in support of this statement. Major Eben Swift, presumably an intelligence officer, was then in Peking, and not having the army code available, he had had United

11 Roosevelt to Root, July 13, 1907, Roosevelt Papers.

States Minister Rockhill send a confidential message for the General Staff through the Department of State. Major Swift was apparently seriously disturbed by the rumors of an impending conflict, for he wired:

Shall I report by cable [the number of] Japanese war vessels now ready, the time when additional Japanese war vessels will be ready, numbers of the army, progress of the new armament, recent movements of naval reserves, arms smuggled into the Philippine islands, character Hawaiian immigration? Report by mail was sent 4th of July.[12]

Roosevelt, refusing to be swept off his feet, promptly informed the Department of State that "there is no need for cabling."[13]

To add to the increasing number of alarming rumors, Ambassador Speck von Sternberg passed on to Roosevelt a report from a German agent in Mexico regarding the large number of Japanese, presumably from eight to ten thousand all together, who were arriving there. Many of them, the agent observed, had knapsacks, arms, and simple uniforms.[14] In his reply to the ambassador, dated July 16, 1907, Roosevelt wrote that the "whole Japanese business is very puzzling. I suppose because there are such deep racial differences that it is very hard for any of us of European descent to understand them or be understood by them." As for the report that Japanese were going to Mexico for military purposes, it was "simply incredible." Then followed a discussion of the number of Japanese of

---

12 Rockhill to Root (telegram), July 12, 1907, in file 1797.

13 Rudolph Foster (assistant secretary to Roosevelt) to Adee, July 13, 1907, in file 1797.

14 Von Sternberg to Roosevelt, July 14, 1907, Roosevelt Papers.

military age who were then in Hawaii; but Roosevelt was not particularly alarmed by this situation. He continued:

Our more unscrupulous, foolish newspapers and certain jingoes and labor leaders, and a corresponding people in Japan, do all they can to cause trouble between the two countries; but as yet there is literally not one reason why war should ensue. I am endeavoring to right every wrong that the Japanese suffer here, and have as yet not received a protest from their government about any conduct of ours. I shall treat them not only with justice but with every courtesy and consideration . . . .

Roosevelt went on to outline his principles in dealing with Japan:

My foreign policy as regards the Japanese (and as regards the rest of the world) is perfectly simple. I shall try to do exact justice to them; to show them every consideration and courtesy; to ask nothing from them that we should not be willing to grant them in return ourselves; and at the same time to make it evident that in following out this course I am not in the slightest degree influenced by fear of them, and that I will no more permit my country to be wronged than I will sanction its committing wrong in return.

The President then condemned Senator Hale, chairman of the Senate committee on naval affairs, the New York *Nation,* and the New York *Evening Post* for their extreme pacifism. He was afraid that because the American people were suffering from all the luxuries of a pleasure-loving civilization they had lost the fighting edge.

From my point of view the fool who continually screams against war and for peace, without regard to whether one or the other is righteous, is as noxious as the wealthy man in whom the desire to achieve wealth has swallowed up all thoughts of patriotism, and of pride in the exercise of the manlier virtues. I am so utterly disgusted with the nonsense chattered by the extreme advocates of peace here that it was difficult for me to take a proper interest in the Hague proceedings.

Nevertheless, even though the American people had grown soft, Roosevelt believed that they still had, fundamentally, good sense and manliness. And he concluded:

In short, I do not believe that there will be trouble, and I am taking all the steps possible for me to take both to prevent it and to prevent its being disastrous if it should come. But of course the situation gives me some concern; for the Japanese are a formidable military power and have unknown possibilities both as regards their power and as regards their motives and purposes.[15]

It was while in this mood that Roosevelt replied to overtures from Andrew Carnegie.

I am sorry to say that I am more concerned about keeping the peace with Japan than I am about advancing the cause of peace in the Hague just at the moment, for the former represents the "instant need of things." I have almost as much trouble with our own people, like Senator Hale, who are always giving the impression to Japan that we are afraid of them, as with the other people, who insult the Japanese. Moreover, I regret to say that the Japanese jingoes seem to be quite as bad as our own.[16]

Another disquieting report, however, was yet to come. On July 17, 1907, Major General Bell, chief of staff of the United States army, forwarded a letter to Roosevelt which had come from a retired American army officer then living in St. Petersburg. This officer had been told of a dinner in the Russian capital at which a Japanese diplomat, having imbibed too freely of liquor, had outlined Japan's plans for taking and making colonies of the Philippines, Hawaii, Alaska, California, and the Pacific Coast. In his covering letter, however, General Bell made it clear that he did not attach much importance to this

[15] Roosevelt to von Sternberg, July 16, 1907, Roosevelt Papers.
[16] Roosevelt to Carnegie, July 15, 1907, Roosevelt Papers.

report.[17] He did not have the slightest doubt but that such thoughts had occurred to "mighty nearly every Jap official, either high or low, now in existence"; and he pointed to the obvious conclusion that the United States was the most likely enemy of Japan in the event of war. But he added that the inclosed letter sounded like boasting, of which some of the Japanese were capable on occasion, and that it did not seem possible that it could be authoritative. He was careful to point out, moreover, that the communication from St. Petersburg did not agree with the reports of American intelligence officers sent to the Far East.[18]

In his reply to General Bell, Roosevelt revealed that he was little disturbed by the alleged indiscretion of the Japanese diplomat. He regarded it as impossible that the Japanese could ever get possession of California.

However, whatever I may think of the Japanese intentions will not in the slightest degree alter the course of conduct I shall try to follow. I shall do my best to prevent any kind of wrong being done the Japanese here. I shall try to show them every courtesy and consideration, and to see that they are not afforded even a pretext for hostilities. On the other hand I shall do my best to keep everything ready for any hostility that may come; and I shall do my best to impress upon the nation that this is the only safe course for the nation to pursue.

In concluding, Roosevelt paid his respects to men like Senator Hale who did not favor the building and maintenance of a powerful navy; and although he was sure that difficulties lay in the future, he was confident that the United States would be able to surmount them.[19]

[17] Pringle, *Roosevelt,* pp. 401–402.

[18] The St. Petersburg letter was dated June 11, 1907. See Bell to Roosevelt, July 17, 1907, Roosevelt Papers.

[19] Roosevelt to Bell, July 23, 1907, Roosevelt Papers.

Early in July, 1907, Charles Denby, American consul general at Shanghai, then in Germany, wrote to Secretary Root of developments in Europe with respect to a possible war with Japan. He reported that popular sentiment in France and Germany had definitely decided that war between the United States and Japan was inevitable within a few years. This opinion was even more strongly held in Germany than in France. German officers, among whom the American consul general had many friends, regarded the conflict as certain, and German merchants with Oriental connections agreed with them. Denby was informed that the outcome of such a conflict had received technical consideration in military circles in Germany and Great Britain, and that the probability of Japan's success was regarded as being represented by the ratio five to four. Moreover, several Japanese, said to be naval officers, were staying in a Hanoverian hotel, and they had visited and inspected factories for uniforms.

Denby's own interpretation of developments, which was doubtless colored by an obvious anti-Japanese bias, is of more than passing interest. He remarked that there was much to indicate that Japan was willing to start a war and that her position with regard to the California difficulty was merely a pretext. He further observed that the attitude of Japan was similar to that which she had evidenced just before the Sino-Japanese War of 1894–95. At that time Denby had been at the American legation in Peking, and at the outbreak of hostilities had been placed in charge of Japanese interests in China. In these circumstances he had been in a good position to observe the war and its causes. It seemed clear to him at the time, he added, that notwithstanding Japan's assurances and in spite of her ostentatious maintenance of friendly relations with China until the last moment, she had in fact carefully planned her course and had struck with deadly precision.[20]

This letter, which was shown to Roosevelt, is paraphrased at length because it illustrates strikingly the sort of thing with which the President had to deal. Although Denby probably was somewhat arbitrary in interpreting the currents of European opinion, he appears to have been correct in stating that in official military and naval circles a war was expected (the wish may well have been the father to the thought), and that Japan was regarded as having a five-to-four chance of defeating the United States. Many of the other observations of the American consul general, however, were ludicrously wide of the mark, and it was indeed fortunate that Roosevelt had authoritative reports from experts like Major Reber to offset such misinformation.

About this time the Department of State received a dispatch from the American ambassador to Germany, Charlemagne Tower, which confirmed with disheartening detail some of the rumors that had been pouring into Washington. Tower stated that the current reports of a possible breach between the United States and Japan were attracting a great deal of attention in Europe, especially in Germany, where the subject had suddenly assumed a place of prime importance among the international questions of the day. The idea was prevalent throughout

[20] Denby to Root, July 2, 1907, in file 1797.

Europe that the Japanese were aggressively belligerent, and that if the United States did not find a remedy for existing difficulties an outbreak would soon come. The American ambassador then went on to say that in the opinion of the highest authorities in Germany and England the contest was not merely a local California problem but one that "involves the great question of the control of the Pacific Ocean which the Japanese claim to be theirs and which they are determined to assert against us, the only great Power that can dispute it with them." The California troubles, these foreign officials believed, were merely a symptom, and the difficulties over the children in San Francisco were being emphasized merely for the purpose of inflaming public sentiment against America. "Military and naval observers," continued Tower, "incline to the belief that it is only a question with the Japanese as to the moment most favorable to them to open hostilities with us." The American ambassador attached considerable significance to the fact that the English officers, who as allies came in closer contact with the Japanese than other foreigners, held this same view.[21]

Tower then proceeded to discuss the possible outcome of such a war. He noted that this problem had been worked out by the German General Staff in Berlin and by the Admiralty in London. Although these calculations had been made quite separately, they pointed to the same conclusion: the odds favored Japan five to four. Tower attached more than ordinary significance to these figures because the Germans did not like the Japanese, whom they viewed with suspicion and distrust, and because in

[21] Tower to Root, July 10, 1907, in file 1797.

the event of war the sympathy of Germany would be unequivocally on the side of the United States.

It will be remembered that Denby, also in Berlin, had communicated some alarming information, or misinformation, in a dispatch dated eight days earlier. Certain details and conclusions in Tower's communication are so similar to those of Denby's as to suggest collaboration rather than corroboration. This is not strange, for it would have been curious indeed if these two officials had refrained from discussing a problem of such great concern to the nation which they were representing. Nevertheless, the cumulative force of the two dispatches is somewhat weakened by the fact that the witnesses probably did not arrive at their conclusions independently of each other.

Secretary Root transmitted these two dispatches from Germany to the President on July 21, 1907, and in his covering letter wrote:

Send you a clear headed letter from Denby which I wish you would read carefully with a question in the back of your head whether the transmittal of some such letter—perhaps this very one—to Governor Gillette [sic] with the inevitable result of its publication might not have a good effect. There would probably be the devil to pay over it; but as things are going now he is sure to present his bill sometime.

Root then continued:

I have a good letter from Tower corroborating this of Denby so far as German opinion goes—the 5:4 estimate and all. There is the more food for thought in this because the Germans do not like the Japs.

We must certainly look to the basis of that estimate and see that it is not justifiable.[22]

22 Root to Roosevelt, July 21, 1907, Roosevelt Papers.

Roosevelt, however, refused to be alarmed. He promptly wrote back to Secretary Root:

All that Denby says I have already gathered from various sources, including the exact ratio of the chances against us in the German mind, 5 to 4. My own judgment is that the only thing that will prevent war is the Japanese feeling that we shall not be beaten, and this feeling we can only excite by keeping and making our navy efficient in the highest degree. It was [*sic*] evidently high time that we should get our whole battle fleet on a practice voyage to the Pacific.[23]

Roosevelt's advance information as to what the German and English naval experts thought of Japan's chances of defeating the United States appears to have come through private advices indirectly transmitted from the Berlin representative of the Associated Press. This German correspondent had talked with an officer in the British naval intelligence service who had recently been in London, where in high naval circles he had heard Japan spoken of as a five-to-four favorite over the United States. The Associated Press representative had then talked with an official in the German Foreign Office who was inclined to attach great weight to the estimates of the British Admiralty.[24] Roosevelt had also received a letter from Sir Ian Hamilton, an Englishman well informed as to military and naval matters, who evidently feared that there would be war with Japan and that the United States would be beaten.[25]

[23] Roosevelt to Root, July 23, 1907, Roosevelt Papers.

[24] Elmer Roberts to Melville E. Stone, July 10, 1907, cited in Pringle, *Roosevelt*, p. 402. Stone was head of the Associated Press, and he sent a copy of the communication from his correspondent to Roosevelt.

[25] Roosevelt to Root, July 23, 1907, Roosevelt Papers. See also Bishop, *Roosevelt*, II, 249–50.

At about this time Roosevelt entered into a discussion with Ambassador Speck von Sternberg over the alleged immigration of large numbers of Japanese reservists to Mexico. The ambassador wrote the President that he would have dismissed as quixotic the reports of the German agent, the gist of which he had already transmitted to Roosevelt, had they not come from so responsible a source. Von Sternberg, however, attempted to console the President with the observation that war seemed to create a restless spirit among the fighters and that after the Sino-Japanese War of 1894–95 there was a strong desire among the Japanese soldiers to emigrate upon their return home. In fact, the Germans had noticed the same tendency among their men in 1871.[26] Roosevelt was inclined to agree with von Sternberg:

I believe that one reason why so many veterans of the Japanese army are to be found in Mexico, Hawaii, and elsewhere is simply that they have found that a return to the humdrum, hard-working conditions of peace would be intolerable after the excitement they have experienced. I think it is this feeling and no deep-laid machination of the Japanese Government that is responsible for their appearance in the region referred to.[27]

On July 26, 1907, Roosevelt's concern over the Japanese problem appears to have neared the high-water mark. On that day he dictated letters regarding the situation to Secretary Root, Dr. W. S. Bigelow, Melville E. Stone, general manager of the Associated Press, Whitelaw Reid, American ambassador to England, and Rear Admiral W. H. Brownson.

[26] Von Sternberg to Roosevelt, July 19, 1907, Roosevelt Papers.
[27] Roosevelt to von Sternberg, July 24, 1907, Roosevelt Papers.

To Root the President sent a letter recently received from Baron Kaneko, Roosevelt's Japanese friend who had stood steadfastly by America during the school difficulty. Now, however, Kaneko was beginning to show bitterness as a result of what he regarded as repeated affronts to the Japanese. In forwarding this communication the President remarked: "I like Kaneko, and he is a good fellow. But he is a fox, and a Japanese fox at that. He recapitulates all the causes of complaint." A few days later Secretary Root returned Kaneko's letter with this cryptic comment: "It produces a disagreeable impression."[28]

But the significant portion of Roosevelt's covering letter to his secretary of state is to be found in the following passage:

The other side of the matter is that nothing that has been done affords the slightest justification or excuse for the Japanese thinking of war. Undoubtedly these irritating articles in the newspapers and irritating actions may arouse a bitter feeling in Japan which will make the Japanese people feel hostile to us and predispose them to war should the occasion arise. But not so much as a shadow of pretext exists for going to war. If the Japanese attack us now, as the German, English and French authorities evidently think that they will, it will be nakedly because they wish the Philippines or Hawaii—or, as their heads seem to be swollen to a marvelous degree, it is possible they may wish Alaska. *I do not think they will attack us. I think these foreign observers are in error.* But there is enough uncertainty to make it evident that we should be very much on our guard and should be ready for anything that comes.[29]

In his letter to Dr. W. S. Bigelow, Roosevelt expressed in forceful terms what he thought of those who were re-

[28] Root to Roosevelt, Aug. 8, 1907, Roosevelt Papers.
[29] Roosevelt to Root, July 26, 1907, Roosevelt Papers. Italics mine.

sponsible for the jingo campaign then in progress, and at the same time he revealed a growing sympathy for the aspirations of the Pacific Coast.

I . . . . would like to trepan the various editors who are striving to cause trouble with Japan. The Japanese, however, seem to have their own yellow press, and it seems to be about as obnoxious as ours. Our people act infamously when they in any way wrong the Japanese who are here. But they are absolutely within their rights when they announce that they will restrict immigration hither en masse of any people which they think for economic or other reasons will not make a good addition to our citizenship.[30]

Roosevelt's letter to Melville Stone contained a number of significant passages. The President was glad that an Associated Press correspondent was going to be sent to Tokyo who would do his best "to prevent any aggravation of the already existing irritation among the Japanese, and who perhaps can gain some information of the real designs of the Japanese statesmen." The purpose of the United States, however, was "genuinely to keep the peace, and there exists literally no possible ground for hostile action against us by Japan. The conduct of certain people in San Francisco, and above all of certain yellow newspapers in San Francisco and elsewhere, has been outrageous." All of this was doubly unfortunate because such "conduct undoubtedly tends to excite hostile feeling in Japan; but it in no way or shape affords justification for hostile action by Japan. I shall not believe until I have to that . . . . hostile action is contemplated . . . . but most assuredly I shall do my best to keep the nation prepared for every emergency." Roosevelt then betrayed his concern over the need for strengthening the navy:

[30] Roosevelt to Bigelow, July 26, 1907, Roosevelt Papers.

Are you a friend of Senator Hale [chairman of the Senate committee on naval affairs]? If so, you ought to tell him the information you have, and point out that the whole chance of war, if
Japan has any such intention . . . . hinges upon the Japanese
belief in our naval preparedness. There will be no war if they
know that we are amply prepared. I think I have gone too far
in yielding to Senator Hale . . . . Senator Hale should be made
to understand that in his extreme anxiety for peace and in his
extreme animosity to the navy and army lie the chief dangers of
a warlike future for this country.[31]

To Ambassador Whitelaw Reid the President wrote:
"My chief concern in foreign affairs now is over the
Japanese situation." Roosevelt did not "know whether
we have most to dread from the wanton levity, brutality
and jingoism of certain California mob leaders and certain yellow journals," or from "the downright cowardice
as well as shortsighted lack of patriotism of men like
Senator Hale in trying to keep the navy weak." Apparently the latter "really believes that this course of his
tends to avoid war. Of course it tends to invite it."[32]

On this same day, July 26, 1907, Roosevelt sent a
striking letter marked "confidential" to Rear Admiral
W. H. Brownson. He began by asking: "Is there any
way in which we can hurry up the building of our big
battleships? Of course any inquiry about this must be
very quiet." The President also wanted to know if any
inquiry could be started "by which I would ascertain how
soon it would be possible in case of dire emergency to
build new battleships."

What I want to know is whether, if a war was started, we could
build battleships during the course of a year or eighteen months,

[31] Roosevelt to Stone, July 26, 1907, Roosevelt Papers.
[32] Roosevelt to Reid, July 26, 1907, Roosevelt Papers.

so that if the war lasted that length of time we would begin to have ships take the place of those we should lose. In the *improbable* event of hostilities with Japan, for instance, it might turn out that the difficulty would be to get the Japanese to engage. This might not be the difficulty at all; but the German and English experts evidently believe that in the event of war, which they (as I hope and believe, wrongly) think inevitable, the Japanese would at first avoid a general engagement and trust to torpedo attacks and the like, and the long distance from our base, gradually to wear our fleet down. Under such circumstances I should like to know whether we could not ourselves play a waiting game by taking advantage of the delay and of our enormous wealth to build up the fleet.

I would also like information as to the amount of powder, projectiles, and so forth, we need, and have on hand.[33]

Admiral Brownson's reply was forthcoming on July 30, 1907. He reported that work on the battleships could be hurried and that it would be possible to rush through a three-year contract in about two years. Such haste, however, would add about fifty per cent to the cost. There was ample space in the United States to build twelve battleships at once, but the big question was that of skilled labor. It would be extremely difficult to find enough properly trained workmen to construct twelve vessels at one time, but high wages probably would attract the necessary skill from abroad. In any event, if the United States were forced to play a waiting game, large outlays for ships could be made without much trouble. As for himself, Admiral Brownson did not believe that there would be a war with Japan. Such a conflict would mean either the loss of the Japanese navy or the wiping out of their all-important merchant marine. The latter would cer-

[33] Roosevelt to Brownson, July 26, 1907, Roosevelt Papers. The italicizing of "improbable" is mine. As originally dictated the word was "probable," which Roosevelt changed to "improbable" with pen.

tainly be the result if the Japanese pursued a Fabian
policy and locked up their battleships. This would mean
the loss of their markets and an unbearable strain on the
resources of a country already overburdened with debt; and
all the fight would be taken out of them for many years
to come. Admiral Brownson felt that the prospect before
the Japanese of becoming bitter enemies, burdened with
defeat, instead of remaining good friends, would act as
an effective brake upon the nation and its leaders.[34]

On the same day that Roosevelt wrote this series of
letters, Secretary of War Taft returned to him certain
inclosures relating to the alleged intention of the Japanese
to force a war with the United States. Taft admitted that
Japan had a jingo party, the leaders of which were known
to be younger army officers, whose views were regarded
as unworthy of consideration by the Elder Statesmen.
Although recognizing that Japan was unlikely to fight
because of her straitened financial circumstances, Secretary Taft admitted that the situation was grave—so grave,
in fact, that he was inclined to believe that it might be
well to make known recent developments in the hope of
getting more money from Congress for the fortification
of the Philippines. As for his own views, Taft remarked
tersely: "Personally I never have been able to believe
that Japan is serious about war with us the next three or
four years."[35]

In the meantime, excitement in the public press over
the possibilities of war continued intense. In its issue of
July 27, 1907, the *Literary Digest* printed a number of

[34] Brownson to Roosevelt, July 30, 1907, Roosevelt Papers.
[35] Taft to Roosevelt, July 26, 1907, Roosevelt Papers.

excerpts from French newspapers, the burden of which was that a clash with Japan was inevitable.[36] On July 29 Roosevelt sent Root a copy of the mischievous and incendiary Tokyo *Puck,* and in his covering letter struck a note which appears frequently in his correspondence during this period: "Our yellow press is now surpassed by the Japanese yellow press in the effort to do mischief and stir up war."[37] About this time, July 26, Ambassador Wright reported on conditions in Japan, but his dispatch, sent by mail, did not reach Washington until some time later. He observed that the accounts in the Japanese newspapers of the recent cordial reception of Admiral Yamamoto in the United States, together with the frank exchange of views with the President on the general situation, had been received with great satisfaction in Japan, and "may be said to have closed the discussion of 'the American affair' for the present." Wright pointed to the failure of a joint meeting in Japan of the organizations interested in keeping alive the question, at which Count Okuma was plainly on the defensive, as conclusive evidence in support of his view.[38]

By the first of August, 1907, the concern in official Washington circles over the possibility of war with Japan appears to have been definitely on the wane.[39] Although

36 *Literary Digest,* July 27, 1907, p. 114.

37 Roosevelt to Root, July 29, 1907, Roosevelt Papers.

38 Wright to Root, July 26, 1907, in file 1797. There was also some excitement at this time over the reported arrest of a Japanese army officer at San Diego while making plans of Fort Rosecrans; the Japanese minister of war strongly denied that any Japanese officer was engaged in such activity.

39 Throughout this month, as contrasted with July, there were only a few communications in the Roosevelt correspondence dealing with the Japanese situation.

Roosevelt did not feel that the United States could hold the Philippines in the event of hostilities with the Japanese, he assured Root that he did "not believe that we are going to have war."[40] To his friend Bishop M. C. Harris, the President remarked that war with Japan was "unthinkable," and if it did come it would stamp all those responsible for it with "eternal infamy."[41] And on August 8, 1907, Root wrote to the President: "On the whole I am convinced that our European friends are over excited. I think the tendency is towards war—not now but in a few years. But much can be done to check or divert the tendency."[42]

Late in August, 1907, probably as a result of lack of public interest in the navy, Roosevelt gave way to a fit of despondency when he wrote to Taft suggesting the possibility of a graceful abandonment of the Philippine Islands. Such a proposal was certainly not Rooseveltian, and probably would have been roundly denounced if it had been forthcoming from any other source. He concluded:

The Philippines form our heel of Achilles. They are all that makes the present situation with Japan dangerous . . . . I think that to have some pretty clear avowal of our intention not to permanently keep them and to give them independence would remove a temptation from Japan's way and would render our task at home easier . . . . I would rather see this nation fight all her life than to see her give them up to Japan or any other nation under duress.[43]

Although Roosevelt continued to show deep concern

[40] Roosevelt to Root, July 31, 1907, Roosevelt Papers.
[41] Roosevelt to Harris, Aug. 6, 1907, Roosevelt Papers.
[42] Root to Roosevelt, Aug. 8, 1907, Roosevelt Papers.
[43] Roosevelt to Taft, Aug. 21, 1907, Roosevelt Papers. Pringle quotes more fully from this letter. Pringle, *Roosevelt,* pp. 408–409.

over the failure of the Gentlemen's Agreement to exclude a satisfactory number of Japanese,[44] it is evident by the latter part of August, at least as far as the administration officials were concerned, that the tension had become appreciably eased. Then, early in September, 1907, there occurred a riot against the Orientals in Vancouver which opened the eyes of the British to the seriousness of the race problem on the Pacific Coast. Aroused by the lieutenant-governor's veto of an exclusion measure passed by the provincial parliament, a mob estimated at 1,000 men attacked Hindus, Chinese, and Japanese on the evening of September 7, 1907, and wrecked over fifty Oriental stores. The Japanese defended themselves vigorously, numerous wounds of a more or less serious nature were sustained by both sides, and a dozen Japanese were thrown off the wharves into the harbor. The well-informed British journalist, Sydney Brooks, wrote that "English opinion was shocked, humiliated, and surprised" by the outbreak. "After all these months spent in chastising the San Francisco mob, and in expressing an amused, tolerant, slightly hypocritical, and still more hypercritical sympathy with the American government in its difficulties," this had to happen.[45]

Among the more interesting aspects of the affair it was observed that the Japanese had come to British Columbia at the recent and express invitation of the Dominion government; that the local and provincial authorities

[44] Roosevelt to Sargent (commissioner-general of immigration), Aug. 29, 1907, Roosevelt Papers.

[45] Sydney Brooks, "The Real 'Pacific Question'," *Harper's Weekly,* Oct. 12, 1907, p. 1484; San Francisco *Chronicle,* Sept. 9, 1907; London *Times,* Sept. 11, 1907; *Literary Digest,* Sept. 21, 1907, p. 394; Oct. 5, 1907, p. 465.

appeared to have been lukewarm in their efforts to subdue the mob; and that the attackers were British subjects, and the attacked Great Britain's allies. Although some details of the first reports were doubtless in error, it was readily apparent on both sides of the Atlantic that the race riot in Vancouver was far more serious, both as regards the intensity of feeling and the size of the demonstration, than anything that had taken place against the Japanese on the American Pacific Coast. The British derived what comfort they could from the thought, which appears to have contained a considerable measure of truth, that the people of Vancouver had been inflamed by American labor agitators.[46]

One does not need to have a profound knowledge of human nature to understand why official Washington reacted as it did to the unfortunate affair at Vancouver. Lodge wrote chucklingly to Roosevelt:

I do not wish ill to my neighbors but I cannot help feeling a certain gentle interest in the performances now going on in Vancouver in regard to the Japanese and other Asiatics. It is a demonstration of the fact that the white peoples will not suffer Asiatic competition in their own country and I think it will perhaps make England a little less inclined to preach in a patronizing way at us about San Francisco.[47]

Roosevelt felt as Lodge did, and he particularly enjoyed the lesson that had been read to British publicists who had been comparing the British and American forms of government to the disadvantage of the latter. The Presi-

[46] Brooks, *loc. cit.*, p. 1484; London *Times*, Sept. 10, 11, 1907. On Sept. 5, 1907, there had been an anti-Hindu riot in Bellingham, Washington, as a result of which six Hindus were badly beaten. San Francisco *Chronicle*, Sept. 6, 1907.

[47] Lodge to Roosevelt, Sept. 10, 1907, Roosevelt Papers.

dent believed that this development would bring home sharply to the British and to their allies, the Japanese, that the problems facing English-speaking peoples along the Pacific Coast were the same. Roosevelt prided himself on having "prevented such outrages . . . . by the fact that I was much quicker to take preventive steps than the British officials were . . . ."[48]

Secretary Root noted facetiously what a "fix the British press is in over the Vancouver riots. I think Loeb [Roosevelt's secretary] must have sent some one there to make the demonstration and relieve our Japanese situation." Root's concluding comment is of the greatest significance: "It is not logical but it is certain that the strain is off. I had a talk with [Ambassador] Aoki the other day and without a word being said the atmosphere was different."[49] Taft, then in Japan, and the American chargé at Tokyo both agreed that the ill-treatment of the Japanese in British Columbia had worked to the advantage of the United States.[50] Roosevelt probably had this development in mind when he wrote to Arthur Lee a number of weeks later: "In the Japanese matter our Pacific States and Australia and British Columbia feel exactly alike, and fundamentally their attitude is proper; but its manifestations are often exceedingly improper."[51]

It is in connection with the Vancouver riots that a new San Francisco outburst, which occurred on October 14, 1907, must be considered. On that day a drunken logger crashed through a Japanese laundryman's window. The

[48] Roosevelt to Lodge, Sept. 11, 1907, Roosevelt Papers.
[49] Root to Roosevelt, Sept. 25, 1907, Roosevelt Papers.
[50] Taft to Root, Oct. 5, 1907; Dodge to Root, Oct. 11, 1907, in file 1797.   [51] Roosevelt to Lee, Dec. 26, 1907, Roosevelt Papers.

proprietor attempted to hold the man until the police could arrive; whereupon the logger's friends came to his rescue. This time, at least, the police appear to have acted energetically, and they used their clubs vigorously to break up the riot. When the mêlée was over, two Japanese were in a hospital, a number of others were less seriously hurt, and a score or so of whites were nursing bruises inflicted by the police. The first reports of the affair that came to New York stated that a dozen Japanese had been killed; and the stock market reacted unfavorably. This was apparently the most violent demonstration against the Japanese that San Francisco had yet witnessed.[52] But, strangely enough, the Japanese appear to have made no diplomatic representations whatsoever regarding it. The reasons for their failure to act on this occasion, when they had previously remonstrated against less serious outbursts in the past, may be surmised. In the first place, the riot was started by a drunken man, and was not the result of deliberate forethought on the part of either the mob or the city officials. In the second place, the police had acted vigorously in defense of the Japanese. In the third place, the fleet was shortly to leave for Pacific waters. And, finally, this flare-up, although serious, was so much less formidable than the Vancouver affair that the Japanese government probably did not feel called upon to lodge a protest.

If by the middle of September the diplomatic strain had been eased, the same cannot be said of the jingo out-

[52] Boston *Evening Transcript,* Oct. 15, 1907 ; London *Times,* Oct. 16, 1907. The San Francisco press viewed this affair with its customary insouciance.

burst in the press. Late in the month the newspaper campaign then being carried on in the United States came to a head. The dignified New York *Times,* which hitherto had regarded the whole situation with more or less indifference, published in its magazine section a lurid article which included incendiary references to alleged Japanese designs on the Philippines.[53] The New York *Tribune* began running in its illustrated supplement a syndicated serial story describing in detail the impending war between the United States and Japan. The New York *Sun* stated bluntly: "The navy is going to the Pacific Ocean for war with Japan, and Japan recognizes that fact and is energetically preparing for it. Once the operation of transferring our ships to Pacific waters has been accomplished, war is inevitable."[54] In the light of these alarmist statements it is not surprising that the well-informed New York correspondent of the London *Times,* referring to Hearst and the Spanish-American War, should have written: "Is the Press of the United States going insane? It is no use trying to minimize the gravity of its attitude or its ability to stir trouble."[55]

In the meantime, Roosevelt had sent Taft, "the trouble shooter," on a good-will mission to the Far East with orders to see what he could do to straighten out the situation.[56] It was indeed fortunate that Secretary Taft was

[53] New York *Times,* Sept. 29, 1907.

[54] Quoted in London *Times,* Sept. 30, 1907. Another English observer remarked that the United States seemed to be as completely under the thumb of the newspapers as in 1898. *Fortnightly Review,* Oct., 1907, p. 645.

[55] London *Times,* Sept. 30, 1907.

[56] Straus, *Under Four Administrations,* p. 225.

in Japan at the time when the jingo campaign was nearing its height. He was warmly received, and at Tokyo
made an extremely felicitous speech in which he blamed
the newspapers of the United States for stirring up the
trouble and expressed confidence that the existing difficulties could be ironed out by diplomacy.[57] It would be
difficult to overestimate the soothing effect of this speech
on public sentiment in Japan, and the London *Times* remarked editorially that sensible observers the world over
were now confident that the fleet would make the trip
without firing a shot.[58] The jingo newspapers of the
United States bitterly resented the strictures of Taft and
blamed Roosevelt's precipitate sending of the fleet for the
war scare,[59] but from this time on their power to stir up
trouble was distinctly on the wane. Furthermore, the
severe financial crisis which came to a head in October,
1907, did much to divert public attention in the United
States to other matters.

One other important aspect of this good-will mission
to Japan must be considered. After discussing existing
problems with a number of Japanese officials, including
Minister Hayashi, Taft dispatched to Roosevelt a cablegram so lengthy that it cost the government $1,500. The
minister for foreign affairs had told him that it was impossible for the Japanese in their present temper to consent to any kind of restriction other than one by adminis-
trative arrangement. But, most important of all, Taft
observed that the Japanese were in no financial condition
to consider hostilities with the United States, and he was

[57] London *Times*, Oct. 2, 3, 1907.
[58] *Ibid.*, Oct. 8, 1907.   [59] *Ibid.*, Oct. 3, 1907.

satisfied that the Japanese government was "most anxious to avoid war."[60] Writing a few days later, the new American ambassador to Japan, Thomas J. O'Brien, agreed substantially with Taft. He noted, however, that the Japanese chagrin over the Peace of Portsmouth still lingered, and that recent articles in the New York *Sun,* Hearst's jingoistic outburst, and the sending of the battleships, "along with rumors that they receive from time to time, give them concern." As nearly as he could judge, however, the "Japanese Government would be found very reluctant to have difficulty with the United States, and the tone of the Press seems to bear out this view." On the other hand, they "would like to believe that our intentions are equally pacific, and for the most part they do believe it, and yet they are some times in doubt as to our real intentions."[61]

Although the war scare appears to have reached its peak late in September or early in October, 1907, several interesting developments occurred before the departure of the fleet on December 16, 1907. Late in October the President's son, Theodore, wrote for the purpose of securing parental permission to volunteer in the event of war with Japan. "I do not think," Roosevelt replied, "there is any chance of war with Japan at this time or in the immediate future . . . . But of course if there was a war I should arrange to have you go." He then expressed the opinion that if the conflict turned out to be a small one his son would have to go as a private in the ranks; but if a major war developed Roosevelt believed that he might secure

60 Taft to Roosevelt, Oct. 18, 1907, Roosevelt Papers.
61 O'Brien to Root, Oct. 25, 1907, in file 1797.

for him a second lieutenant's commission in the volun-
teers.[62]

Early in November, 1907, if a dispatch sent to the
German Foreign Office can be credited, Roosevelt made
overtures to Ambassador von Sternberg that could be
interpreted as a thinly veiled invitation to a naval alliance
between the two powers against Japan. Von Sternberg
countered by sounding the President on his willingness
to use German troops in the event of a Japanese invasion
of the United States by way of Canada or Mexico. Roosevelt, however, saw a number of practical objections to
such a scheme, and the matter appears to have been
dropped.[63] Although such overtures may not have been
made, or at least not properly understood, it is clear that
Roosevelt had his eyes open to a great many possible
contingencies.

About the middle of November, 1907, Roosevelt received another disquieting letter from Ambassador Tower,
in Germany. The latter reported that he had had a conversation with a high official who was in a position to speak
for the German navy. From information that the Imperial
Government had been able to gather from military and
naval agents, especially in the Far East, "it looks upon the
situation between ourselves and Japan as exceedingly criti-

[62] Roosevelt to Theodore Roosevelt, Jr., Oct. 29, 1907, Roosevelt
Papers.

[63] Von Sternberg to von Bülow, *Die Grosse Politik,* XXV, 79. The
British minister to Japan learned that the Japanese Foreign Office knew
that the Kaiser had offered to lend Roosevelt the entire German fleet for
guarding the Atlantic Coast while the American fleet was in the Pacific,
and that at a later date the Kaiser had offered to place an entire army
corps at the disposal of Roosevelt. Sir C. MacDonald to Grey (telegram), Nov. 27, 1908, G. P. Gooch and Harold Temperley, eds., *British
Documents on the Origins of the War, 1898–1914* (1932), VIII, 461.

cal,—that it is believed here that we do not sufficiently realize this at home." This German official remarked that the Japanese, who had their eyes on Hawaii, the key to the Pacific, were armed to the teeth and were almost "ready now to go to war . . . ." Tower added that this information was given spontaneously during a conversation on other subjects, and that it "had all the marks of a conviction arrived at after full deliberation, and was evidently sincere." This opinion, the Ambassador concluded, no doubt represented that of the highest military and naval authorities in Germany. They believed that it was Japan's policy to strike before the Panama Canal was finished.[64]

In reply Roosevelt assured Tower that his letter impressed him "very much, as do similar letters coming from the Naval Attachés to Secretary Metcalf. I have shown your letter to Root. I can hardly believe that Japan is intending to strike us, but I am taking and have taken every step to be ready." The President then turned to the approaching departure of the battleships. "The fleet is in good condition; [Admiral] Evans is a good man; it starts for the Pacific inside of a month. The wisdom—indeed, I may say the absolute need—of going there has been amply demonstrated. I should hardly suppose that the Japanese would hit us while the fleet was there, but of course I can not be sure."[65]

This leads us to a consideration of what was undoubtedly the most significant peace-time naval demonstration of modern times—the world cruise of the American battleship fleet.

---

[64] Tower to Roosevelt, Nov. 2, 1907, Roosevelt Papers.
[65] Roosevelt to Tower, Nov. 19, 1907, Roosevelt Papers.

CHAPTER XII

The World Cruise and Its Results

"In my own judgment the most important service that I rendered to peace was the voyage of the battle fleet round the world."—Roosevelt, *Autobiography*, p. 563

THE STAGE was now set for the departure of the fleet. Preparations for the event had been going steadily forward, and certain unforeseen technical difficulties indicated that valuable lessons were to be learned from the experience.[1] Finally, on December 16, 1907, sixteen battleships, described by Secretary Metcalf as the strongest force ever assembled as a unit,[2] steamed out of Hampton Roads. The armada was under the command of the picturesque "Fighting Bob" Evans, who had assured his listeners at a farewell banquet given by the Lotus Club of New York that they would not "be disappointed in the fleet, whether it proves a feast, a frolic, or a fight."[3]

Unfortunately, the departure of the battleships was the signal for a renewed outburst of predictions of war, particularly by the continental European press.[4] Roosevelt was confident, however, that "Japan knew my sincere friendship and admiration for her and realized that we could not as a Nation have any intention of attacking

[1] A. T. Mahan, "The True Significance of the Pacific Cruise," *Scientific American*, Dec. 7, 1907, p. 412; London *Times*, Oct. 3, 1907.

[2] *Annual Report of the Secretary of the Navy, 1907*, p. 6.

[3] Edwin A. Falk, *Fighting Bob Evans* (New York, 1931), p. 424.

[4] London *Times*, Dec. 24, 1907; Jan. 3, 18, 1908; New York *Times*, Jan. 19, 1908.

her . . . ." Accordingly, in a personal interview with the officers before they left he had said that the trip "would be one of absolute peace, but that they were to take exactly the same precautions against sudden attack of any kind as if we were at war with all the nations of the earth. . . . ." He later observed that "if my expectations had proved mistaken, it would have been proof positive that we were going to be attacked anyhow, and that in such event it would have been an enormous gain to have had the three months' preliminary preparations which enabled the fleet to start perfectly equipped."[5]

Two factors, generally overlooked, operated to make Roosevelt's venture less rash than it would otherwise have been. First, the United States was, in July, 1907, the second naval power in the world, ranking below England. Japan was in fifth place, and the American fleet probably could have given an excellent account of itself against the entire Japanese navy.[6] Secondly, in spite of generally believed rumors of a world cruise, San Francisco was repeatedly and officially designated as the destination of the fleet.[7] The Japanese could not legitimately

[5] Roosevelt, *Autobiography*, p. 564.

[6] On Nov. 1, 1907, the United States had 29 vessels of 10,000 tons or over built or building, as compared with 13 for Japan. The tonnage figures as of June 1, 1907, were:

England	1,633,116
United States	611,616
France	609,079
Germany	529,032
Japan	374,701

Senate Documents, 60 Cong., 1 sess., no. 100, pp. 587–88; *Scientific American*, Dec. 7, 1907, p. 414.

[7] Occasional remarks of the officers and certain details in the equipping of the ships indicated that a world cruise was definitely in view. New York *Times*, Dec. 15, 1907.

take offense at the transfer of ships from one American port to another,[8] but the brandishing of the big stick would have been a little too obvious had it been proclaimed in July, 1907, that the fleet was steaming directly to Far Eastern waters. It was not only good diplomacy to defer the announcement until the ships reached the Pacific, but it might also avoid embarrassment to see how the vessels behaved before making known the more ambitious project. Not until February 21, 1908, therefore, did an intimation come from a "responsible source," in this case from Secretary Root, that the fleet might continue on around the world;[9] and not until the battleships had reached Magdalena Bay, Lower California, in March, 1908, was the world cruise officially announced.[10]

The first stop of the fleet was at Port of Spain, Trinidad. There the official British welcome was courteous, if not cordial, but the populace, to whom warships were no novelty, showed "profound indifference."[11] At Rio de Janeiro, however, there occurred the first of those amazing outbursts of competitive hospitality that were to greet

[8] Roosevelt to Bourne, Aug. 13, 1907; Roosevelt to E. A. Hayes, Sept. 19, 1907; Roosevelt to Lodge, July 10, 1907, Roosevelt Papers.

[9] London *Times,* Feb. 22, 1908.

[10] After the fleet had put out to sea, an unofficial signal from the flagship informed the officers and men, on December 16, 1907, that it was the "President's intention to have the fleet return to the Atlantic Coast by way of the Mediterranean." Franklin Matthews, *With the Battle Fleet* (New York, 1909), p. 14. This writer, a special correspondent for the New York *Sun,* was one of the few civilians who accompanied the fleet on its entire cruise. The book consists of a series of letters, written immediately after the events described and checked by naval officers, which were originally published in the *Sun. Ibid.,* p. xi.

[11] *Ibid.,* pp. 38, 184; W. W. Handley (consul at Trinidad) to the Assistant Secretary of State, Dec. 31, 1907, in file 8258. See also New York *Times,* Dec. 25, 1907.

the Americans from the South American coast to China.
An English edition of the Rio *Journal of Commerce*
stated that "never was a heartier or more spontaneous
welcome extended to any representatives of any nation
than that which yesterday Brazilians extended to their
brothers of the North;"[12] and Admiral Evans testified
that the warmth of the reception surpassed anything in
his experience.[13] Lavish entertainment was provided; special editions of the great dailies were printed in English;
and felicitous messages were exchanged between Roosevelt and President Penna of Brazil.[14] The latter took
occasion to announce a reduction of import duties on certain American products, a gesture of friendship that made
a most favorable impression in the United States;[15] and
the entire visit unquestionably had a happy effect on the
relations between the two countries.[16]

The fleet was unable to stop at Buenos Aires,[17] but the

[12] Quoted in New York *Times,* Jan. 14, 1908.

[13] Evans to Root, Jan. 17, 1908, in file 6072, Bureau of Navigation,
Navy Department.

[14] New York *Times,* Jan. 13, 14, 16, 1908.

[15] *Ibid.*

[16] I. B. Dudley (ambassador to Brazil) to Root, Jan. 27, 1908, in
file 8258. One Brazilian journal, the *Diario de Noticias,* remarked that
the stay of the fleet was "worth another trip of Mr. Root." Translated
inclosure in *ibid.* President Penna, in a message to Congress, dwelt particularly on the "cordial manifestations of esteem" which had resulted
from the visit. *Papers Relating to the Foreign Relations of the United
States, 1908,* p. 43. Hereafter cited as *Foreign Relations.*

[17] Few important nations of the world failed to extend to the United
States, directly or indirectly, an invitation to send the fleet to their
shores. The Department of State was subjected to no little embarrassment in refusing these requests, but if they had all been accepted the
fleet would have been drawn far from its course and would have returned home dangerously behind schedule. Coaling and harbor facilities
also had to be taken into consideration. Consequently, few changes were
made in the original itinerary, and those for very good reasons.

Argentine government paid its respects in a striking manner by sending a squadron out to sea to salute the American vessels.[18] A Chilean cruiser escorted the fleet through the Straits of Magellan,[19] where a brief stop was made at Punta Arenas. Although Valparaiso was not a scheduled port of call, Admiral Evans swung the fleet into the harbor to salute the Chilean President and flag, and then continued on his way. This unusual courtesy made a deep impression on the people of Chile, particularly when it was remembered that Evans, then in command of the *Yorktown,* had last seen Valparaiso during the days following the "Baltimore" riot, and that his stay there had been marred by extreme bitterness of feeling on the part of the populace.[20] John Hicks, United States minister to Chile, was "decidedly of the opinion that the visit of the fleet . . . . has served to create in this country a more friendly feeling toward the United States and it will have a vast influence for good in the future."[21]

At Callao and Lima the Peruvians made a determined attempt to outdo the welcome of the Brazilians. President Pardo declared Washington's birthday a legal holiday, and a special bullfight was held at Lima, which thou-

[18] Matthews, *With the Battle Fleet,* pp. 115 ff.

[19] Because of the numerous rumors regarding Japanese mines, Roosevelt had enjoined Evans to take every possible precaution in the harbor of Rio de Janeiro and in the Straits of Magellan. Bryce to Grey, Feb. 14, 1908, *British Documents on the Origins of the War,* VIII, 456; Falk, *Fighting Bob Evans,* p. 433.

[20] See Robley D. Evans, *A Sailor's Log* (New York, 1901), pp. 258 ff.

[21] Hicks to Root, Feb. 21, 1908, in file 8258. In his annual message to Congress, President Montt of Chile stressed "the demonstration of international courtesy made to us lately by a great fleet of the United States" as a manifestation "of sincere friendship which ought to inspire confidence in the Government and people of the Great Republic." *Foreign Relations, 1908,* pp. 58, 59.

sands of appreciative sailors attended.[22] Leslie Combs, United States minister to Peru, wrote in glowing terms of the good feeling engendered by the event, and Samuel M. Taylor, consul general at Callao, asserted that nothing "save the visit of Mr. Root, has been of so much advantage to the United States as the recent visit of the Atlantic fleet . . . . and I feel certain the results will be beneficially far reaching."[23]

As the battleships steamed away from South America it was evident that their visit had done much to cement the happy results of Secretary Root's good-will tour through the Latin American countries in 1906.[24] Perhaps equally important was the vivid impression which the fleet left behind as to the ability of the United States to guarantee the stability of the Western Hemisphere against European aggression. The *Zig-Zag,* a Santiago weekly, remarked that the outcry of jubilation at the visit of the battleships was like that of "a person who, in danger of a blow from a strong enemy, sees himself unexpectedly helped by a friendly athlete of Herculean proportions."[25]

[22] Matthews wrote that the Callao reception, though less demonstrative than that of Rio de Janeiro, was probably the most heartfelt encountered in Latin America. Matthews, *With the Battle Fleet,* pp. 213–14, 312. See also New York *Times,* Feb. 25, 1908.

[23] Combs to Root, Mar. 4, 1908; Taylor to the Assistant Secretary of State, Mar. 12, 1908, in file 8258. Felicitous messages were exchanged between Roosevelt and Pardo, and the latter, in a message to Congress, referred to the visit of the fleet as "evident proof of the cordial relations which unite the two Governments, and in which the people of the one and the other country fully share. . . . ." *Foreign Relations, 1908,* p. 683 ; see also New York *Times,* Feb. 25, 1908.

[24] See Matthews, *With the Battle Fleet,* p. 99. It should be noted that the torpedo-boat flotilla visited a number of Latin American ports not touched by the fleet. Roosevelt, *Autobiography,* pp. 566–67.

[25] Quoted in *Review of Reviews,* XXXVII (May, 1908), 609.

It was perhaps with this thought in mind that Roosevelt stated, in an address on July 22, 1908, before the Naval War College, that the cruise was the most instructive object lesson that had ever been afforded as to the reality of the Monroe Doctrine.[26]

Ever since the departure of the fleet, Roosevelt, although repeatedly expressing his disbelief in the probability of war,[27] had kept a wary eye on the international situation. Three days after the beginning of the cruise, Captain William S. Sims, in response to a verbal request from Roosevelt, submitted information regarding three battleships then being built in England, ostensibly for Brazil. He reported that in design they were exactly like others under construction for Japan, and he raised the question as to whether they were really intended for Brazil.[28] Shortly thereafter Roosevelt asked Root to look over the data provided by Sims, adding: "It certainly looks as if there was an even chance that these ships might not go to Brazil. If so, we ought to be exceedingly careful that they do not go to Japan. Would it not be possible to make some arrangement with the Brazilians on the subject?"[29] Nothing, however, appears to have come of this rumored transfer.

[26] New York *Times*, July 23, 1908.

[27] Roosevelt wrote to Cecil Spring Rice that it was "national folly" on the part of the United States both to permit outrages against the Japanese and to decline to keep the navy up to the highest point of efficiency. Such a course "might result in a bitterly humiliating and disastrous war which would turn over not only the Philippines but Hawaii to Japan. I do not anticipate any such war, and I think I am taking the best possible measures to prevent it and to get the two races or nations on a footing which will permit a policy of permanent friendliness or at least mutual toleration." Roosevelt to Rice, Dec. 21, 1907, Roosevelt Papers.

[28] Sims to Roosevelt, Dec. 19, 1907, Roosevelt Papers.

[29] Roosevelt to Root, Feb. 15, 1908, Roosevelt Papers.

During January, 1908, Ambassador Tower contributed further information as to the official German view
of Japanese-American relations. The American diplomat
had had a long talk with Chancellor von Bülow, who had
just received a dispatch from the German ambassador to
Japan. The latter described a dangerously bitter feeling
against the United States among the masses and newspaper writers of Japan. The lower classes appeared to contemplate war; but, added von Bülow, the government was
wise and would not allow itself to be carried away. The
Elder Statesmen were conservative and strong enough to
control the policy of the country. They knew that their
resources had been drained by Russia, and that in the end
they would be beaten down by the energy and immense
wealth of the Americans. The German chancellor therefore believed that the Japanese "have no intention whatever of going to war" and he looked upon "the situation
with tranquillity." But this unwillingness to attack, both
von Bülow and the German ambassador to Japan held, was
not because of friendship for the United States "but because they have no money to fight with and they are afraid
of the battleship fleet which is just going around Cape
Horn [*sic*]."[30]

Late in January, 1908, Tower transmitted a message
to Roosevelt from the Kaiser, who had just heard from
one of his agents in Mexico. This observer claimed that
he had seen thousands of Japanese, with "brass buttons on
their coats," drilling after hours with staves. Moreover,
the German ministers in Peru and Chile had reported substantially the same thing from those countries. The Kaiser

[30] Tower to Roosevelt, Jan. 8, 1908, Roosevelt Papers.

did not doubt, Tower added, that the Japanese contemplated war with the United States, and that in such an event they intended to move in upon the Panama Canal from both sides.[31]

Roosevelt had previously evidenced skepticism regarding some of the German estimates, but this was just a bit too much. He wrote to Tower that he had already known of large numbers of Japanese in Mexico, but the fact that many of them were soldiers did not necessarily indicate design but might well be evidence of dissatisfaction with life in the Orient.[32] About this time, too, von Sternberg wrote to Roosevelt that the German military attaché in Peking was convinced that Japan did not then contemplate war with the United States, and that her warlike preparations were for trouble with China. In sending this information on to Root, Roosevelt indicated that he did not attach much value to the Kaiser's wild stories, for he wrote: "It helps to correct the imperial pipe dream forwarded thru Ambassador Tower."[33]

Some further light is thrown upon the situation by the dispatches which Ambassador Bryce sent from the United States to the British Foreign Office. In a conversation with the British ambassador in February the President stated that he did not himself think that the Japanese could mean to provoke war. Nevertheless, Roosevelt asserted, anything might happen with the public mind on both sides

[31] Tower to Roosevelt, Jan. 28, 1908, Roosevelt Papers. A considerable portion of this letter is reproduced in Pringle, *Roosevelt*, pp. 403–404.

[32] Roosevelt to Tower, Feb. 12, 1908, Roosevelt Papers.

[33] Roosevelt to Root, Feb. 17, 1908, Roosevelt Papers. Von Sternberg forwarded further information of a similar nature several weeks later. Von Sternberg to Roosevelt, Apr. 14, 1908, Roosevelt Papers.

of the Pacific inflamed as it was. There might be a riot on the Coast in which a Japanese might be killed; there might be an outbreak in Japan aroused by the passing of American exclusion legislation. Yet, in spite of the widespread predictions in Germany, France, and Russia regarding the inevitability of war, Roosevelt did not feel that there would be hostilities; and he again referred contemptuously to the Kaiser's "pipe dreams."[34]

On March 19, 1908, Bryce wrote of a conversation with Baron Takahira, the new Japanese ambassador to the United States. He had asked the Japanese diplomat to what he attributed the war-scare talk "so constantly renewed in the Press—though less frequently in the United States in the last six weeks. . . . ." Takahira had replied, confidentially, that this jingoism might be the deliberate work of persons or governments who were anxious to disrupt or weaken the Anglo-Japanese alliance by forcing Great Britain into the uncomfortable position of having to choose between the friendship of her kin and that of her ally. The Japanese ambassador had also suggested that those groups in America which were interested in pushing a big navy might to some extent be responsible for the war talk.[35]

Early in February, 1908, Roosevelt received some disquieting news relating to the failure of the Gentlemen's Agreement to operate satisfactorily, when MacKenzie King, the Canadian commissioner of labor and immigration, visited him. The latter, who had "hold of a num-

[34] Bryce to Grey, Feb. 14, 1908, *British Documents on the Origins of the War,* VIII, 455.
[35] *Ibid.,* VIII, 459.

ber of Japanese documents such as we on this side of the line had never seen," was able to convince the President that the Japanese officials had overissued two or three times the number of passports which they claimed they were issuing. Roosevelt was much perturbed over this apparent violation of a solemn promise, and he pointed out to Arthur Lee that if the existing arrangement proved unsatisfactory Congress would doubtless proceed to exclude the Japanese by statute. It is interesting to note that the Canadians, deeply disturbed over the situation, were looking to the United States for support in their anti-Japanese policy, for, wrote Roosevelt, King "thanked me very earnestly for having sent our fleet to the Pacific."[36] Four members of the British Columbian parliament who were then visiting Washington did the same thing.[37]

Roosevelt did not hesitate to communicate to Ambassador Bryce the details of his visit with King, emphasizing the strength of feeling against the Japanese in British Columbia. The President remarked that if war with Japan came and the Pacific Coast should be invaded, the British Columbians would doubtless rush into the fray on the side of the United States. Bryce concluded his dispatch to Grey with these words:

The impression left on my mind is that he [Roosevelt] entertains some doubt of the bona-fides of the Japanese Government, believing that the Emigration Companies interested in keeping up the outflow of Japanese labour are very powerful in Japan, and that without attributing to that Government an intention so obviously wild and hazardous as that of provoking a war, he thinks

[36] Roosevelt to Arthur Lee, Feb. 2, 1908, Roosevelt Papers.
[37] Bryce to Grey, Feb. 14, 1908, *British Documents on the Origins of the War, 1898–1914*, VIII, 455.

the contingency of a breach not too remote to be provided against.[38]

In the meantime the fleet, having left South American waters, continued its triumphant voyage up the Pacific Coast. On March 12, 1908, two days ahead of schedule, it dropped anchor in Magdalena Bay and, with the permission of the Mexican government, began preparations for target practice.[39] Admiral Evans reported to the Navy Department that the fleet was in better condition than when it had left Hampton Roads, and that it was ready to enter upon active service.[40] The American press thrilled with pride at the successful completion of what had been widely regarded as an exceedingly difficult feat of navigation, and the voices of the Cassandras were hushed.[41] Even the New York *Nation,* which had regarded the cruise as "ill-timed and rather hazardous," observed that the safe arrival at Magdalena Bay was a "legitimate cause for national gratification," and it was pleased that "our ships, so far, have been much more active for peace than for war in leaving a trail of international good will along both coasts of Latin America."[42] And the European press, which, together with foreign naval experts, had followed the voyage with the keenest interest, was generous in its expressions of admiration and praise.[43]

[38] *British Documents on the Origins of the War, 1898–1914,* VIII, 455–56.

[39] *Annual Report of the Secretary of the Navy, 1908,* p. 5.

[40] New York *Times,* Mar. 13, 1908.

[41] See the *Argonaut,* San Francisco, May 9, 1908, p. 305; *Harper's Weekly,* July 11, 1908, p. 30; *World's Work,* XVI (May, 1908), 10177.

[42] *Nation,* Mar. 19, 1908, p. 250; Feb. 25, 1909, p. 181.

[43] London *Times,* Mar. 9, 1908; *Literary Digest,* Mar. 21, 1908, p. 393; *Review of Reviews,* XXXVII (Apr., 1908), 402; *Spectator,* Aug. 15, 1908, p. 218.

However much public opinion in Europe and America may have been impressed with the achievement of the fleet, Japanese officialdom evidenced no great warmth. This was not unnatural, for the Japanese, although having greeted the original announcement of the cruise with characteristic self-restraint and courtesy, doubtless were not overjoyed at the rôle they were having to play. It was obvious to everyone that the big stick was being flourished for Japan's benefit. The British minister to Japan, Sir Claude M. MacDonald, threw some light on the reaction of the Japanese government in his dispatch of March 17, 1908. In referring to Roosevelt's reported intention to "impress" the Japanese with the seriousness of the situation, MacDonald wrote:

. . . . the arrival of the fleet in the Pacific has certainly failed to impress Japan. The Japanese Government are fully impressed with the seriousness of the emigration question, and sooner than imperil friendly relations with America they would, I know, themselves prohibit emigration; *but a menace such as the sending of a fleet, leaves them absolutely cold.*[44]

Whether as a result of the triumphant progress of the fleet or some other cause, it is evident that Roosevelt's concern over the tension between Japan and the United States had already been greatly relieved. On March 19, 1908, Bryce reported an interesting conversation with the President.[45] Although expressing displeasure with the workings of the Gentlemen's Agreement, and dwelling on the possibility that mob action might cause a rupture, Roosevelt "did not show the same eagerness to discuss the subject

[44] *British Documents on the Origins of the War, 1898–1914,* VIII, 458. Italics mine.

[45] Bryce to Grey, Mar. 19, 1908, *ibid.,* VIII, 459.

as when he had introduced it a month ago; and he referred to it with much more calmness."

The day after the arrival at Magdalena Bay, Secretary Metcalf announced that the fleet would return home by way of Australia, the Philippines, and the Suez Canal.[46] Not only did this statement officially confirm the widely believed rumors of a world cruise but it also announced the acceptance of the Australian invitation, which had been received during the previous month.[47] Roosevelt later wrote that it had not been his intention to send the fleet to Australia but he had acceded to this request "for I have, as every American ought to have, a hearty admiration for, and fellow feeling with, Australia, and I believe that America should be ready to stand back of Australia in any serious emergency."[48] When Prime Minister Deakin read the good news to a Sydney audience, the call went forth for three cheers for the United States, and the crowd arose *en masse* and responded with "deafening hurrahs."[49] Preparations were then begun to make good the boast that if the fleet came to Australia the South American reception would be eclipsed.[50]

On March 18, 1908, five days after the announcement of the world cruise, Baron Takahira, Japanese ambassador

[46] New York *Times,* Mar. 14, 1908.

[47] Prime Minister Deakin had approached the American consul general at Melbourne on this subject as early as December, 1907. John Bray to the Assistant Secretary of State, Dec. 24, 1907, in file 8258. Deakin used his influence with Whitelaw Reid, American ambassador to England, and the invitation was finally presented by Ambassador Bryce, who was friendly to the scheme. Deakin to Reid, Jan. 7, 1908, copy; Reid to Root, Mar. 3, 1908; Bryce to Root, Mar. 2, 1908, in file 8258.

[48] Roosevelt, *Autobiography,* p. 568; see also Roosevelt to Metcalf, Feb. 21, 1908, Roosevelt Papers.

[49] Melbourne *Argus,* Mar. 16, 1908.

[50] London *Times,* Feb. 24, 1908.

to the United States, delivered to the Department of State an invitation for the fleet to visit Japan.[51] After a discussion in the cabinet, which was reported to have hinged on the question of whether or not the American sailors were sufficiently well disciplined for such a mission, an acceptance was announced the following day. Takahira expressed his pleasure at the prompt decision and intimated that the invitation would have been forthcoming sooner had the United States not delayed announcing the world cruise.[52] Ambassador O'Brien was somewhat alarmed by the news that the entire fleet was coming to Japan, and he immediately suggested to Root that the effect might be better if only one squadron were sent. But subsequent inquiries among Japanese officials, including the minister of marine and the minister for foreign affairs, convinced O'Brien that the Japanese were sincerely anxious to be honored by a visit of the largest possible fleet, and that they well understood the moral value of such a friendly demonstration.[53]

The Japanese people expressed great satisfaction over the acceptance, and the Tokyo correspondent of the London *Times* reported that the Japanese press was "profoundly gratified."[54] The reaction of public opinion in the United States was no less favorable, and even journals

[51] Takahira to Root, Mar. 18, 1908, in file 8258.

[52] New York *Times*, Mar. 21, 1908; Bacon (assistant secretary of state) to Takahira, Mar. 20, 1908, in file 8258. The matter of granting shore leave occasioned a considerable amount of discussion in official circles. Roosevelt to Metcalf, Apr. 17, 1908, Roosevelt Papers.

[53] O'Brien to Root, Apr. 16, May 20, June 19, 1908, in file 8258. Takahira made inquiries and reported that the Japanese would "be greatly disappointed in case the whole fleet could *not* visit Japan." Takahira to Root, May 15, 1908, Roosevelt Papers.

[54] London *Times*, Mar. 26, 1908.

like the New York *World* and the New York *Sun,* both
bitter foes of the cruise, were pleased with this development; and the latter rejoiced "to see a feeling of distrust
succeeded by one of international good will and mutual
confidence."[55] Beyond question the Japanese invitation
was a disarming stroke of diplomacy, the far-reaching effects of which cannot be overestimated.[56] Rumors of war,
which had greatly decreased since Taft's Tokyo speech,
almost disappeared, distrust gave way to cordiality, and
the voyage of the fleet henceforth was to be regarded as a
guaranty of peace.

These evidences of friendliness on the part of the Japanese, however, did not completely banish Roosevelt's ap-
prehensions. In writing to Root of information that had
come to him through von Sternberg from a German consul and a military attaché, the President pointed to "the
matter-of-course way in which the Japanese accept the
view that in the event of war they will obtain the naval
supremacy of the Pacific." He further observed that "this
statement of the German Military Attaché corroborates
the information we have both had through the Austrian
Embassy at Tokio and the French Embassy at St. Petersburg, to the effect that many of the Japanese generals . . . .
accept as a matter of course the view that they would land
a strong army on the Pacific Slope." Roosevelt then re-

[55] Quoted in London *Times,* Mar. 23, 1908. The New York correspondent of the *Times* wrote: "Few events have been hailed with more
genuine satisfaction by the entire people and Press of the country than
the proposed visit of the American fleet to Japan. . . . . It should be
regarded as putting the seal of real international friendship upon the
final settlement of the differences between the two nations."

[56] The suggestion was made in certain quarters that the invitation
might have been prompted by Japan's ally, England. See Bristol *Western Daily Press,* Mar. 23, 1908; Bristol *Times and Mirror,* Mar. 21, 1908.

marked that "the German Consul takes exactly your [Root's] view, that the Japanese can restrict immigration hither if they wish to." In concluding, the President returned to the familiar theme of the "one-sided folly" of not preparing. "I think the probabilities are that war will not take place; but there is sufficient likelihood to make it inexcusable for us not to take such measures as will surely prevent it. If we have adequate coast defense and a really large navy, the war can not take place."[57]

Two days later, on April 19, 1908, Roosevelt repeated somewhat the same observations to his son Kermit. He began by speaking of the futile fight he was making to get four battleships from Congress. "I cannot give in public my reasons for being apprehensive about Japan, for of course to do so might bring on grave trouble; but I said enough to put Congress thoroly on its guard, if it cared to be on its guard." He did not believe there would be war, but there was "enough chance of war to make it eminently wise to insure against it by building such a navy as to forbid Japan's hoping for success." He happened to know that "the Japanese military party is inclined for war with us and is not only confident of success, but confident that they could land a large expeditionary force in California and conquer all of the United States west of the Rockies." Roosevelt was convinced "that they would in the end pay dearly for this, but meantime we would have been set back at least a generation by the loss of life, the humiliation, and the material damage."[58]

It is clear to us now that by the middle of April the war

[57] Roosevelt to Root, Apr. 17, 1908, Roosevelt Papers.
[58] Roosevelt to Kermit Roosevelt, Apr. 19, 1908, Roosevelt Papers.

scare had ceased to be a factor to be reckoned with. Even the reports from biased German sources which Roosevelt was still receiving indicated that the Japanese were in no mood for hostilities with the United States. During these weeks, however, Roosevelt suggests a man who has firmly resisted alarmist rumors during a period of great trial and who, when the danger is almost over, is beginning to succumb to the cumulative effect of what he has heard. Perhaps the strain of keeping his head throughout almost a year of the most frenzied jingoism was proving a bit too much for him. Perhaps in his efforts to secure the four battleships from Congress he was convincing himself that much of what he had heard was fact. It is probably true that by the middle of April, 1908, Japanese-American relations were less strained than they had been at any time since May, 1907, or even October, 1906. Yet, on April 19, 1908, Roosevelt could write as follows to his secretary of the treasury, George B. Cortelyou:

I do not at all like having so much gold in San Francisco. Have you yet shipped much of it to Denver? If not please take steps to get at least the bulk of it there during the next six months. San Francisco is on every account an undesirable place in which to leave it; a fatal place should there be war.[59]

It was about this time, however, that Roosevelt received information which to a large extent quieted his fears as to the impracticability of the Gentlemen's Agreement. In March, 1908, he had noted that over one hundred and fifty Japanese laborers had come in during the previous month. "It is certainly to be regretted that as large a number came

[59] Roosevelt to Cortelyou, Apr. 19, 1908, Roosevelt Papers. The last two words of this quotation are not distinct in the letter press copy.

in . . . . more . . . . than I like to see, having in view the future good relations between Japan and the United States."[60] In April, 1908, he had observed that coolies were still pouring in at the rate of about five hundred a month, a flow large enough to keep alive the ill-feeling. It was "possible that in the future the bricks will fly."[61] In May he had learned that over one thousand steerage passengers had left for the United States and Hawaii during the previous month. Roosevelt was plainly irritated: "The Japanese might as well be given to understand that if this thing goes on an exclusion law will be past."[62] In June the President could write Root that, although the total Japanese immigration for May, 1908, was nearly 900, as against nearly 2,300 for May, 1907, this was not nearly so great a falling off as for other countries. "I do not feel that satisfactory results have been achieved yet, and I think the Japanese Government should be notified in the plainest manner that they have nothing to expect but a Japanese exclusion law unless the figures soon begin to show a totally different complexion."[63]

By July, 1908, however, the situation was markedly improved. As a result of more drastic restrictions imposed by the Japanese government, Roosevelt was able to note with satisfaction that "the number of Japanese who left the United States much exceeds the number who remained here."[64] Then, on August 1, 1908, Root wrote Roosevelt

---

[60] Roosevelt to Root, Mar. 28, 1908, Roosevelt Papers.
[61] Roosevelt to Arthur Lee, Apr. 8, 1908, Roosevelt Papers.
[62] Roosevelt to Root, May 4, 1908, Roosevelt Papers.
[63] Roosevelt to Root, June 18, 1908, Roosevelt Papers.
[64] Roosevelt to Takahira, July 8, 1908, Roosevelt Papers.

a remarkably sane letter, and from that time on references to the unworkability of the Gentlemen's Agreement drop out of the President's correspondence. The secretary of state observed that "performance is the only real test of sincerity." He thought, however, that "we must not be too extreme in our expectations of perfection in the working of a new system of repression on the part of the Japanese—a system in which, however good the faith of the Government may be, they cannot, in the nature of things, have the really hearty cooperation and sympathy of the great body of Japanese officials." Secretary Root then made the point that naturally "a little time must be necessary to make such a system work satisfactorily." The United States had had ample experience with the difficulty of accomplishing results through unwilling subordinates. "Time and patience and persistence will doubtless be necessary, but I am sure that the subject is being dealt with in the right spirit and in the right way, and that if what is now being done does not obviate further legislation on our part, it will create a situation where there can be further legislation with infinitely less offence to Japan than would have been the case a short time ago."[65]

In the meantime, Admiral Evans' armada had not been idle. Concluding extended target practice at Magdalena Bay, the fleet left for the California coast on April 11, 1908. The officers and men were received with great enthusiasm in Southern California, and when they reached San Francisco, on May 6, 1908, they were greeted with frenzied rejoicing. It was estimated that 300,000 visitors

[65] Root to Roosevelt, Aug. 1, 1908, Roosevelt Papers.

were drawn from every Western state to that port alone.[66] The fleet then proceeded to Puget Sound, where it was warmly received and where it remained for several weeks for refitting.[67] By July 7, 1908, the battleships were back at San Francisco, and on that day steamed out of the harbor for the Far East under the command of Admiral Sperry, who had relieved Evans.[68]

After a week in Hawaii, during which the picturesque hospitality of the islands was lavished upon the officers and men,[69] the fleet began its long voyage to Auckland, New Zealand, which was reached on August 9, 1908. The overwhelming exuberance of the reception there led an eyewitness to write: "California went mad; New Zealand not only went fleet mad but it developed a new disease— fleetitis."[70] Admiral Sperry told the London *Times* correspondent that the Auckland reception was more enthusiastic than any encountered on the western coast of America.[71] The welcome of Sydney, where the fleet arrived on August 20, 1908, was even more unrestrained.[72] By the time the ships had left Melbourne and Albany,

[66] *Argonaut,* San Francisco, May 23, 1908, p. 338; Matthews, *With the Battle Fleet,* p. 318.

[67] San Francisco *Chronicle,* May 22, 1908.

[68] Evans was in extremely poor health and would have reached the retirement age before the return of the fleet. He retired with honors. See Roosevelt to Evans, Mar. 23, 1908, Roosevelt Papers. Sperry was a singularly happy choice for a position which required a speechmaker, a diplomat, and a naval officer. Roosevelt was highly appreciative of his services. Roosevelt to Sperry, Oct. 28, 1908; Feb. 27, 1909; Roosevelt to Mahan, Oct. 1, 1908; Roosevelt to Admiral J. E. Pillsbury, Oct. 23, 1908, Roosevelt Papers.

[69] San Francisco *Chronicle,* July 18, 19, 1908; Franklin Matthews, *Back to Hampton Roads* (New York, 1909), pp. 1–27.

[70] *Ibid.,* p. 29. This expression took hold. See *Literary Digest,* Feb. 27, 1909, p. 327; *Harper's Weekly,* Feb. 20, 1909, p. 9.

[71] London *Times,* Aug. 10, 1908.   [72] See *ibid.,* Aug. 21, 1908.

Admiral Seaton Schroeder could write that "no possible vehicle of greeting was left unharnessed";[73] and Roosevelt later described as "wonderful" the "considerate, generous, and open-handed hospitality" of these people.[74]

The Australian welcome was so overwhelming as to cause speculation elsewhere as to the weakening bonds of empire. These rumors, which appear to have had their origin in the United States, were promptly disavowed by the Australians, and England did not appear to be seriously disturbed by them.[75] The general explanation given for the outburst was that these isolated people, hungering for excitement, were electrified by the sight of the most impressive fleet ever to visit the Pacific, and the subsequent outpouring was in large part an attempt to congratulate these American cousins on their splendid achievement.[76] Certain other factors, however, undoubtedly lay behind the exuberance of the Australian welcome. There was some evidence of a desire to make the situation as attractive as possible in the hope of attracting immigrants from the United States.[77] Furthermore, Prime Minister Deakin, who later admitted that one of his objects in inviting the fleet had been to secure support for his pet project of a separate Australian navy,[78] saw to it that as many people

[73] Seaton Schroeder, "America's Welcome Abroad," in *Independent*, Mar. 4, 1909, p. 478.

[74] Roosevelt, *Autobiography*, p. 568.

[75] London *Times*, Aug. 10, 11, Sept. 5, 8, 1908; Melbourne *Age*, Aug. 12, 1908.

[76] London *Times*, Sept. 5, 1908; *Argonaut*, San Francisco, Sept. 26, 1908, p. 195; Matthews, *Back to Hampton Roads*, p. 129.

[77] London *Times*, Sept. 5, 1908; Matthews, *Back to Hampton Roads*, pp. 128–29.

[78] Melbourne *Age*, Sept. 9, 1908; *Literary Digest*, Aug. 22, 1908, p. 242.

as possible were given an opportunity to witness this great naval demonstration. Then there was the white Australian ideal, which was widely interpreted in the United States as the fundamental reason for the hysterical greeting. Such a conclusion was so obvious that certain American observers viewed the unrestrained Australian welcome with alarm lest the Japanese, the next foreign hosts, should take offense.[79] As a matter of fact, some uneasiness was expressed in Japan over this development.[80]

Facing the teeming Orient, the Australians had for some time lived in dread of a yellow inundation, and this fear accounted for their "white Australia" policy and the recently developed emphasis on national defense.[81] The renewal of the Anglo-Japanese alliance in 1905 had led to some misgivings in Australia that England was weakening in her support of the white ideal,[82] and the greeting given the Americans may well have been an attempt to remind the mother country of her imperial obligations.[83] In July, 1908, the Prime Minister of New Zealand, Sir Joseph Ward, made a speech in which he expressed the belief that in the future fight to determine white or Oriental supremacy the United States would stand shoulder to shoulder with the Australians.[84] Shortly after the Australian invitation had been extended, the Melbourne *Age,* perhaps the most influential newspaper in Australia, observed:

[79] *Japan Weekly Mail,* Sept. 5, 1908, p. 278 ; *Literary Digest,* Aug. 22, 1908, p. 239.

[80] O'Brien to Root, Oct. 25, 1908, in file 8258.

[81] London *Times,* Dec. 14, 1907 ; Feb. 1, 1908 ; New York *Times,* July 8, 1907.

[82] London *Times,* Jan. 4, 1908, quoting the Sydney *Morning Herald.*

[83] See Matthews, *Back to Hampton Roads,* p. 87.

[84] London *Times,* July 22, 1908.

Ever since the renewal of the Anglo-Japanese alliance the naval supremacy of the Pacific has been in the hands of Japan . . . . the effect . . . . has been to place our rich, sparsely settled, and as yet undefended country more or less at the mercy of a colored race whom our "white Australian" ideal has bitterly offended.

The amazing advance of Japan into the rank of a first class Power and her newly conceived colonising ambitions, fortunately for us, have aroused our American cousins, and persuaded them to make a bid to recapture for the Anglo-Saxon blood the naval predominancy in the Pacific which Britain lately relinquished. Japan is at present our Imperial ally . . . . Nevertheless we are unfeignedly glad that America has invaded the Pacific. It is a move that cannot help but lessen our danger of Asiatic aggression and strengthen the grounds of our national security.[85]

It is not surprising, then, that the Australians should have welcomed, with a view to possible future assistance, the battleships of a people whose views on Japanese immigration coincided with theirs. The Australian, however, was too perfect a host to dwell upon such a selfish theme, and the emphasis was consequently placed upon the desirability of Anglo-Saxon solidarity.[86] This avoidance of the subject naturally led to the conclusion in some quarters that fear of the Japanese had nothing whatever to do with the overwhelming welcome. It has already been noted, however, that before the arrival of the fleet the newspapers and the leaders of public opinion were less guarded in their utterances,[87] and even while the fleet was in port a sufficiently large number of expressions leaked out, in speeches or in the press, to indicate what the people

[85] Melbourne *Age,* Feb. 25, 1908.

[86] *Ibid.,* Aug. 25, 1908; London *Times,* Sept. 5, 1908; Matthews, *Back to Hampton Roads,* p. 67.

[87] See also Melbourne *Argus,* Mar. 17, 1908.

were thinking.[88]   The Wellington *Post,* the Wellington *Times,* and the Melbourne *Age,* for example, were not averse to discussing the relation of the visit to the white Australian ideal even after the fleet had reached Australian waters.[89] It is difficult, therefore, to avoid the conclusion that the alleged Oriental peril did bear an important relation to the extravagance of the reception.

From Australia the fleet went to Manila, arriving on October 2, 1908. Although preparations had been made for entertainment, the epidemic of cholera then raging resulted in the withholding of shore leave from all except officers.[90] This development resulted in considerable dissatisfaction in the city, but the precaution taken by the naval authorities appears to have been fully justified.

The prows of the battleships were now turned toward Japan, and the crisis of the cruise was at hand. Despite the manifestations of mutual esteem that had followed the acceptance of the Japanese invitation, there was the possibility that a fanatic, or a drunken sailor, or some other irresponsible person might cause the worst to happen. Several months earlier Roosevelt had advised Admiral Sperry of the delicacy of the situation in the Far East, and had instructed him to extend shore leave to only those enlisted men who were thoroughly dependable. In addition, he had urged him to make every effort to avoid giving offense to the Japanese and to guard the ships carefully against pos-

[88] For expressions in speeches see London *Times,* Aug. 13, 1908; Matthews, *Back to Hampton Roads,* p. 66.

[89] London *Times,* Aug. 10, 1908, quoting Wellington *Post* and Welington *Times;* Melbourne *Age,* Aug. 10, 19, 1908. See also Sperry to Edith Sperry, Aug. 16, 1908, Sperry Papers, Library of Congress.

[90] San Francisco *Chronicle,* Oct. 2, 3, 1908; Matthews, *Back to Hampton Roads,* pp. 156–57.

sible attack by fanatics.[91] In spite of these warnings, some
of which he openly disregarded, Sperry did not expect
trouble, although he reported that "Even such wise men
as Wainwright and some of my staff were stubbornly confident that a row with Japan was imminent. . . . ."[92]

On October 18, 1908, the battleships arrived at Yokohama and were immediately accorded an overwhelming
reception, which Roosevelt later described as the "most
noteworthy incident of the cruise . . . ."[93] Officers, men,
and correspondents were unanimous in describing the welcome of the Japanese as the warmest and most enthusiastic encountered on the entire voyage;[94] and Ambassador
O'Brien was assured that it outdid in magnificence even
that accorded to Admiral Togo when he returned from
his brilliant victory over the Russian fleet.[95] Not only had
the arrangements been worked out with marvelous precision, as was evidenced by the teaching of American national songs to tens of thousands of school children, but
the spontaneous outpouring of the people was unrestrained
and whole-hearted.[96] Whatever the cause—whether a

[91] Roosevelt to Sperry, Mar. 21, 1908; Sperry to Charles Sperry,
Apr. 5, 1908, Sperry Papers.

[92] Sperry to Charles Sperry, Jan. 6, 1909, Sperry Papers.

[93] Roosevelt, *Autobiography*, p. 568.

[94] Matthews, *Back to Hampton Roads*, p. 183; San Francisco *Chronicle*, Oct. 19, 20, 25, 1908; New York *Times*, Oct. 20, 24, 1908. A thousand English-speaking Japanese students and sailors were provided as
guides. Sperry memorandum, Sperry Papers. Sperry wrote to his wife:
"You cannot imagine the perfection of the details of our reception and
their generosity." Sperry to Edith Sperry, Oct. 21, 1908, Sperry Papers.
To his son he stated: "There was literally nothing in the way of comfort or convenience that was not provided." Sperry to Charles Sperry,
Oct. 30, 1908, Sperry Papers.

[95] O'Brien to Root, Oct. 25, 1908, in file 8258.

[96] *Ibid.;* Matthews, *Back to Hampton Roads*, p. 187; *Japan Weekly
Mail*, Oct. 24, 1908, p. 487; Oct. 31, 1908, p. 519; San Francisco *Chronicle*, Oct. 19–25, 1908.

desire to outdo the Australians, whether an impulse to show that the attitude of Japan toward the United States had been misrepresented, whether relief at the recent disappearance of all war talk, whether a genuine feeling of friendship for the United States—the unstinted hospitality of the Japanese made a profound impression on the officers and men, and the reaction of the press of the United States was appreciative to a high degree.[97] Well could O'Brien report the "extraordinary success" of the visit, the "universally favorable" tone of the Japanese press, and his belief that "the effects of the visit will be material and far-reaching for good."[98]

The British minister to Japan corroborated the enthusiastic report of Ambassador O'Brien. He observed that the visit of the American battleships "has been an unqualified success and has produced a marked and favourable impression on both officers and men of the fleet—in fact it has had the effect that our Allies [the Japanese] wanted it to and has put an end to all nonsensical war talk." Nor, as Minister MacDonald further observed, had the event been without its humorous aspects.

Speaking to the Prime Minister who is also for the moment Finance Minister I said, to entertain 14,000 men for seven days must have cost a lot of money—not so much he replied with a twinkle in his eye as they have left behind them. As the men were not allowed ashore at Manila on account of the cholera they

[97] See *Literary Digest,* Oct. 31, 1908, p. 614; New York *Times,* Oct. 20, 1908.

[98] O'Brien to Root, Oct. 25, 1908, in file 8258. O'Brien inclosed with this dispatch long extracts from ten of the leading Japanese newspapers showing the extreme gratification of the Japanese over the visit. It is also significant that the Tokyo stock market was stronger during the first week of October than it had been for the past two years. *Review of Reviews,* XXXVIII (Nov., 1908), 539.

had lots of back pay to dispose of and I understand Tokio and Yokohama are now full of Uncle Sam's gold. The Japanese have therefore got what they wanted, and are not out of pocket in the getting.[99]

Here and there a voice was raised in the United States to warn the people that the demonstration of the Japanese had merely been a subterfuge to hide their true feelings.[100] This reaction, however, was the exception rather than the rule. The officers and men came away thoroughly convinced of Japan's sincerity;[101] and the New York *Times* observed: "No nation teaches its children to sing the songs of a people for whom it has unfriendly feelings."[102] Perhaps the most convincing refutation of the charge of insincerity was written by Admiral Schroeder:

I call upon all good Americans not to let any germs of doubt enter their minds as to the whole-heartedness of that greeting. The unstudied eloquence of careless attitude revealed at every turn cannot be controverted by a distant view possibly tinged with prejudice. . . . . When it is said that thousands of school children lined the hedges along the highways and waved in unison the flag of the stars and stripes and the flag of the rising sun, it has been retorted, "That is easily done by imperial command." So it is . . . . But when crowds lining the thorofares . . . . five, ten, even fifteen files deep, day after day at all hours from morning until late at night . . . . are smiling with lips unmistakably framing the "Banzais" that rend the air in one continuous thundering chorus—no such retort is possible.[103]

Of the various explanations that have been advanced for the overwhelming nature of the reception, that given

[99] MacDonald to Grey, Oct. 26, 1908, *British Documents on the Origins of the War, 1898–1914*, VIII, 459–60.

[100] *Argonaut*, San Francisco, Oct. 31, 1908, p. 276.

[101] Matthews, *Back to Hampton Roads*, p. 184.

[102] New York *Times*, Oct. 30, 1908.   [103] Schroeder, *loc. cit.*, p. 479.

by Admiral Sperry appears to be the most plausible. When the fleet arrived in Japan, Sperry was surprised to find the Japanese officials extremely nervous, as if they feared the consequences of what some fanatic might do or what might happen if the sailors should misbehave or the officers fail to observe certain diplomatic niceties.[104] In fact, Sperry described this nervous tension as being so great as to be "almost unendurable."[105] But the exemplary conduct and the manifest friendliness of the Americans, which were fully reciprocated by their Japanese hosts, together with Sperry's felicitous remarks and the exchange of courtesies between the Emperor of Japan and President Roosevelt, resulted in a feeling of relief in Japan which Sperry described as "almost hysterical."[106] Once the ice was broken, everything went off so smoothly, he reported, "that one wonders what all the fuss was about." But prior to that time the atmosphere had been such that Sperry had found it necessary "to walk on eggs" and carefully avoid "several first rate opportunities to make a mess."[107]

For the happy outcome of the whole affair the commander of the American fleet deserves no small share of the credit. Aside from his skilful handling of a delicate

[104] Sperry to Edith Sperry, Nov. 10, 1908, Sperry Papers.

[105] Sperry to Edith Sperry, Nov. 1, 1908. To his son he wrote: "*Everybody* had a scare and if I had blundered with that fleet back of me it would have been bad business." Sperry to Charles Sperry, Jan. 6, 1909, Sperry Papers.

[106] Sperry to Charles Sperry, Jan. 6, 1909, Sperry Papers. Admiral Sperry wrote to his wife: "Mr. Denison [adviser to Japanese Foreign Office] has just been here and had a long talk. He says the satisfaction with the way the visit has gone is unalloyed, from the emperor down and that absolutely nothing has occurred to mar the smoothness of things: that it has certainly killed the war foolishness and made friendship closer." Sperry to Edith Sperry, Oct. 23, 1908, Sperry Papers.

[107] Sperry to Charles Sperry, Oct. 30, 1908, Sperry Papers.

situation while on the ground, one important piece of fore-sighted diplomacy must be noted. Several months prior to the visit to Japan, Admiral Sperry had written to a friend, an American named Denison who was an adviser to the Japanese Foreign Office, and had described in detail the type of entertainment which would be best calculated to keep the American sailors out of mischief, emphasizing particularly the desirability of having an abundance of tables and rest places available.[108] Denison had communicated this letter to the Japanese officials; and it is not to detract from the cordiality of their welcome to say that they followed and improved upon many of these suggestions. Thus, as Sperry wrote to his wife, "all of the most perplexing matters had been arranged in advance of any official communications." He then went on to say:

> I cannot help smiling a little satirically to myself because things have gone so smoothly that apparently they ran themselves. They talk of the "splendid behavior" of the men but they were picked men—that is the small percentage of loafers and drunkards did not go ashore at all—and they had been encouraged to be good.[109]

After leaving Japan on October 25, 1908, the fleet divided, part returning to Manila for maneuvers and part proceeding to Amoy in response to an invitation of the Chinese government accepted in March, 1908.[110] Fear was expressed by American officials in China that the appearance of this powerful armada might have the unfortunate effect of leading the Chinese to believe that the United

[108] Sperry to Charles Sperry, Oct. 30, 1908, Sperry Papers.
[109] Sperry to Edith Sperry, Oct. 30, 1908, Sperry Papers.
[110] Root to Wu Ting Fang, Mar. 24, 1908, in file 8258.

States was prepared to back their claims against those of Japan in Manchuria, but Root instructed Minister W. W. Rockhill to remove any such misinterpretation.[111] As a result of the recent remission of the Boxer indemnity, as well as other developments, the relations between the United States and China were particularly cordial at that time, and the appropriation by the Chinese government of 400,000 taels for the Amoy entertainment was regarded as an expression of appreciation.[112] A number of adverse factors, however, among them a typhoon, caused such great difficulties that the best the Chinese were able to do could be only an anti-climax after the Japanese reception.[113] Nevertheless, friendly feelings were aroused by the visit, and the American consul at Amoy could report that among the numerous telegrams of felicitation which poured into his office from all parts of China were two from newspapers that three years before had taken a leading part in the anti-American boycott.[114]

After uniting at Manila for extended target practice,

[111] Charles Denby (consul general at Shanghai) to Root, Apr. 18, 1908; Rockhill to Root (telegram), Apr. 18, 1908; Rockhill to Root, Apr. 21, 1908; Root to Rockhill (telegram), Apr. 28, 1908, in file 8258.

[112] See London *Times*, July 20, Oct. 31, 1908. Early in October, 1907, Taft had written: "The truth is that the Chinese are now very favorable to us. Indeed they are growing more and more suspicious of the Japanese and the English and the French in their desire for exclusive concessions and they turn to us as the only country that is really unselfish in the matter of obtaining territory and monopolies. I think it therefore worth while to cultivate them and accept courtesies at their hands." Taft to Roosevelt, Oct. 5, 1907, in file 1797.

[113] *North China Herald,* Oct. 31, 1908, p. 248; *Japan Weekly Mail,* Nov. 7, 1908, p. 552; Nov. 14, 1908, p. 585; San Francisco *Chronicle,* Oct. 26, 1908. Sperry reported that a nervous tension similar to that encountered in Japan was noticeable in China. Sperry to Edith Sperry, Nov. 10, 1908, Sperry Papers.

[114] J. H. Arnold to the Assistant Secretary of State, Nov. 27, 1908, in file 8258.

the fleet left on December 1, 1908, for home waters. On the day before, an exchange of notes known as the Root-Takahira agreement had taken place at Washington.[115] This diplomatic achievement was the culmination of a series of treaties or conventions that had been negotiated during the general clearing of the air following the acceptance of the Japanese invitation in March, 1908. On May 5, 1908, an arbitration convention had been signed at Washington between representatives of the two powers;[116] and, although this agreement was not intrinsically of great importance, the Washington correspondent of the London *Times* noted that it was expected greatly to accelerate "the decided improvement that has recently taken place in American public sentiment towards Japan."[117]

Fourteen days later, on May 19, 1908, two treaties were signed providing for the protection of trade marks in Korea and in China.[118] Then, on November 30, 1908, came the Root-Takahira agreement, a diplomatic understanding of the first importance, which provided, among other things, for the preservation of the *status quo* in the Pacific and the open door in China.[119] Ambassador Bryce wrote home that the important consideration was not the agreement itself but the fact that it had actually been concluded.

---

[115] *Foreign Relations*, 1908, pp. 510–12.   [116] *Ibid.*, pp. 503–505.

[117] London *Times*, May 8, 1908. In response to Takahira's request for advice Ambassador Bryce replied that his own view was that the conclusion of such a treaty "would have a good moral effect and help to dispel the rumours so persistently repeated of strained relations between Japan and the United States." Bryce to Grey, Mar. 19, 1908, *British Documents on the Origins of the War, 1898–1914*, VIII, 458.

[118] *Foreign Relations*, 1908, pp. 518–23.

[119] For text see *ibid.*, pp. 510–12.

It "marks a period in the Pacific policy" of the United States and "silences the last echoes of the war cries of last year."[120] Nor can the fact be overlooked that Ambassador Aoki, more than a year previously and before the sending of the fleet, had independently proposed an understanding along precisely the same lines, but his government had discouraged his efforts and had shortly thereafter recalled him.[121] Yet, in the light of recent developments, the Root-Takahira agreement was received with great satisfaction in both the United States and Japan, and it was generally regarded as an achievement growing out of the visit of the fleet.[122] Roosevelt himself shared this view, for in writing to Arthur Lee of this understanding he observed that his "policy of constant friendliness and courtesy toward Japan, *coupled with sending the fleet around the world,* has borne good results."[123]

The return voyage by way of Colombo, Suez, and Gibraltar was uneventful, except for a short stay at Messina, Sicily, to help earthquake sufferers. Because the Roosevelt administration was anxious to get the fleet home without any further delay, it was necessary to refuse

[120] Bryce to Grey, Dec. 1, 1908, *British Documents on the Origins of the War, 1898–1914,* VIII, 464.

[121] See Roosevelt to Aoki, Dec. 19, 1908, Roosevelt Papers; O'Brien to Root, Nov. 3, 1907, in file 1797; O'Brien to Root, Dec. 12, 1908 (inclosure), in file 16533.

[122] The London *Times* spoke of the agreement as "a remarkable diplomatic achievement to which the visit of Mr. Taft to Japan and the reception of the American fleet in Japanese waters doubtless contributed." Nov. 30, 1908. The New York *Times* observed: "It may be regarded as the echo in diplomacy of the splendid manifestation of friendship in Japan on the occasion of the visit of the fleet." Nov. 29, 1908. See also *Independent,* Dec. 24, 1908, p. 1558.

[123] Roosevelt to Arthur Lee, Dec. 20, 1908, Roosevelt Papers. Italics Roosevelt's.

all invitations from European powers; and because large centers of population were avoided, the tremendous receptions of Pacific and Far Eastern waters were not duplicated. So, after its 46,000-mile cruise the fleet reached Hampton Roads on February 22, 1909, just in time, as certain unfriendly critics observed, to usher out the Roosevelt era in a blaze of glory.[124] The President welcomed the officers and men with great enthusiasm, and complimented them on bringing the fleet home "a much more efficient fighting instrument than when it started sixteen months before."[125] A chorus of praise arose from the press of the United States, even from those newspapers that had condemned the venture. The New York *Sun,* which had been most bitter in its denunciation, lauded this "achievement without precedent or parallel" as "spectacularly splendid."[126] The New York correspondent of the London *Times* wrote: "President Roosevelt's judgment in ordering this venturesome naval movement has been splendidly vindicated. It is impossible even for his enemies to begrudge him the genuine satisfaction and pleasure of tendering to the battle fleet the nation's welcome . . . ."[127]

Perhaps the most damaging criticism directed against the fleet after its return was that it had awakened in for-

---

[124] *Argonaut,* San Francisco, May 23, 1908, p. 338; New York *Nation,* Sept. 3, 1908, p. 199. In spite of the receptions, Sperry stated that the fleet stayed at no place longer than was necessary to coal the ships. Sperry memorandum, Sperry Papers.

[125] Roosevelt, *Autobiography,* p. 566.

[126] Quoted in *Literary Digest,* Mar. 6, 1909, p. 366.

[127] London *Times,* Feb. 22, 1909. Shortly after the return of the fleet Roosevelt wrote that at first "it seemed as if popular feeling was nearly a unit" against him, and that after the safe return it was "nearly a unit in favor of what I did." Roosevelt to Taft, Mar. 3, 1909, Roosevelt Papers.

eign peoples a lamentable spirit of envy and emulation.[128] It is true that after the cruise had been announced the English and German fleets engaged in impressive demonstrations; that Austria launched out upon a three-dreadnaught program; and that Spain began a renovation of her navy.[129] Much of this activity had been planned in advance, and it would be extremely difficult to prove that it was influenced to any appreciable extent by the move of the United States. It must be admitted, however, that the visit of the fleet, as Deakin had hoped, did encourage the Australians to go ahead with their plans for a separate navy; but the movement in this direction had already assumed considerable proportions before the announcement of the cruise.[130] On the other hand, this demonstration cannot be blamed for the Anglo-German naval race, which had begun in all earnestness several years before.[131] Shortly after the South American visit, Brazil placed orders for a number of warships with European builders; and Argentina countered by voting a $55,000,000 naval increase.[132] Pacifists pointed to these developments as direct results of the cruise;[133] yet the fact was overlooked that the Brazilian program had been in contemplation for a number of years and that it had actually been adopted prior to the departure

---

[128] See *Advocate of Peace*, Jan., 1908, p. 2; Apr., 1908, p. 73.

[129] *Annual Report of the Secretary of the Navy, 1907*, pp. 8–10; *ibid., 1908*, p. 10; *Literary Digest*, May 8, 1909, p. 788; London *Times*, June 29, July 8, Nov. 13, 1908.

[130] *Ibid.*, Aug. 21, Oct. 2, 1908; *Harper's Weekly*, July 11, 1908, p. 30; *Literary Digest*, Apr. 10, 1908, p. 589.

[131] See Winston S. Churchill, *The World Crisis, 1911–1914* (London, 1923), p. 38.

[132] *Annual Report of the Secretary of the Navy, 1908*, p. 10.

[133] *Advocate of Peace*, July, 1908, p. 154; Nov., 1908, p. 240.

of the fleet; and the Argentine appropriation was probably dictated by what was regarded as the necessity of following the lead of Brazil.[134] It should further be observed that during 1908 Japan slashed her naval expenditures and that the Russian Duma refused to accept an ambitious program for a new fleet.[135]

Most notable of all, the American people, while applauding the exploits of their navy, refused to be swept off their feet. Not satisfied with having "more than doubled the navy of the United States,"[136] Roosevelt vigorously demanded four new battleships; but Congress ruthlessly pared the administration program down to two.[137] Because of the impossibility of securing American colliers to accompany the fleet, despite the willingness of the naval authorities to pay fifty per cent more to home industry, the battleships presented to the world the highly incongruous spectacle of being accompanied by more than a score of vessels flying foreign flags. Alarmists throughout the United States were quick to point out that in the event of hostilities a strict observance of neutrality would deprive the battleships of their colliers, with a consequent paralysis of the naval arm.[138] In spite of this unmistakable

---

[134] *Annual Report of the Secretary of the Navy, 1908,* p. 10.

[135] *Advocate of Peace,* May, 1908, p. 98.

[136] Roosevelt to Brooks, Dec. 28, 1908, Roosevelt Papers.

[137] Roosevelt confessed privately that he had demanded four so as to be sure of two. Roosevelt to White, June 30, 1908, Roosevelt Papers.

[138] *Congressional Record,* 60 Cong., 1 sess., pp. 2372 ff.; New York *Times,* Sept. 27, Oct. 5, 1907; London *Times,* Oct. 4, 1907; Roosevelt to Lodge, Sept. 29, 1907; Roosevelt to Knox, Feb. 8, 1909, Roosevelt Papers. Sperry was greatly annoyed in Australia when the foreign colliers failed to deliver 27,000 tons of coal on schedule. Sperry to Charles Sperry, Oct. 1, 1908, Sperry Papers.

object lesson as to the need of a larger merchant marine for auxiliary purposes, Congress stubbornly repeated its previous action and refused to approve a subsidy bill. It may well be doubted, therefore, whether the cruise gave any dangerous stimulus to naval construction in the United States or elsewhere. It was a day when the idea of having big navies was in the air, and the United States, far from leading the procession, was content to follow along.

In summarizing the results of the cruise certain important developments of a purely technical nature must be mentioned briefly. The general efficiency, discipline, and morale of the fleet was markedly improved; new standards of economy in coal consumption were established as a result of competitive awards; valuable lessons in self-sustenance and in handling all needed repairs were learned; training was afforded in holding the vessels accurately in formation and in operating them as a unit; and a great improvement in target practice was recorded.[139] In addition, experiments were carried on with wireless telephony, and the necessity of securing a supply of high-grade coal on the Pacific Coast led to an investigation of the Alaska and British Columbia coal fields.[140] Furthermore, the demonstrated need of better bases and adequate dry-dock facilities on the Pacific Coast resulted in agitation for additional improvements at Mare Island, California, and Bremerton, Wash-

[139] Sperry memorandum; Sperry to Charles Sperry, Mar. 5, 1908, Sperry Papers; *Annual Report of the Secretary of the Navy, 1908*, p. 6; *ibid., 1909*, p. 29; Sperry to Pillsbury, July 25, 1908, in file 6072, Bureau of Navigation, Navy Department; Roosevelt, *Autobiography*, pp. 571, 572; New York *Times*, Jan. 17, 1908; *Scientific American*, Feb. 20, 1909, p. 146.

[140] *Annual Report of the Secretary of the Navy, 1911*, pp. 59–60; *ibid., 1913*, p. 16. Roosevelt, *Autobiography*, p. 571.

ington, and the inauguration of long-delayed improvements at Pearl Harbor.[141]

In its larger aspect perhaps the most significant result of the cruise was that it marked the further emergence of the United States not only as a Pacific but as a world power.[142] The American public, which had followed the course of the fleet with intense interest, lost much of its provincialism by studying the geography of other parts of the world and the people, as described in detail by special correspondents, who lived there. One prominent Australian wrote: "The delusions of distance and ignorance and the caricatures of humor have been corrected by the reality of contact."[143] To some extent sectionalism was broken down by focusing attention on the needs and strategic opportunities of the Pacific Coast and on the commercial opportunities that might be developed in the Pacific. As Roosevelt said after the return of the fleet, "nobody after this will forget that the American coast is on the Pacific as well as on the Atlantic."[144] The visits to Hawaii and the

[141] *Annual Report of the Secretary of the Navy, 1908*, p. 33; *ibid., 1909*, p. 30; *ibid., 1910*, p. 36; *Argonaut*, San Francisco, June 6, 1908, p. 370; San Francisco *Chronicle*, July 5, 1907; May 8, 22, July 18, 1908.

[142] A recent writer described the event as "an incident of America's coming of age in the family of nations." Mark Sullivan, *Our Times: Pre-War America* (New York, 1930), III, 514.

[143] G. H. Reid, "An After-Glance at the Visit of the American Fleet to Australia," *North American Review*, CLXXXIX (Mar., 1909), 409. Sperry thought that accounts of the friendly greetings which were written home by thousands of sailors promoted peace. Sperry memorandum, Sperry Papers.

[144] New York *Times*, Feb. 23, 1909. One of the results of the voyage was a persistent attempt on the part of an element on the Pacific Coast to secure a permanent battleship fleet in the Pacific, but Roosevelt, more convinced than ever of the folly of dividing the fleet before the completion of the Panama Canal, steadfastly resisted these efforts. See Roosevelt to Knox, Feb. 8, 1909; Roosevelt to Taft, Mar. 3, 1909, Roosevelt Papers.

Philippines emphasized the value of these places to a nation that essayed to set itself up as a naval power in the Pacific, and demonstrated to the natives, as well as to investors, that the United States was prepared to defend its outposts. It was also assumed—a thing difficult to prove—that the good-will tour, by introducing the Americans favorably to foreign peoples, stimulated the demand for American goods. Beyond question the Monroe Doctrine took on an added significance, and it became increasingly evident that the United States was to be no idle spectator in the midst of international developments.

In looking back over the events of his administration, Theodore Roosevelt wrote that "the two American achievements that really impressed foreign peoples during the first dozen years of this century were the digging of the Panama Canal and the cruise of the battle fleet round the world." He further observed, presumably not overlooking the Nobel Prize which he had won in 1906, that the dispatching of this armada was "the most important service that I rendered to peace . . . ."[145] After examining this entire episode in detail, one has no disposition to quarrel with Roosevelt's appraisal. Prior to 1908 no fleet approaching in strength that of the United States had ever made a voyage so far as the distance between Hampton Roads and San Francisco.[146] Many foreign experts were confident

[145] Roosevelt, *Autobiography*, pp. 563, 565. Contemporaneously the President stated his conviction that nothing had "occurred in the history of the navy of greater and more fortunate significance to this country . . . ." Roosevelt to G. H. Grosvenor, Jan. 28, 1908, Roosevelt Papers. He also wrote that he had "anticipated good in every way . . . . but it has far more than come up to my anticipations." Roosevelt to Sperry, Dec. 5, 1908, Roosevelt Papers.

[146] The voyage of the ill-fated Rozhestvenski from the Baltic to Far Eastern waters, 1904–1905, was most frequently compared with that of

that it could not be done successfully.[147] Yet the fleet arrived at Magdalena Bay in fighting trim and ahead of schedule, and then proceeded to circumnavigate the globe. Without serious mishap or delay, despite several terrific storms, and with unqualified success, the battleships arrived at Hampton Roads ready to start out again. Judged by every standard of naval efficiency, the fleet returned home, collectively and individually, a more effective fighting force than when it had started.[148] Henceforth it was evident that the United States could defend both of its coasts with vigor and dispatch, and that as a naval power it was not to be trifled with. From France Ambassador Henry White wrote glowingly of the impression created, and he described how wonderful it was, in contrast with the old days when he had no fleet at his back, to represent a nation with such a formidable navy.[149]

In the light of the evidence presented, it would also seem as if Roosevelt had good grounds for asserting that the cruise of the fleet was his most notable contribution to peace. The trail of friendliness and good-will that followed the fleet undoubtedly had permanent effects, especially upon the tens of thousands of impressionable children who welcomed the sailors in Japan. Barriers of ignorance and misunderstanding were broken down, and

---

the Americans. The Russian fleet, however, was much less formidable, did not travel nearly so far, and arrived in wretched condition.

[147] Von Tirpitz told Roosevelt in 1910 that he had not believed that the cruise could be made successfully, and that the English Naval Office and Foreign Office held the same view. Bishop, *Roosevelt*, II, 249.

[148] See Roosevelt to Kaiser, Jan. 2, 1909, Roosevelt Papers.

[149] White to Roosevelt, Mar. 20, 1908; Jan. 31, 1909, Roosevelt Papers.

throughout the cruise the function of the navy as a police force and not as a threat was constantly emphasized. But with reference to peace Roosevelt was probably thinking particularly of Japan. At the time the cruise was announced war was a distinct possibility, and, with the jingoes of both countries warming to their task, was fast becoming a probability. This impressive exhibition of naval power had a quieting effect upon the yellow press of Japan, and, most important of all, gave the Japanese an opportunity to invite the fleet to their shores and demonstrate that their feelings toward the United States were those of the sincerest friendship. The ensuing reception dispelled all war clouds and paved the way for a diplomatic *rapprochement* which, a year before, had been thought impossible. Whether or not the situation would in time have righted itself it is not within the province of the historian to determine; but it must be admitted that, however untimely and ill-advised the cruise may have been regarded by unfriendly critics, Roosevelt's decision set in motion a series of events which undoubtedly hastened the understanding that followed.[150] Referring in this connection to the Venezuelan episode and his use of the big stick on the Kaiser, Roosevelt wrote:

The recent voyage of the fleet around the world was not the first occasion in which I have used it [big stick] to bring about prompt resumption of peaceful relations between this country and

[150] In 1910, Von Tirpitz and the Kaiser both told Roosevelt that the voyage had "done more for peace in the Orient than anything else that could possibly have happened." Bishop, *Roosevelt*, II, 250–51. Ambassador Tower reported that the Kaiser had told him that in his opinion the fleet prevented an immediate attack by Japan and "the dismemberment of China." The Kaiser's estimates during this period, however, were unreliable. Tower to Roosevelt, Jan. 28, 1908, Roosevelt Papers.

a foreign Power. But of course one of the conditions of such use is that it should be accompanied with every manifestation of politeness and friendship—manifestations which are sincere, by the way, for the foreign policy in which I believe is in very fact the policy of speaking softly and carrying a big stick. I want to make it evident to every foreign nation that I intend to do justice; and neither to wrong them nor to hurt their self-respect; but that on the other, I am both entirely ready and entirely able to see that our rights are maintained in their turn.[151]

The world cruise was characteristically Rooseveltian, done in the grand manner that Roosevelt loved. At the time it was announced the possibilities of misunderstanding and danger were great. The Japanese might have been goaded into a declaration of war; the fleet might have been wrecked in the Straits of Magellan; it might have been pounced upon by the Japanese in Far Eastern waters; it might have been stranded in Australia while a European squadron was ravaging the Atlantic Coast.[152] Cautious statesmanship would have dictated a further postponement of the venture. But like a skilful gambler Roosevelt carefully weighed the chances and decided to send the fleet. His correspondence abundantly reveals that he went into this enterprise with his eyes open. He knew the ships and the men, and he was confident they could go around in safety—a confidence shared by the officers high in command.[153] He had reason to believe that the odds were

---

[151] Roosevelt to Whitelaw Reid, Dec. 4, 1908, Roosevelt Papers.

[152] Roosevelt considered this point carefully and concluded that relations with all of the European powers were so good that "it seems in the highest degree unlikely that trouble will occur pending the absence of the fleet" and that he "could not send it to the Pacific at a better time . . . ." Roosevelt to L. F. Abbott, Sept. 13, 1907. See also Roosevelt to Newberry, Aug. 6, 1907, Roosevelt Papers.

[153] Roosevelt, *Autobiography*, p. 566.

decidedly against war and that, if he won, the cruise would have a most salutary effect. Had he lost, the condemnation of posterity would deservedly be heaped upon his head. But he won, as he was accustomed to win when the stakes were high. Some have called it Rooseveltian luck; others have called it statesmanship. Call it what you will, the historian must admit that this venture, harebrained though it may have been regarded by contemporaries, was far-reaching in its results for good.

CHAPTER XIII

The Final Flare-Up

"By George! I wish I could get California to call a halt in its proposed Japanese action. The whole business has been most unfortunate, and I am more concerned over it than any of the other rather stormy incidents during my career as President."—Roosevelt to Kent, January 22, 1909

ROOSEVELT had used the big stick with effect on the California legislature in 1907, but the evil day had merely been postponed. In January, 1909, while the fleet was nearing the Atlantic on its homeward voyage and while the cheers of the Japanese people were ringing in the ears of the American nation, the California legislature began to show signs of restiveness. There was still a large and perhaps growing anti-Japanese element in the state, as was evidenced by the introduction of a number of resolutions and bills in the legislature which were aimed at the Japanese residents. The agitation was brought to a head on January 15, 1909, when the assembly judiciary committee reported favorably Drew's alien land bill. This measure provided that an alien acquiring title to land within the state would have to become a citizen within five years or dispose of his holding. Although the Japanese were not mentioned by name, their ineligibility to citizenship made it clear that they were being aimed at.[1]

[1] Franklin Hichborn, *Story of the Session of the California Legislature of 1909* (San Francisco, 1909), p. 203, hereafter cited as Hichborn, *Legislature of 1909*; San Francisco *Chronicle*, Jan. 16, 1909.

Roosevelt was genuinely disturbed by these new developments, all the more so because his term was nearing its end and because Japanese-American relations, largely as a result of the cruise of the fleet, were in a happier posture than they had been since October, 1906. He therefore wired Governor Gillett:

We are greatly concerned at newspaper reports of anti-Japanese legislation . . . . Have written you at length on subject. Earnestly hope that no progress will be made on bills until you have chance to receive my letter, and if necessary to discuss its contents with the leaders of the two houses. My knowledge of the international situation, particularly with reference to emigration of Japanese laborers from United States, satisfies me that passage of proposed legislation would be of incalculable damage to State of California as well as to whole Union.[2]

In his letter to Gillett of January 16, 1909, written the same day that the telegram was sent, Roosevelt stated that these anti-Japanese bills were "in every sense most unfortunate," largely because at "last we have in first class working order the arrangement which with such difficulty we succeeded in getting thru two years ago." The President then went on to show that the Japanese government was "obviously acting in entire good faith," for during the six months ending October 31, 1908, the total number of Japanese coming to the mainland of the United States had been 2,074, and the total number departing for Japan 3,181. It was evident, then, that "the whole object nominally desired by those who wish to prevent the incoming of Japanese laborers has been achieved." More Japanese were leaving the country than entering, and "by present indications in a very few years the number of Japanese

[2] Roosevelt to Gillett (telegram), Jan. 16, 1909, Roosevelt Papers.

here will be no greater than the number of Americans in Japan; that is, the movement will be as normal in one case as in the other, which is just what we desire." Roosevelt concluded:

There is, therefore, no shadow of excuse for action which will simply produce great irritation and may result in upsetting the present agreement and throwing open the whole situation again. These agitators have themselves to thank if trouble comes from what they do, if there is a fresh influx of Japanese hither. They hamper the National Government in what it has now so efficiently accomplished—the agreement by peaceful means, and thru the friendly initiative of the Japanese Government, to keep Japanese immigrants out of the United States save as Americans themselves visit Japan. Is it not possible to get the legislature to realize the great unwisdom from the standpoint of the country at large, and above all from the standpoint of California, of what is being done?[3]

Roosevelt was evidently determined to see what he could do to marshal American public opinion behind him in his efforts to quiet the California legislature and at the same time convince the Japanese that he was still the champion of international fair play, for on January 19, 1909, three days after he sent the telegram and the letter to Gillett, he gave copies of these communications to the press. In fact, practically all of the private correspondence that will be considered in this connection was made public shortly after it was sent. In a sense this was unfortunate, for such expressions as "incalculable damage," "great irritation," and "great unwisdom" gave to the country at large the impression that the situation was much more serious than it actually was. Indeed, as we shall have occasion to observe, Roosevelt greatly overestimated the concern of the Japa-

[3] Roosevelt to Gillett, Jan. 16, 1909, Roosevelt Papers.

nese. Nevertheless, he seems to have been sincere, for on January 22, 1909, he wrote to William Kent, later Congressman from California: "By George! I wish I could get California to call a halt in its proposed Japanese action. The whole business has been most unfortunate, and I am more concerned over it than any of the other rather stormy incidents during my career as President."[4]

The situation with regard to the California legislature was further complicated by the introduction of an anti-Japanese school bill on January 22, 1909.[5] This measure was designed to extend and strengthen the provisions of the state law under which the San Francisco Board of Education had attempted to segregate the Japanese in 1906. But the supporters of the bill received a serious blow when Governor Gillett, acting upon the vigorously expressed suggestions of Roosevelt, sent a special message to the legislature, on January 25, 1909, in which he urged that body to do nothing that would disrupt cordial relations with Japan.[6] This evident disposition on the part of the governor to veto undesirable measures relating to Orientals did much to improve the complexion of affairs.[7]

The President expressed his warm gratitude to Governor Gillett for what he had done, and continued to acquaint him with the views of the federal government. Roosevelt made it clear that the alien land bill would not be objectionable if it was amended in such a way as to remove

---

[4] Roosevelt to Kent, Jan. 22, 1909, Roosevelt Papers.
[5] *Assembly Journal* (California), 1909, p. 222.
[6] *Senate Journal* (California), 1909, pp. 254–57.
[7] *Japan Weekly Mail*, Jan. 30, 1909, p. 124.

the discriminatory features and apply to all aliens alike. In fact, several states already had such statutes on their books. But the President considered the anti-Japanese school bill and a recently introduced measure providing for the segregation of Japanese in the cities as highly pernicious, and he remonstrated strongly against them.[8] This vigorous intervention on the part of the federal executive, to say nothing of parliamentary maneuvering in the California legislature, appears to have accomplished definite results; for, by February 4, 1909, it seemed as if the three important anti-Japanese bills had either been shelved or defeated outright.

In the meantime, two unpleasant incidents had threatened to inflame the situation. The Japanese consul at San Francisco had called upon Governor Gillett to make certain representations regarding the pending legislation. But State Senator Anthony, regarding this action as objectionable interference, introduced a resolution in the legislature to the effect that the Japanese official should be recalled. Governor Gillett made it clear, however, that no improper influence had been brought to bear, and the matter was not pressed further.[9] The *Japan Weekly Mail* passed the affair off gracefully when it rejoiced that this development had occurred because it had injected an element of humor into the situation.[10]

The other disagreeable incident occurred on January 30, 1909, when a Japanese university graduate was attacked in Berkeley, apparently without provocation, by a group of

8 Roosevelt to Gillett (telegram), Jan. 25, 1909; Roosevelt to Gillett (telegram), Jan. 26, 1909; Roosevelt to Gillett, Jan. 26, 1909, Roosevelt Papers.   9 San Francisco *Chronicle,* Jan. 28, 1909.
10 *Japan Weekly Mail,* Feb. 6, 1909, p. 154.

young men thought to be University of California students. It later developed that town rowdies, not students, were responsible for the assault, and the victim requested the president of the university to drop the investigation.[11] It was indeed fortunate that these two unpleasant developments were smoothed over so quietly; and it was noted that the international situation was decidedly improved when, on February 2, 1909, Minister for Foreign Affairs Komura made a most pacific speech before the lower house of the Diet.[12]

But almost overnight the complexion of affairs changed. The assembly suddenly turned on February 4, 1909, and by a vote of 45 to 29 passed the anti-Japanese school bill.[13] Roosevelt at once wired Gillett: "This is the most offensive bill of all and in my judgment is clearly unconstitutional and we should at once have to test it in the courts. Can it not be stopt in the legislature or by veto?"[14] Gillett immediately sent a special message to the legislature in which he strongly advised against the passage of the school bill.[15] But neither the efforts of Roosevelt nor those of the governor would have availed to stop the bill had it not been for the support of Speaker Stanton. Evidencing extreme perturbation and with the restrained manner of one who knew of an impending disaster which he was not at liberty to reveal, he took the floor and said in part:

I believe—I know—that a grave crisis has been reached in this question. My lips have been sealed. I wish I could take you into

[11] *Independent,* Feb. 4, 1909, p. 216; Feb. 11, 1909, p. 282.
[12] San Francisco *Chronicle,* Feb. 3, 1909.
[13] Hichborn, *Legislature of 1909,* p. 208.
[14] Roosevelt to Gillett, Feb. 4, 1909, Roosevelt Papers.
[15] *Senate Journal* (California), 1909, p. 477.

my confidence and tell you what I know, but I cannot. I will tell you, however, that you are treading on dangerous ground. Already I feel it slipping from under my feet . . . . It is a very grave problem and I think it would be a serious mistake to vote against reconsideration at this time.[16]

This speech paved the way for reconsideration of the measure,[17] and Roosevelt promptly sent his warm thanks to Stanton.[18] Henceforth, except for a few rumblings, there was little danger that the anti-Japanese bills would pass during this session of the legislature. But Roosevelt was still worried, as is indicated by a letter of February 6, 1909, to his son Theodore:

I have spent my usual lively week; but the troubles I have with Congress don't count at all when compared with the trouble I am having with California over Japan. I have been vigorously holding the lid down for the last three weeks, with varying success. I think I shall succeed but I can not be sure.[19]

On February 8, 1909, Roosevelt summed up his Pacific Coast Japanese policy in a communication to Speaker Stanton, which was intended for publication and which, he confessed to Philander Knox, was "really meant almost as much for Japan as for California, and sets forth, seemingly as incidental, what our future policy must be."[20] At the beginning of his letter the President made it clear that the federal government was "jealously endeavoring

16 San Francisco *Chronicle,* Feb. 6, 1909.

17 Hichborn, *Legislature of 1909,* pp. 211–12.

18 Roosevelt to Stanton (telegrams), Feb. 6, 10, 1909, Roosevelt Papers.

19 Roosevelt to Theodore Roosevelt, Jr., Feb. 6, 1909, Roosevelt Papers.

20 Roosevelt to Knox, Feb. 8, 1909, Roosevelt Papers.

to guard the interests of California and of the entire West in accordance with the desires of our Western people." Roosevelt pointed out that he had inaugurated a policy, namely the Gentlemen's Agreement, which was working to the satisfaction of all parties concerned, and with mutual good feeling. He then observed that the school bill would accomplish nothing with respect to cutting down the number of Japanese in California, and "gives just and grave cause for irritation." But the policy of the Administration "is to combine the maximum of efficiency in achieving the real object which the people of the Pacific Slope have at heart, with the minimum of friction and trouble, while the misguided men who advocate such action as this against which I protest are following a policy which combines the very minimum of efficiency with the maximum of insult, and which, while totally failing to achieve any real result for good, yet might accomplish an infinity of harm." If, at the end of a year or two, it should develop that the Gentlemen's Agreement was not accomplishing the desired results, then it would be possible for the federal government to take appropriate action to exclude the Japanese. But as things then stood the Californians were getting the exclusion for which they had been clamoring.[21]

We have already noted that Roosevelt's words, including those written for private consumption alone, would indicate that he was more alarmed over the developments in the California legislature than he had been by some of the earlier and apparently more serious troubles with the

[21] Roosevelt to Stanton, Feb. 8, 1909, Roosevelt Papers. This letter is printed in full in Roosevelt's *Autobiography*, pp. 397–98.

Japanese. The reasonableness of his attitude, however, can be determined only after reference has been made to the reaction of Japanese public opinion, a subject to which it is now necessary to turn.

On January 16, 1909, the *Japan Weekly Mail* regretted that a telegram had been sent from Tokyo to the effect that a considerable stir had been caused in Japan. "We are at a loss," this journal remarked, "to account for this view of the situation. Short of absolutely ignoring the whole affair, it would scarcely have been possible for the Japanese press to show greater insouciance. Were we asked to analyze the attitude of the Tokyo press we should describe it by the one adjective 'unconcerned'."[22] A week later this same organ observed: "So far as we know no more than two Tokyo journals have commented editorially upon the proposed legislation, and these comments can not by any stretch of the imagination be described as extreme or violent."[23] One of these two newspapers, it may be observed, was the perennial trouble-maker, the *Hochi Shimbun,* but even its remarks were only slightly offensive in tone.[24] The *Japan Weekly Mail* probably voiced majority opinion when it wrote: "There can be little doubt, we think, that the good sense of the American nation and the firmness of the President will devise some exit from the unpleasant situation."[25]

In summarizing press opinion in Japan, the *Japan Weekly Mail,* in its note of January 23, 1909, remarked

22 *Japan Weekly Mail,* Jan. 16, 1909, p. 65.
23 *Ibid.,* Jan. 23, 1909, p. 93.
24 San Francisco *Chronicle,* Jan. 21, 1909.
25 *Japan Weekly Mail,* Jan. 23, 1909, p. 93.

that America "has the whole commotion to herself on this occasion." The Japanese were looking on quietly, but not "without astonishment," while floods of telegrams poured in from the United States indicating uneasiness in official circles. This weekly observed that, although Japan was peaceful and quiet, "her reward is to be brutally vilified by lunatics like this person Hearst." After paying its respects to the latter, who, this journal felt, could not be adequately described by the phrase "reckless liar," the *Japan Weekly Mail* concluded that the "California agitators and Mr. Hearst have a monopoly of the excitement." Then came a remarkable observation: "The only really discouraging feature of the situation is that the President evidently attaches considerable importance to it." And in its note of January 24, this same weekly observed that "not so much as one Tokyo journal, either in a leading article or in a note, discusses the situation. There is absolute calm in Japan. The nation evidently trusts the President and the great bulk of the friendly American public to protect it against insulting ebullitions of race prejudice."[26]

But by January 25, 1909, so great had become the concern in the United States over what was assumed to be the alarming reaction of Japan that the Tokyo journals began to break their silence and take casual notice of the commotion. These newspapers, although regretting such developments, recognized that the trouble was local and that the federal government was doing its best to handle a difficult situation. Roosevelt's communications to the California authorities were printed at length in Japan, and although the Japanese press may not have approved of the

[26] *Ibid.*, Jan. 30, 1909, pp. 122–23.

President's methods it realized that his efforts were well-meaning.[27]

Unfortunately, however, at this time the legislatures of several other Western states took such action as to make it clear that they sympathized with California in its campaign of prejudice. An anti-Japanese resolution, which in its original form censured the President for his interference with California, was introduced into the Nevada legislature and was passed by the lower house. Roosevelt, however, succeeded in having the offensive resolution squelched through intervention on the part of the United States Senators from Nevada.[28] And in the legislatures of Oregon and Montana action was taken, none of it decisive, which also evidenced hostility to the Japanese.[29]

Up to this time the Japanese had derived much comfort from the presumed fact that the agitation in America was highly localized and was confined to only a few agitators in one part of California. Such a flurry in a number of other Western states did much to dispel this illusion. Nevertheless, public opinion in Japan remained calm.[30] This somewhat unexpected absence of resentment cannot be definitely explained, but it would seem as if the fleet demonstration and satisfaction with the Root-Takahira agreement were not altogether dissociated from the Japanese reaction.

[27] *Japan Weekly Mail*, Jan. 30, 1909, p. 123.

[28] San Francisco *Chronicle*, Feb. 2, 1909; *Japan Weekly Mail*, Feb. 6, 1909, p. 154; Feb. 13, 1909, p. 186; *Literary Digest*, Feb. 13, 1909, pp. 239–40.

[29] *Japan Weekly Mail*, Feb. 13, 1909, pp. 186, 187; Feb. 20, 1909, p. 220; Mar. 13, 1909, p. 329.

[30] The *Japan Weekly Mail* remarked that "everything tends to show that Japan may implicitly trust the United States to do the right thing in the end." Feb. 20, 1909, p. 220.

In the state of California, strangely enough, there appears to have been much less sympathy with the activity of the legislature than one would expect to find there in the light of the previous anti-Japanese manifestations. Chambers of Commerce and merchants' associations were opposed to the aggravation of a problem which for the time appeared to have been satisfactorily solved.[31] Even the San Francisco *Chronicle* was found in the unaccustomed rôle of opposition to anti-Japanese legislation. It regarded the bills that had been introduced as foolish because unnecessary, and it asserted that any such measures as were being contemplated were directly at variance with the treaty with Japan.[32]

In the eastern part of the United States there was the usual unfavorable reaction to the trouble-making of the California legislature.[33] Professor G. T. Ladd, of Yale University, probably voiced the sentiments of a good many when he remarked that one way to put an end to the war talk was to man a battleship with the editors and staff of the yellow press, put it under the command of Captain Hobson (perhaps the outstanding Japanese baiter in America), and send it out to the central Pacific to meet a Japanese vessel similarly manned. The survivors of the battle would all be banished to a desert island.[34]

As in 1907, when Roosevelt had felt it necessary to interfere with the legislature of California, the press of the country engaged in a warm discussion of the wisdom

[31] *Senate Journal* (California), 1909, pp. 235, 279–80.

[32] San Francisco *Chronicle,* Jan. 22, 1909.

[33] See *Literary Digest,* Jan. 23, 1909, pp. 127–28 ; *Japan Weekly Mail,* Jan. 23, 1909, p. 93 ; Feb. 13, 1909, p. 187 ; Feb. 20, 1909, p. 220.

[34] *Ibid.,* Mar. 6, 1909, p. 288.

of direct interference by the President. States' rights advocates were naturally not pleased with this increased activity on the part of the chief executive, and their perturbation may perhaps be better appreciated when the extent of Roosevelt's intervention is analyzed. All together, during this 1909 flurry, the President sent twelve letters or telegrams to Governor Gillett, four letters and telegrams to the speaker of the assembly, and two telegrams to the president of the senate.

Nevertheless, a considerable amount of commendation of the President's course appeared in the press of the United States;[35] but there were some who felt, with reason, that Roosevelt had become unnecessarily wrought up and that he had made the situation more serious than it would have normally become. The New York *Nation* regretted that the quiet methods of suasion had been thrown to the winds and that Roosevelt's slapdash and sensational methods, by concentrating attention on the California legislature and emphasizing the possibility of war, had added fuel to the flames.[36] The San Francisco *Chronicle,* which had not rejoiced over Metcalf's mission in 1906, remarked that the President would have done better to send some official across the continent to reason with the legislature.[37] The *Japan Weekly Mail* wrote in the strain of one who was in need of being delivered from the zeal of his friends.

Speaking as outsiders, we can not but think that the President might easily find gentler ways of dealing with great questions

[35] *Literary Digest,* Jan. 30, 1909, p. 159.
[36] New York *Nation,* Feb. 11, 1909, p. 127.
[37] San Francisco *Chronicle,* Jan. 22, 1909.

than the methods he habitually resorts to. It may be that he appeals to public opinion only after private suggestions have failed, but the interval which usually elapses between the appearance of a question and its reference to the whole nation is too short to permit the hypothesis that diplomacy is fully tried before publicity is courted. It is the inevitable habit of human nature to develop resistance in the direct ratio of the pressure brought to bear, and really tactful rulers know how to exercise pressure without letting its [sic] subjects feel that they are restrained. However, nothing succeeds like success. President Roosevelt certainly succeeds, and the only possible conclusion is that he knows his public better than any outsider can know it.[38]

One unhappy feature of this last flare-up was not overlooked. Although Roosevelt was able to bring his administration to a close with the Japanese problem in a reasonably satisfactory posture, it was pointed out, with prescience, that the California legislature would probably be heard from again, for the bills had been defeated by so narrow a margin that the anti-Japanese element was obviously far from discouraged.[39] This anticipated difficulty again focused the attention of the nation on the possibilities of war with Japan, and the approaching return of the battleship fleet from its world cruise gave renewed strength to the cry that the fleet be divided in such a way as to provide for the permanent stationing of a respectable force in Pacific waters.[40] Roosevelt continued to insist, however, that to divide, and consequently to weaken, the navy in this fashion would be to invite disaster.[41]

This final tilt with the California legislature produced,

[38] *Japan Weekly Mail*, Jan. 30, 1909, p. 122.
[39] *Ibid.*, Feb. 20, 1909, p. 220.
[40] *Ibid.*, Jan. 30, 1909, p. 123; Feb. 27, 1909, p. 251.
[41] Roosevelt to Knox, Feb. 8, 1909, Roosevelt Papers.

incidentally, two important results. First of all, through the statements of Roosevelt and the figures that were published at the time, it was made clear to the American people that the Gentlemen's Agreement, as to the workability of which there had been grave doubts, was operating with a reasonable degree of satisfaction.[42] In the second place, the President took this opportunity to outline in considerable detail and make public his views regarding the Japanese problem. Inasmuch as he was shortly to retire from office, these communications take on added significance as representing his matured policy.

On February 5, 1909, the President wrote to William Kent, of California: "Our line of policy must be adopted holding ever in view the fact that this is a race question, and that race questions stand by themselves." Then Roosevelt made a significant admission: "I did not clearly see this at the outset; but for nearly three years I have seen it, and thruout my treatment of the question have shaped my course accordingly." The important thing to him was that the Japanese as a race should be excluded by an arrangement which should be reciprocal, and that there should be complete freedom of movement for the upper classes of both races. This policy, although the best one, would have to be phrased with extreme care, for it was "peculiarly apt to be misunderstood and to cause intense humiliation and bitterness and arouse intense resentment; especially in the case of a people very sensitive and at the same time very self-confident in their warlike strength, as is true with the Japanese." Roosevelt went on to say:

[42] *Outlook,* Jan. 30, 1909, p. 227.

In such circumstances the wise policy is to insist on keeping out Japanese immigration; but at the same time to behave with scrupulous courtesy to Japan as a nation and to the Japanese who are here; and also to continue to build up and maintain at the highest point of efficiency our navy. This three-fold policy is precisely the policy of the administration of the past two years.

In spite of Senator Hale of Maine and Senator Perkins of California, who had the "backbone of a sea-anemone," Roosevelt pointed out that he had built up the navy; and he had made an agreement under which Japanese immigration was decreasing, as well as the total number of Japanese in the United States. Yet he had treated the Japanese with studied politeness, and he had shown respect and admiration for them. The demagogues of California, he remarked, were wicked and foolish. The laws they were proposing could not prevent the Japanese from coming in; all that they could do would be to irritate the Japanese in California and profoundly offend Japan. This was combining the maximum of irritation with the minimum of efficiency, which was precisely the reverse of his own policy.[43]

On February 7, 1909, Roosevelt elaborated these ideas in letters to Frederic Remington and Arthur Lee.[44] To the former he described at some length his minimum-maximum policy, and to the latter he wrote in even greater detail. He observed that the "thing that gives me serious uneasiness is the friction with Japan. I have been reluctantly forced to the conclusion that it is indispensable for the Japanese to be kept from coming in any numbers as settlers . . . ." The feeling against them on the Ameri-

[43] Roosevelt to Kent, Feb. 5, 1909, Roosevelt Papers.
[44] Both letters are in the Roosevelt Papers.

can Pacific Coast, which was just as strong as in Australia and British Columbia, should not be disregarded and, in fact, simply could not be disregarded. If Washington and London were to throw open the gates "we should the following week see our Pacific States and British Columbia declare their independence as a separate republic, in close alliance with Australia." His policy, then, was (1) to keep out the Japanese masses, (2) to do it with the minimum of friction and the maximum of courtesy, and (3) to build up the navy. The demagogues, however, were trying to keep the navy weak and drive the country into disaster.

The next day, February 8, 1909, Roosevelt wrote a remarkable long letter of admonition and advice to Philander C. Knox, who was shortly to become secretary of state under Taft. The President was taking this step because at the outset the new secretary would be overwhelmed with every kind of work and because "there is one matter of foreign policy of such great and permanent importance that I wish to lay it before the President-to-be and yourself. I speak of the relations of the United States and Japan." Roosevelt then discussed the possibility of trouble with Germany, England, and the other European powers, and pointed out that the difficulties with them had been reasonably well ironed out. "But with Japan the case is different." The Japanese, with their expanding population, were a formidable and warlike nation of fighting men. Furthermore, they were proud, self-confident, sensitive, and touchy. During the past three years Roosevelt had become convinced that the Americans would not tolerate them in the mass, and he had "reluctantly come to feel" that this opposition to their presence in numbers "is entirely warranted" and must be heeded by the national government. As long as they were here in large bodies, he observed, there was always a chance for violence. They must therefore be kept out with courtesy; and the United States must arm. Japan was reluctant to fight the United States because of her financial condition and because such a step would weaken her for her policy in the Far East. But Japan would fight if sufficiently hurt. There was, in fact, always danger of a mob outbreak in both countries.

Roosevelt then repeated the three cardinal points in his policy. He added that the Japanese must be made to feel that, unless the Gentlemen's Agreement worked well, it would be impossible to prevent drastic legislation in California. The navy must be kept strong, especially in auxiliary vessels; and the fleet must not be divided. The Japanese should be continually reminded that unless they themselves controlled coolie immigration, "in the end this country is certain to stop it, and ought to stop it, no matter what the consequences may be." Roosevelt concluded:

There is no more important continuing feature of our foreign policy than this in reference to our dealing with Japan; the whole question of our dealings with the Orient is certain to grow in importance. I do not believe that there will be war, but there is always the chance that war will come, and if it did come, the calamity would be very great, and while I believe we would win, there is at least a chance of disaster.[45]

[45] Roosevelt to Knox, Feb. 8, 1909, Roosevelt Papers.

CHAPTER XIV

Conclusions

OUR STORY has been told. There remain, however, certain observations and conclusions of a more general nature. In the first place, the attitude of the Japanese government during the period under review was characterized, outwardly, at least, by a high degree of patience, forbearance, and courtesy. It is difficult to see how the Japanese Foreign Office could have conducted itself with a greater regard for the historic friendship which had long existed between the two powers. And this attitude was all the more noteworthy because the Japanese, as the aggrieved parties, were on the defensive throughout. Confronted with repeated indignities, most of which were clearly the result of race prejudice, the Japanese government consistently refused to take high ground; and such measures as it did adopt were largely designed to save its face and to quiet the opposition at home. On a number of occasions the Japanese authorities went out of their way to discourage their subjects from emigrating to places where they were not wanted; voluntarily adopted other measures to prevent friction with the United States; refused to lodge protests when they would have been fully justified; and made such representations as were necessary in the least offensive language and form.[1]

---

[1] On April, 19, 1907, Secretary Root stated in a public address: "It is a pleasure to be able to say that never for a moment was there as between the government of the United States and the government of Japan, the slightest departure from perfect good temper, mutual confidence, and

The position of the Japanese people, however, was somewhat different. The less conciliatory group, stimulated to an unusual degree by the recent smashing victories over the Russians, were unable to see why they should submit tamely to repeated insults and discriminations at the hands of the Americans on the Pacific Coast. This element was led to some extent by young army officers and representatives of the emigration companies, but chiefly by the opposition party, which did its best to make political capital out of the embarrassments of the government. The mouthpiece of these malcontents was an irresponsible and dangerously inflammatory jingo press. Nevertheless, it is clear that a majority, probably a great majority, of the Japanese people supported their government in its attitude of moderation. They perceived that isolated outbursts of certain groups on the Pacific Coast were by no means representative of the American people; they reposed great confidence in the fairness of Roosevelt; and above all they were still attached to the ideal of historic friendship. It should further be noted that the calmness of the Japanese on a number of occasions was in large part due to a deep preoccupation with developments nearer at home in Korea and Manchuria.

The attitude of the United States government, like that of Japan, was all that could have been desired. It is a curious fact that in general the controversy lay not between the United States and Japan but between Japan and California, with the federal government seeking to

kindly consideration. . . . ." Elihu Root, "The Real Questions under the Japanese Treaty," *American Journal of International Law,* I (Apr., 1907), 276.

secure justice for the aggrieved foreign power and at the same time endeavoring to convince the state of its obligations to the rest of the Union. The Department of State was prompt to convey its regrets to the Japanese Foreign Office when any untoward event occurred on the Coast; and every conceivable kind of pressure was brought to bear on federal, state, and local officials to straighten out the resultant difficulties. It would, in fact, be difficult to point to any practicable step that the federal government failed to take in its attempt to protect the Japanese in their treaty rights. A knowledge of this solicitude doubtless accounts in large measure for the willingness of the Japanese to go slowly in seeking redress.

It is probably correct to say that a majority of the people of the United States favored, or at least acquiesced in, the general policy of Roosevelt and the national government. This was particularly true of the East and Middle West, but the South, fearing for its white schools and its states' rights, was disposed to show a considerable degree of sympathy for the Californians. On the Pacific Coast, however, particularly in California, the situation was different. Although the so-called better element there deplored the anti-Japanese agitation, the masses, led chiefly by the labor unions, were bitterly opposed to the immigration of hordes of Orientals. This feeling appears to have been grounded largely on fear of a lowered standard of living, although race prejudice pure and simple was not lacking. But Congress, far removed from the problem, turned a deaf ear to the demands of California for exclusion; and the resulting discrimination and violence on the Coast were largely the result of a determination on the part of the exclusionists to take matters into their own hands and at the same time arouse the lethargic and pharisaical East. These direct methods were successful, for they drove the national government into securing a relatively satisfactory type of exclusion much sooner than would otherwise have been the case.

President Theodore Roosevelt entertained a sincere friendship and a deep admiration for the Japanese people —and they knew it. He viewed with great displeasure the offensive discrimination and the brutal violence of certain elements in California, and he was fully prepared to use federal troops to protect the property and lives of the Japanese. But his vigorous, at times almost hysterical, use of the big stick on the California authorities did not produce uniformly satisfactory results. Such methods tended to give undue prominence to certain rather minor developments and unnecessarily aggravated the already ugly temper of the Pacific Coast. Indeed, at times the Japanese could well have prayed to be delivered from the zeal of their friend. Yet, on the whole, Roosevelt's intervention probably did more good than harm in tiding over a number of serious situations. This does not mean, however, that the results would not have been happier if Roosevelt had resorted to less spectacular devices. In any event, he gave the Japanese unmistakable evidence that they had a powerful friend at court—and this did much to quiet the troubled waters.

In pursuing his policy of the square deal Roosevelt took unprecedented liberties with what were regarded as states' rights. Under the federal constitution it is quite possible for one of the forty-eight states, particularly in its treatment of aliens, to provoke a war which the other forty-seven will have to fight. Such an insane course California, during the Roosevelt period as well as during the alien land difficulties of 1913,[2] seemed bent on following. But Roosevelt was not the man to make a fetish of states' rights while the house appeared to be about ready to tumble about his ears. He ordered his secretary of commerce and labor to San Francisco to investigate the situation and bring pressure to bear on the local authorities, a move which remained without precedent until, in 1913, President Wilson sent Secretary of State Bryan to California to remonstrate with the legislature. Not only did Roosevelt send Metcalf to San Francisco, but he brought eight San Francisco officials at government expense to Washington, where they might be made more amenable to the big stick. These third-rate politicians, headed by a bassoon-playing mayor then under indictment for graft, afforded a grotesque commentary on the weaknesses of our federal form of government. In addition, Roosevelt, alternately threatening and cajoling, sent dozens of letters or telegrams to the legislature of California, to the officials of that body, and to the governor of the state, to say nothing of communications to the federal officials already on the ground. Although the old states'

---

[2] President Taft, like his predecessor, Roosevelt, was able to bring pressure to bear on the Republican California legislature to prevent the passage of obnoxious anti-Japanese measures. But President Wilson's Democratic administration could do nothing with the Progressive Republican legislature, which, in spite of a trip to California and a personal appeal by Secretary of State Bryan, approved an alien land bill directed at the Japanese. The author has discussed this critical situation at considerable length in a previous study. See Thomas A. Bailey, "California, Japan, and the Alien Land Legislation of 1913," *Pacific Historical Review,* I (1932), 36–59.

rights school mourned the passing of local autonomy, Roosevelt's methods seemed to get results and at the same time to command the acquiescence, if not the approval, of a majority of the American people.

The Japanese immigration problem well illustrates Roosevelt's ability to change his mind when confronted with disagreeable facts, and his unwillingness to attempt to drive his head against a stone wall. Starting off in 1905 with a thorough lack of sympathy with the obvious prejudice of the Californians, he swung around to the conclusion that he was confronted with a condition and not a theory. However reprehensible the methods of the Californians were to him personally, and however sincere he was in his belief that whites ought to live in harmony with their colored neighbors, he quickly learned to his sorrow that race prejudice cannot be reasoned or argued out of a people, and that the policy of the national government had to be based upon a recognition of that fact. Indeed, he soon came to the point where he was willing to admit that the Californians, as well as the Canadians and other whites in the Pacific, were right in opposing mass immigration from the Orient; that economic and social problems of a most serious nature inevitably arise when East and West meet in numbers; and that the American people already had enough vexatious and insoluble race problems without deliberately adding another. But he believed in securing the desired exclusion through courtesy and fair-dealing.

Throughout the years from 1906 to 1909 a half-dozen or so situations developed which, under different circumstances and treatment, might easily have resulted in war.

The school incident of 1906 injected the first serious difference into the traditionally amicable relations between the two powers. Although the immediate reaction of the Japanese bore on the surface dangerous symptoms, the agitation was quieted by judicious handling on the part of the American federal government and by a habitual deference in Japan to the ideal of historic friendship. But the pin-pricks and evidences of violent race prejudice continued, and by the end of the period it is evident that Japanese patience was wearing thin. Widespread cynicism had developed in Japan regarding the United States and her so-called friendship, and an evident unwillingness to turn the other cheek more than the proverbial seventy times seven was becoming manifest. It was indeed fortunate that the school incident occurred early in this period rather than after the Japanese pride had suffered from a series of disillusioning shocks, for otherwise the danger would have become far more serious than it did.

The situation was unfortunately complicated by the activities of the professional jingoes and the big navy men on both sides of the Pacific. In addition, the attitude of the nations of continental Europe was not conducive to a peaceful settlement. They were not at all averse to seeing the two parvenus among the powers of the world come to grips and waste their strength on each other. The Kaiser, in particular, was eager to weaken the Anglo-Japanese alliance by egging the United States on against Japan and possibly involving the United States in serious difficulties with the mother country. It would probably not be going too far to say, without attempting to heap further coals on the head of a much-maligned sovereign, that the Kaiser emerges as the evil genius of the period. The quality and quantity of misinformation with which he deluged Roosevelt suggest ulterior motives, and this propaganda might well have been more effective had it been fabricated with a greater regard for realities. But in the end the Kaiser overplayed his hand, and Roosevelt began to speak disparagingly of "imperial pipe dreams."

The real danger spot during this period was the yellow press of both the United States and Japan. Most of the responsible journals of both countries kept their heads reasonably well, but at times they showed signs, particularly in the United States, of yielding to the hysteria of the sensational newspapers. The jingo press of the United States was led by William Randolph Hearst, who strove mightily to bring on hostilities with Japan. When one remembers the success which attended his efforts to precipitate the Spanish-American War, it is difficult to understand why he and his imitators were unable to produce the desired explosion. The whole period is a vivid commentary on the appalling power for evil which may be lodged in the hands of an unprincipled few.

Fortunately, however, certain powerful factors were operating for peace. In the first place, both governments were unquestionably anxious to avoid hostilities. In the second place, the great majority of the population of both countries did not want war, although neither nation was quite sure of the pacific intentions of the other until the visit of the fleet to Japan. The ideal of the historic friendship, on which two generations had been reared, could not be entirely swept away in the space of a few months. And, finally, Japan had not yet recovered from the exhaustion of her recent conflict with Russia, a fact which was widely known in the United States and which to some extent probably accounted for the unreasonable attitude of the Pacific Coast.

In conclusion, it seems fair to say that the two nations during this period were probably never so near to war as the yellow journals would have liked to believe. None the less, there were many combustibles lying about, lacking only the necessary spark. The Japanese did not want to fight and they were not prepared to fight, but a proud people can be pushed only so far. Roosevelt, himself, was not particularly concerned about ordinary diplomatic developments, but he was afraid that a lynching party or a similar disturbance would cause the situation to get out of hand. In fact, one of the noteworthy features of these years was the manner in which Roosevelt, whose love for a fight was notorious, kept his head in the midst of alarms that might easily have swept a less self-assured man off his feet. Although he showed signs of weakening after the crises had passed, his touch was surest when the danger seemed greatest. He took chances, to be sure, when he sent the fleet around the world; but this venturesome move gave the Japanese an opportunity to demonstrate their friendship for the United States, with a resultant clearing away of the war clouds.

The Roosevelt era marks a transition in the relations between the United States and Japan. The days when America could manifest a more or less parental interest in her Far Eastern protégé had passed. Within the space of a decade both nations had emerged as world powers, and as a consequence their interests had begun to come more and more into conflict. Suspicion and jealousy, not unmingled with fear, were bound to be the unhappy products of this changed status. The golden age in Japanese-American relations was gone, and although men might continue to speak of the traditional friendship as if nothing had happened, the attitude of the two peoples toward each other was no longer the same, and never could be. It was the price that both Japan and America had to pay for coming of age.

BIBLIOGRAPHY

I. MANUSCRIPT COLLECTIONS

Department of State. Division of Communications and Records. Files 1797, 8258, 16533.

> Dispatches, instructions, memoranda, etc., on Japanese-American relations, 1906–1909.

Navy Department. Bureau of Navigation. File 6072.

> Correspondence relating to cruise of battleship fleet, 1907–1909.

Papers of Charles J. Bonaparte, 1906–1909. Library of Congress, Washington, D.C.

Papers of David Starr Jordan, 1906–1909. Stanford University, California.

Papers of Theodore Roosevelt, 1906–1909. Library of Congress, Washington, D.C.

> Where it has been possible to refer to published copies of certain letters, this has been done.

Papers of Elihu Root, 1906–1909. Library of Congress, Washington, D.C.

Papers of Admiral Charles S. Sperry, 1907–1909. Library of Congress, Washington, D.C.

II. UNITED STATES GOVERNMENT DOCUMENTS

Annual Report of the Secretary of Commerce and Labor, 1908. Washington, D.C., 1908.

Annual Report of the Secretary of the Navy, 1907. Washington, D.C., 1908.

Annual Report of the Secretary of the Navy, 1908. Washington, D.C., 1908.

Annual Report of the Secretary of the Navy, 1911. Washington, D.C., 1912.

Annual Report of the United States Commissioner General of Immigration, 1908. Washington, D.C., 1908.

Congressional Record. 56th, 57th, 58th, 59th, and 60th Congresses.

House Documents, 59 Cong., 2 sess., no. 251.

> Relating to the raid of Japanese poachers on the seal rookeries.

Information Relative to the Voyage of the United States Atlantic Fleet around the World. Washington, D.C., 1910.

MALLOY, W. M., comp. *Treaties, Conventions, International Acts, Protocols and Agreements between the United States of America and Other Powers, 1776–1909.* 2 vols. Washington, D.C., 1910.

Papers Relating to the Foreign Relations of the United States, 1908. Washington, D.C., 1912.

Senate Documents, 59 Cong., 2 sess., no. 104.

> Metcalf's letter in response to Senate resolution.

Senate Documents, 59 Cong., 2 sess., no. 147.

> Metcalf's report of his San Francisco investigation.

III. FOREIGN GOVERNMENT DOCUMENTS

GERMANY, AUSWÄRTIGES AMT. *Die Grosse Politik der Europäischen Kabinette, 1871–1914,* Sammlung der diplomatischen Akten des Auswärtigen Amtes (im Auftrage des Auswärtigen Amtes, herausgegeben von Johannes Lepsius, Albrecht Mendelssohn-Bartholdy, Friedrich Thimme). Vol. XXV. Berlin, 1925.

GOOCH, G. P., and HAROLD TEMPERLEY, eds. *British Documents on the Origins of the War, 1898–1914.* Vol. VIII. London, 1932.

IV. CALIFORNIA GOVERNMENT DOCUMENTS

The Journal of the Assembly during the Thirty-sixth Session of the Legislature of the State of California, 1905. Sacramento, 1905.

The Journal of the Assembly during the Thirty-seventh Session of the Legislature of the State of California, 1907. Sacramento, 1907.

The Journal of the Assembly during the Thirty-eighth Session of the Legislature of the State of California, 1909. Sacramento, 1909.

The Journal of the Senate during the Thirty-sixth Session of the Legislature of the State of California, 1905. Sacramento, 1905.

The Journal of the Senate during the Thirty-eighth Session of the Legislature of the State of California, 1909. Sacramento, 1909.

School Law of California. Sacramento, 1902.

V. NEWSPAPERS

Boston *Evening Transcript*, 1906–1909, *passim.*
London *Times*, 1906–1909.
Melbourne *Age*, 1908, *passim.*
Melbourne *Argus*, 1908, *passim.*
New York *Times*, 1906–1909, *passim.*
Sacramento *Union*, 1906–1907, *passim.*
San Francisco *Bulletin*, 1906–1907.
San Francisco *Call*, 1906–1907.
San Francisco *Chronicle*, 1905–1907.
San Francisco *Examiner*, 1906–1907.

Newspapers cited in the text but not mentioned here were used through the medium of clippings or translations found in the diplomatic correspondence.

VI. PERIODICALS

Advocate of Peace, 1908–1909. Boston.
Argonaut, 1906–1909. San Francisco.
Current Literature, 1906–1909. New York.
Fortnightly Review, 1907–1908. London.
Harper's Weekly, 1906–1909. New York.
Independent, 1906–1909. New York.
Japan Weekly Mail, 1906–1909. Yokohama.
Literary Digest, 1906–1909. New York.
Living Age, 1908. Boston.
Nation, 1906–1909. New York.
North China Herald, 1907–1909. Shanghai.
Outlook, 1906–1909. New York.
Review of Reviews, 1906–1909. New York.
Scientific American, 1907–1909. New York.
Spectator, Aug., 1908. London.
World's Work, 1906–1909. New York.

VII. PUBLISHED LETTERS

"Letters written by John P. Irish to George F. Parker," *Iowa Journal of History and Politics*, XXXI (July, 1933), 421–512.

Selections from the Correspondence of Theodore Roosevelt and Henry Cabot Lodge, 1884–1918. 2 vols. New York, 1925.

VIII. AUTOBIOGRAPHIES

EVANS, ROBLEY D. *A Sailor's Log.* New York, 1901.

JORDAN, DAVID STARR. *The Days of a Man.* 2 vols. Yonkers-on-Hudson, 1922.

MATTHEWS, FRANKLIN. *Back to Hampton Roads.* New York, 1909.

———. *With the Battle Fleet.* New York, 1909.

ROOSEVELT, THEODORE. *An Autobiography.* New York, 1916.

STRAUS, OSCAR S. *Under Four Administrations: from Cleveland to Taft.* Boston, 1922.

IX. SECONDARY ACCOUNTS

CHURCHILL, WINSTON S. *The World Crisis, 1911–1914.* London, 1923.

BELL, REGINALD. *Status of Public School Education of Second-Generation Japanese in California.* University Series, Stanford University, 1934.

DENNETT, TYLER. *Roosevelt and the Russo-Japanese War.* New York, 1925.

HICHBORN, FRANKLIN. *Story of the Session of the California Legislature of 1909.* San Francisco, 1909.

ICHIHASHI, YAMATO. *The Japanese in the United States.* Stanford University, 1932.

JOHNSON, HERBERT B. *Discrimination against the Japanese in California.* Berkeley, California, 1907.

LATANÉ, JOHN H. *America as a World Power: 1897–1907.* New York, 1907.

SULLIVAN, MARK. *Our Times: Pre-War America.* Vol. III. New York, 1930.

TREAT, PAYSON J. *Diplomatic Relations between the United States and Japan, 1853–1895.* 2 vols. Stanford University, 1932.

TREAT, PAYSON J. *The Far East: A Political and Diplomatic History.* New York, 1928.
———. *Japan and the United States, 1853–1921.* Revised and Continued to 1928. Stanford University, 1928.

X. BIOGRAPHIES

BISHOP, JOSEPH B. *Theodore Roosevelt and His Time.* 2 vols. New York, 1920.
FALK, EDWIN A. *Fighting Bob Evans.* New York, 1931.
NEVINS, ALLAN. *Henry White.* New York, 1930.
PRINGLE, HENRY F. *Theodore Roosevelt: A Biography.* New York, 1931.

XI. ARTICLES

BAILEY, THOMAS A. "California, Japan, and the Alien Land Legislation of 1913." *Pacific Historical Review,* I (Mar., 1932), 36–59.
———. "The World Cruise of the American Battleship Fleet, 1907–1909." *Pacific Historical Review,* I (Dec., 1932), 389–423.
BALDWIN, SIMEON E. "Schooling Rights under Our Treaty with Japan." *Columbia Law Review,* VII (Feb., 1907), 85–92.
BROOKS, SYDNEY. "The Real 'Pacific Question.'" *Harper's Weekly,* LI (Oct. 12, 1907), 1484.
BUELL, RAYMOND L. "The Development of the Anti-Japanese Agitation in the United States." *Political Science Quarterly,* XXXVII (Dec., 1922), 605–38.
HALL, LUELLA J. "The Abortive German-American-Chinese Entente of 1907–08." *Journal of Modern History,* I (June, 1929), 219–35.
HART, JEROME. "The Oriental Problem, as the Coast Sees It." *World's Work,* XIII (Mar., 1907), 8689–93.
HERSHEY, AMOS. "The Japanese School Question and the Treaty-Making Power." *American Political Science Review,* I (May, 1907), 393–409.
HYDE, CHARLES C. "The Segregation of Japanese Students by the School Authorities of San Francisco." *The Green Bag,* XIX (Jan., 1907), 38–49.
INGLIS, WILLIAM. "The Width of a School Bench." *Harper's Weekly,* LI (Jan. 19, 1907), 82–84.

INGLIS, WILLIAM. "Japan's Preference for Peace with America." *Harper's Weekly*, LI (Mar. 2, 1907), 298–300.

ION, THEODORE P. "The Japanese School Incident at San Francisco from the Point of View of International and Constitutional Law." *Michigan Law Review*, V (Mar., 1907), 326–43.

KENNAN, GEORGE. "The Japanese in the San Francisco Schools." *Outlook*, LXXXVI (June 1, 1907), 246–52.

KUHN, ARTHUR K. "The Treaty-Making Power and the Reserved Sovereignty of the States." *Columbia Law Review*, VII (Mar., 1907), 172–85.

LEWIS, WILLIAM DRAPER. "Can the United States by Treaty Confer on Japanese Residents in California the Right to Attend the Public Schools?" *American Law Register*, LV (Feb., 1907), 73–90.

MAHAN, A. T. "The True Significance of the Pacific Cruise." *Scientific American*, IIIC (Dec. 7, 1907), 407, *et passim*.

REID, GEORGE H. "An After-Glance at the Visit of the American Fleet to Australia." *North American Review*, CLXXXIX (Mar., 1909), 404–409.

ROOT, ELIHU. "The Real Questions under the Japanese Treaty and the San Francisco School Board Resolution." *American Journal of International Law*, I (Apr., 1907), 273–86.

SCHROEDER, SEATON. "America's Welcome Abroad." *Independent*, LXVI (Mar. 4, 1909), 478–80.

XII. MANUSCRIPT THESES

BUTZBACH, ARTHUR G. "The Segregation of Orientals in the San Francisco Schools." Unpublished Master's thesis, Stanford University, 1928.

THOMSON, RUTH HAINES. "Events Leading to the Order to Segregate Japanese Pupils in the San Francisco Public Schools." Unpublished Doctor's dissertation, Stanford University, 1931.

INDEX

339

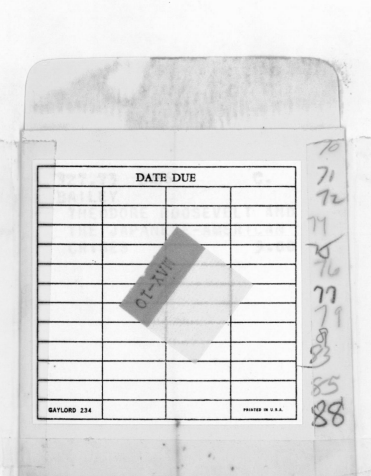